PIONEER BUSH PILOT

PIONEER BUSH PILOT

THE STORY OF NOEL WIEN

By Ira Harkey

UNIVERSITY OF WASHINGTON PRESS
SEATTLE AND LONDON

Library of Congress Cataloging in Publication Data

Harkey, Ira B
    Pioneer bush pilot.

    Includes bibliographical references.
    1. Wien, Noel. 2. Aeronautics—Alaska—History.
3. Alaska—History. I. Title.
TL540.W513H37   629.13′092′4 [B]   74-13213
    ISBN 0-295-95339-X

Dedicated with love to my mother, Flora Broad Lewis,
and to my father, Ira B. Harkey, rest them

With gratitude to Kay Kennedy, Alaskan; Professor Charles J. Keim, University
of Alaska; and Professor Paul Barton, Indiana University

PREFACE

Noel Wien, a self-effacing Minnesota farm boy who arrived in Fairbanks in 1924, was for two summer flying seasons the only aviator in Alaska Territory. As a working pilot he had been preceded in Alaska only by Roy Jones, Carl Ben Eielson, and Art Sampson. Jones flew a seaplane for a while down on the foggy coast of Ketchikan and then gave up. Eielson had gone to Fairbanks as a schoolteacher in 1922, in 1923 had done exhibition, joyhop, and some commercial flying within a fifty-mile radius of Fairbanks, and in 1924 made eight mail flights between Fairbanks and McGrath, 280 miles west.

None of these men was a bush pilot, Jones because the southeastern Alaska coast to which he confined himself is not the bush, Eielson because his short-term exhibition and mail flying was not in the "general practice" tradition of bush flying. Jones had returned to the States by 1924. Eielson and Wien crossed paths in Anchorage where Wien, who had just arrived in June as a twenty-five-year-old ex-barnstormer and stunt flyer, was assembling a Hisso Standard in which he began his Alaska career. Eielson, his mail contract canceled because of three crashes, was on his way Outside, where he would remain for two years. He returned to work for George Hubert Wilkins, the Polar explorer, serving as his pilot in 1928 on the milestone flight from Barrow to Spitsbergen.

Eielson did not enter bush flying until 1929. By that time Wien had pioneered the bush routes they all were later to fly and had already had a mountain officially named for him. Robert Marshall, a forester, drew a reconnaissance map of the northern Koyukuk region that he had explored, and labeled a 6,000-foot prominence in the Brooks Range for Noel Wien, "the first aviator to land in the Koyukuk and to fly over this peak."

The third working pilot, Art Sampson, was in Fairbanks in the summer of 1924 waiting for Wien to arrive and take over his job so that he could return Outside. Sampson could see no future for aviation in a land so sparsely settled, so huge, and so inhospitable to flying. Sampson, with little flying experience, had taken a job with Jimmy Rodebaugh's firm as the only aviator in that infant enterprise. But after he had arrived in the Interior, he made immediate plans to get out. Interior Alaska does that to some people, not just flyers, and the instant turnaround is not uncommon even today.

Wien's list of firsts, which seem so important in the documentation of aviation heroes, is almost endless. As he was the first bush pilot, almost every flight he made was an inaugural. He was the first to fly the 350 miles from Anchorage up the muskeg and through the Alaska Range alongside Mount McKinley's 20,300-foot eminence to Fairbanks in the "Golden Heart" of Alaska. He was the first to fly over and land beyond the Arctic Circle; to fly commercially between Fairbanks and Nome; to pilot a first passenger flight from Seattle to Fairbanks; to fly the Arctic coast commercially; to land at such places as Deering, Taylor, Teller, Wainwright, Point Hope, Kotzebue, Circle Hot Springs, Eagle, and Fort Yukon; to glimpse the Arctic Slope from the air over the Brooks Range. Perhaps of more consequence than all of these, Wien was the first man to attempt scheduled flying through an Alaskan winter, and to be successful at it.

Wien captured world attention by making the first flight across the Bering Strait, during the first round-trip flight ever made from North America to Asia in 1929, and by winning the race to deliver to the Outside world the first photographs of the Wiley Post–Will Rogers fatal crash near Barrow in 1935. His pilotage excellence on that flight gained the applause of flying men everywhere and it remains a classic in aviation history, although far more public acclaim was given to the glamour hops that brought criminals to justice, ill and maimed persons to medical care (and vice versa), and one hundred thousand dollars' worth of fox pelts from an icebound ship off Siberia.

Wien's skill was recognized by Captain Wilkins, who hired him as a pilot. In 1928 Wien preferred to remain in Alaska rather than accept Richard Byrd's offer, through Bernt Balchen, of a job as pilot with his Antarctic expedition. During the 1940s and 1950s, important personages and officials visiting Alaska often asked that their planes be piloted by the famous Noel Wien.

Although other men—notably Eielson and businessman Jimmy Rodebaugh and W. T. Thompson—had envisioned and worked toward this same goal, Wien, as the first bush pilot, was the working flyer who pulled Alaska from the stone age to the age of wings, from transport by dog sled and boat to airplane. His flight from Fairbanks to Nome in 1925, for example, reduced mail delivery time between Seattle and Nome from as much as six weeks to about eight days. Over an area of some three hundred thousand square miles—about half of Alaska—Wien flew miners, adventurers, trappers, romantics, drunks, scientists, light ladies, poets, fugitives, clergymen, stowaways, madmen, prisoners, and corpses, to all of whom but the last the most valuable commodity in the rich endless distances of Alaska was time.

In a day when men practice golf strokes on the moon, it may be difficult to find perspective that properly locates the importance and perils of early Alaska flying and the intrepidity of the men who did it. Astronauts are the final parts added to a scientific, engineering, and technical structure of thousands of men who conceive, draw plans for, and build space vehicles and their systems. In simplest terms, the groundlings run the show while the astronauts take a ride. In Alaska in the 1920s Wien was utterly alone in a giant, undeveloped land. He conceived, planned, and executed his historic flights, depending solely upon his own courage and skills. There was no one to point over a mountain and say with certainty, "It's that way." The triumph of man alone is sublime, and that is the reason why the name Lindbergh is still posted several rungs higher than Armstrong. Wien, too, was a man alone.

While the flamboyant characters among the flyers who followed Wien into the bush gained the publicity, Wien gained the admiration and gratitude of even the show-offs who used his wisdom and the lore he gathered to make their jobs easier. In a day when the typical aviator was—or pretended to be—a sort of cowboy of the air, a hell-for-struts daredevil happy to be referred to in print as "a flying fool," Wien was a cautious, methodical practitioner who carefully planned every flight. In this he was years ahead of his time. He studied the weather, using his own judgment based upon his own observations, because there were no machines or specialists to hand him a print-out. He anticipated the winds; measured, packed, and repacked his load; and checked and rechecked his distances. He never flew the short, direct route if along the way there were no spots to give him an even chance in the emergency landings he knew were inevitable. "Noel won't fly a straight line" was a common complaint of those who did not understand.

He babied his airplanes. He changed oil every five hours. He once quit the only flying job available in Alaska because a fellow worker insisted upon a convenient but dangerous mechanical adjustment. He babied himself. He did not smoke. He drank only water and milk. He was decades ahead of the Canadian Air Force in physical fitness. He exercised daily and, beginning in the 1920s, he jogged every day to maintain the stamina that he needed more than once to stay alive when lost in the quagmire muskeg and the frozen tundra.

Some of the late-coming cowboys of the air ridiculed Wien's caution, and employers and prospective customers often grumbled with impatience because their pilot would not take off into a cloudless sky. On such days, while his competitors were flying, Wien remained on the ground because he knew the weather at his destination likely was foul, or because the blue local sky was due to change and return would be impossible. Only on urgent occasions, such as when one of his scoffing competitors was overdue in bad weather that only Wien had known was coming, would he take off into marginal conditions.

Wien's character is at odds with the stereotyped image of the 1920s cloud buster. Certain of his deeds have been told and retold in newspapers, magazines, and in books ostensibly about other pilots. Yet the man remains an enigma. "One wonders how so mild and quiet a person could have taken part in all of the pioneer flights which he did," wrote Thomas M. Griffiths, head of the University of Denver Department of Geography in 1971.* Griffiths met Wien during a 1941 trip to the Kuskokwim and Yukon. Bob Reeve of Anchorage, the colorful old mud flats flyer who built Reeve Aleutian

* Letter to author, 1971.

Airways, says, "I have never heard Noel Wien raise his voice to any man, and I've seen him take guff that would make the Pope cuss his mother." °

Stoicism allowed Wien to endure reverses that would have crushed other men. There were financial losses, unfair competition, forgiven debtors. Noel, his wife, and his daughter all experienced illnesses that threatened time after time to drain the struggling family of its resources; he himself has lost an eye and been crippled by polio. But there are persons who have been close to the Wiens for decades who will for the first time learn of these crises when they read these pages.

A competitor once arranged for dangerous overloading of a plane Wien was scheduled to fly, and flew ahead to the small field that was Wien's destination in order to watch the hoped-for crack-up. He bragged around Fairbanks about his ingenuity. "We're good friends," Wien says today. "I see him every now and then and tell him hello and we talk a bit." In mature societies what this man did is defined as attempted murder, but Wien does not think of it as that. "It was a long time ago and he was just a young fellow trying to get along," he says.

Four hundred persons attended a banquet in 1964 observing the fortieth anniversary of Wien's arrival in Alaska. Unable to attend was former bush pilot Herman Lerdahl, who wrote his regrets to Wien and added, "Do you remember the first pilot's check you handed me for $257 commission, commenting that this was pretty good for two weeks' work? When I told you it was for a month's flying, you promptly tore it up and scribbled a check for $500 saying this was the least a Wien pilot should be paid for a month. Such a guy to work for!"

Bob Reeve, a tooth-and-nail scrapper of rare competence, still tells in astonishment how once when he was nearly broke he moved in on the tiny aviation business in Fairbanks and received life-saving help from Noel Wien, whose livelihood Reeve was trying to cut into. "It was dog eat dog in those days," Reeve says. "Nobody else would ever have done that. I got there in January of 1941. It was sixty below. I had my old Fairchild and enough money for a month's rent. Noel actually turned over some of his business to me, and he and I flew supplies into a mine in the Chandalar country.

° Interview with author in Anchorage, 1969.

"Noel's generosity to me was like nothing ever seen before in those cutthroat days. Why, I've had twenty-one, forced landings in Alaska and in only three of them was anybody searching for me. When they heard a competitor was down, there was a moment of glee. All except Noel Wien. And he was a tremendous airman. He had perfect timing, perfect coordination."

Sam O. White is a giant of a man who left his home state of Maine in 1922 because "it was getting crowded out there." He went to Alaska and put his foot in just about every square mile of it, walking for the Coast & Geodetic Survey and later for the Alaska Game Commission. "I came down the Yukon in a canoe one time to Eagle," White said, "and started walking to Fairbanks." That is a stroll of about two hundred miles through mountains. "About halfway there this airplane flew over me and I figured, 'You know, that fellow's gonna be in Fairbanks in about an hour and it'll take me about a week.' That was that. I started taking flying lessons from Noel and his brother Ralph and got me a plane." °

White says that he was most impressed by Noel Wien's honesty. "That went right on through the years. This was the basis of his whole life. A man you could rely on. And I don't believe there was ever anyone around here who could get everything out of an airplane like Noel Wien did. It was like the wings were attached to his own shoulders."

Somewhere there is a story about a Ryan mechanic who was at the plant during the building of Lindbergh's plane.

"Did Lindbergh do much talking?" the mechanic was asked.

"Not too much."

"What kinds of things would he say?"

"Come to think of it, well, he didn't talk at all." Some people could say the same about Noel Wien, who is so taciturn as to be a genuine "Yep" and "Nope" man. Wien does not think of the great flights he made as anything but routine workaday flying. Their historical and economic—much less their philosophical—meaning is not for him to ponder. But he still knows the horsepower of every engine he ever heard of, or the temperature off Uelen, Siberia, at 10:30 A.M. on March 9, 1929; and he can look down through a cloud peephole from a jet flying at twenty-eight thousand feet above the featureless muskeg of Minto Flats and tell you exactly where you

_____
° Interview with author in Fairbanks, 1969.

are. He seems to think like the ancient Eskimo, who, it is said, put words only to concrete objects, having a different word for each of the dozens of physical variations in snow and ice but none for any abstraction.

Noel Wien wanted to fly, and only to fly. He did not envision founding an airline that has grown from biplane Standards to Boeing 737 jets, or pulling a primitive land from the stone age to the air age, or becoming a certified international hero. He wanted to fly, only to fly. His gratifications from flying might be what psychiatrist Douglas Bond has described as the "secret experience" of the devoted flyer whose "dependence upon flying becomes virtually an addiction." Such men, Bond wrote, are inarticulate about flying, and their inarticulateness "is indicative of the unconsciousness of those [needs] that are satisfied." ° Perhaps for this reason Wien cannot explain what motivated him to fly and to continue to fly and what yearnings in him were satisfied by flying.

Sir Gordon Taylor has written that "the silent he-man, fearless and therefore upon whom impressions do not register, is a menace in the air. His days are numbered." † Silent, like Wien, he may be, but no unimpressionable man can survive forty years of Alaska flying. Is Wien then a paragon, a flawless man? No. But in two years of research this writer was unable to elicit a negative word from people who knew Noel Wien.

I am a flyer too, although mentioning this in the same breath with the name Noel Wien is like letting drop to Tenzing Norkay that you have conquered the highest peak in New Jersey. I point out the fact merely because Bond also notes that among flyers there is a "separateness of themselves from others" which makes for a "unity of those who fly against those who do not. . . ." Perhaps Noel Wien and I share just a pinch of the secret experiences, enough to permit us to establish a unity for a little while.

IRA HARKEY

Reno, Nevada

° Douglas Danford Bond, *The Fear and Love of Flying* (New York: International Universities Press, 1952).
† *The Sky Beyond* (Boston: Houghton Mifflin, 1963).

CONTENTS

Contents

ILLUSTRATIONS

PART I

I. WHEELS

I liked geography and history better than anything, Noel said, because I could visualize going to all those countries. But I was a poor student in all of it, and the eighth grade was my last. They kept me back and made me do the eighth grade over. I know why. I had a mania for wheels, any kind of wheels, and automobiles and airplanes. As soon as I was old enough to read about automobiles and airplanes, I couldn't think of anything else. The first World War was in 1914, when I was fifteen, and I began to read about those pilots—Richthofen, Mannock, and Fonck. I knew them all from the Duluth *Tribune*.

We took the *Saturday Evening Post* also, and after my father and mother had read it, I would read about the flying and then read the automobile advertisements over and over. To see the pictures of those beautiful cars! How I longed to drive them. I always pretended I was behind the wheel when I drove the team of horses pulling the harrow or plow or hay rake or binder. I had a mania for getting everything on the button, just exactly right. I didn't let the reins go slack, but kept them tight and kept the horses exactly in the right direction so the cutter or binder didn't overlap and didn't miss any grain either, going exactly down the edge of the last swath.

I just wanted to drive things and to drive them perfect. It was in my blood. In my mind I was driving continuously. I didn't concentrate in school. I just sat there waiting for the next automobile or truck to come along, blowing dust. They were the

3

most wonderful things you can imagine, the beautiful shape of the hoods and wheels. I would run out as soon as we were dismissed and study the tire tracks in the dirt of the road. Firestone had "Firestone" written in the treads, and Goodyear had a diamond tread.

The road was put in in 1910, and sometimes cars would come up from the Iron Range, from Virginia, Hibbing, Chisholm, and Evelyth. The fascinating noises they made, too, their motors roaring and popping. It was wonderful. After a rain I could see long streaks of tire treads and wonder if I could do better, if I could drive straighter than they had. And after the first light snowfall in the autumn the tracks would be easy to study. I was used to plain old wagon tracks, and these rounded rubber tires and their patterns left a different impression on the road and certainly left an impression on me.

When I was about eight, the other kids would go up the road and over the bridge to the school and play basketball at the hoop in the yard. I seldom went because I found an old bicycle Pa had had in Wisconsin. I remember working for hours and hours trying to put it into shape to ride. I just had to ride something with rubber tires and pretend it was an automobile. I got the bicycle to where it would move, but the biggest trouble was those rubber tires. They wouldn't hold air long. They would give me a ride of maybe three hundred feet down the road and back and then I'd have to pump them up. Another turn and another pump. Then I'd have to take the tires off and try to stuff them with something—old rags, in the holes in the inner tubes and between the casings—and take off again riding and pumping.

The place where I was born was Lake Nebagamon in Wisconsin, but in 1905 when I was six, Pa moved us and Ma up to land he was homesteading six miles west of Ashawa in northern Minnesota. It's called Cook now. Nebagamon was a drinking, cursing, fighting lumber town and he wanted to get us away from that and onto a farm where he could be his own boss. He got the house built one summer. He had been a finished carpenter in Norway, where he was born in 1869. It was a little different than most log houses, with spruce poles peeled and then stood on end, not laid lengthwise.

We had a main door that went into the kitchen. We used a wood-burning kitchen stove with four covers on top and the oven underneath. The bedroom was divided in two: my folks had one side, and the five kids crowded into the other, sleeping maybe three in a bed at first. Three and two. Later we would sleep in the attic upstairs. We had a drum-type heater in the bedroom that laid over like a fifty-gallon drum. In the attic it was freezing.

Coming up from Wisconsin, we got to the farm by river from Ashawa, in a big wooden scow, Ma and the five children with two men to row and carry over the portages. It was about ten miles. Pa could make the finest skis, but he couldn't find work as a carpenter. For six or seven years he worked for the lumber company in Virginia, about thirty miles south, and would come home every two or three months, walking the last six miles. Before he left again he would lay out all the work he expected to be done by the time he got back. We cleared off about seventy acres before I left the farm. During the winter the temperature could get as low as thirty below. To heat the house we helped our mother cut wood; we sawed down the trees and cut them up with handsaws or bucksaws.

When I was about ten I got to steer a car. A fellow from Cook came out with an Elcar, a little four-cylinder, and tried to get Pa to take a ride with him.

"I'm not ready to buy anything," Pa told him, "and I don't need to go anywhere. So why should I take a ride?"

He didn't want to encourage the fellow to sell him one. The man invited me and Ralph and took us for a little ride. Then he let me get behind the wheel and steer it. He worked the pedals and all I did was steer. I was small. I couldn't tell where I was going. It was one of the great times of my life. For a long time after that I dreamed at night about driving and steering, worrying that I couldn't see and couldn't steer straight and might slip off the rut into the ditch.

Ma was born in Sweden in 1879, in Dollernack or something like that. My dad was born in Dokka, Norway. After they were married, Ma had to speak Norwegian and go to the Norwegian church and cook Norwegian food. She spoke Swedish sometimes at home only to us. When we first went to school, my older brother Ralph and I, the teacher sent home a note after a few days and said my parents would have to do something about helping their children to speak English. She said we couldn't understand anything in school and nobody could understand us. Pa was home then and he announced that from now on only English in the house at any time, only English anywhere. His word was law and we immediately obeyed.

Pa had a big moustache and wide-open blue eyes and looked a little severe. His speech was quick and rough. He meant business. He was about five foot seven and stocky. He was schooled in the old country. You do everything just right, always the same way, in handling a saw, driving a mule, putting a wood planer down. You worked, you didn't talk and giggle, and you didn't ask questions. He didn't have time for foolishness like that. You just did what he said. He didn't spank much but when he did, it was a real whipping. He taught us to work hard, to do things right, and, most of all, never to drink whiskey.

My mother was tall, about five foot six, and quite slender, although she got heavy in her later years—but she always seemed slender to me. She was a blond and nice-looking. Her voice was soft and pleasant and she was very patient. We would run to her when we were in trouble and we weren't afraid to ask her questions. We walked about four miles to the Norwegian Lutheran Church with her. She was a remarkable woman who read the doctor book and understood all of it and cured us of everything we got. Later she got a camera and taught herself how to take pictures and how to develop them herself. She taught me, too.

But she taught us mainly to never take advantage of anybody weaker than us, never to fight, to take care of our health, and to try to be with religious people. She told us this all the time when my dad wasn't there to hear it. You talk too much about making them good, he'd tell her. If we worked hard, did our chores, wiped our feet before coming in the house, and did the things he told us to, that was enough. My mother kept the garden and we boys chopped, grubbed with a grub hoe around the roots of the trees, and when Pa came home, he pulled the stumps with the team or dynamited them.

Fridtjof (Fritz) Wien, two years younger than Noel, said their father was an accomplished musician who made a beautiful violin and also played the cornet. He had traveled Norway as a musician, but could not find a musical job in the United States. "He wouldn't teach us kids," Fritz said, "and he said it was just a bunch of racket. He told my mother to keep us quiet, he wanted to sleep. We'd start tooting the cornet sometimes when he was home from Virginia, and he couldn't stand it. He wanted to sleep. It wasn't more than one or two days he could stay at home. We just loved to hear him play the horn, but he'd lost a tooth and when he'd hit a sour note that was it. He wouldn't play anymore. He was a perfectionist."

When I was seventeen, Noel said, a few years after Pa had quit his job in Virginia and moved to the farm, he was able to get a payment plan from a dealer at Cook and buy a car. Oh, boy, what a car! It was a Model T that had been used a little. It had straight fenders in front with a little dip at the very tip. Four cylinders, three pedals, planetary transmission, open, with a top that would go up and side curtains. The dealer taught Pa to drive, then Pa taught Ralph. Ralph was nineteen then. But he wouldn't let me learn and I nearly died. Later we all learned, but for a time all I could do was look and feel. That brass radiator sure looked wonderful coming down the road, and the whole car would shine in the sun.

So we had a car of our own now, a real car, but I couldn't drive it. I went back into the newspaper and the *Saturday Evening Post* even more, reading about and studying the ads on the Pierce Arrow, Mitchell, Stutz, and the other fine cars. I used to daydream about how great it would be to drive into the yard there on the farm with one of those fine, smooth-running six-cylinder cars with its straight, sweeping lines and the beauty of its paint job. Long, slick, and smooth.

I read all about the airplane flights and the war aces, but I began to be more interested now in the kind of planes they flew and the motors in them. The British S.E.5, the Jenny, the Standard, not like the conversion I first flew in Alaska, but the original. The Hispano-Suiza V-8 motor, the Renault, the rotary LeRhone, the Monosoupape Gnome, the Rolls-Royce, and later the Liberty and the OX-5. My grades in school were low, but I could recite the names of all the airplanes and their engines and what war pilots flew them. I could tell you the name of any car on sight at a distance. I remember talking a lot with Ralph, but he wasn't as enthusiastic about flying as I was then. After the war when Curtiss Jennies and the Standards started flying around the country in flying circuses and carrying passengers and doing stunts, I told Ralph that I was determined to learn to fly and to spend the rest of my life flying.

"It's dangerous, Nonie," Ralph would say, and he'd remind me of the old-timers, the war heroes, who were being killed in stunt flying.

"I wouldn't mind that," I told Ralph. "It would be an honor to be killed in an airplane." This was mighty big talk for a little farmer boy with no money.

Pa would sometimes take us to the Saint Louis County Fair, thirty-five miles over a gravel road to Hibbing. There was exhibition flying, usually in OX-5 Jennies, but Pa was more interested in farm machinery and other farm things, so he'd never drive us out to the flying field. This usually was a farmer's field where the planes landed and took off with passengers after doing stunts. He said it was all foolishness, that an airplane wasn't any use like a tractor or a mule. I never did get to see and feel an airplane then, but I did see flying and stunting in the air and it made me more determined than ever to see and feel an airplane.

The summer I was seventeen I got my first job away from the farm. This was raking rocks on the road, working for the county, making $1.50 a day. Fifteen cents an hour for ten hours. I finished the eighth grade, for the second time, when I was eighteen, and that summer I got a great job driving a GMC dump truck, two-ton, hauling the rocks instead of raking them, and at $2.50 a day, big money.

Fritz Wien said his brother Noel was given the hardest truck to drive. But he studied it and practiced it so he could make a clean shift without grinding the gears. It seemed impossible for anyone else to get those gears to mesh, but Noel managed to do it. He took pride in being able to make the slow old truck keep up with the others.

After a year, I'd saved nearly eight hundred dollars, almost all I'd earned. The day I turned twenty-one, I took all this money and bought a car, a 1920-model Overland touring car, four cylinders, five-passenger, with a folding top. Pa tried hard to get me not to buy this car, but I was twenty-one and had my own money and a job.

"It's not good business," Pa said, "for a young fellow to spend everything he has on a car. You don't need it. You will need that money sometime, to get married on maybe."

But for me there wasn't any choice here, a car or getting married. I'd take the car any day.

Fritz said you didn't find Noel abusing that car, sluing around corners and such. He kept it spotless and shiny, spending all his spare time pampering it. When he sold it, the car was still like new.

I lost my truck-driving job the second winter and had to put the Overland up for sale. I left it with brother Ralph to try to sell. I had itchy feet about then, so I decided to go down to Duluth and see if I could find a job. Duluth was a big city where maybe there was an airplane I could see and touch and think about. I got a job in a harness factory, riveting the buckles on and oiling the leather to make it black. I was back to making $1.50 a day, living in the YMCA and eating one meal a day in a cafe. I never did see an airplane.

Finally Ralph sold the car for me for seven hundred dollars and with that money I went down to Minneapolis and Saint Paul to enter the William Hood Dunwoodie Institute to learn about airplanes. But when I got there, I found out they didn't have an airplane course, just courses for bakers, electricians, and auto mechanics. Nobody there even knew where there were any airplanes or how to get to an airport. I entered the mechanics course and got a room in a cheap rooming house and bought loaves of bread from the baking school to eat. That was in the fall of 1920.

At the auto show a couple of months later, sitting on a stand at the entrance was a shining, wonderful Curtiss OX-5 airplane motor. A sign on it said "Curtiss Northwest Airplane Co., Snelling and Larpenteur Avenue," and that this company had a flying school. I knew there was a streetcar line on Larpenteur, so I didn't lose any time getting on a car. The line ended about a mile away from the airfield, and I walked the rest of the way.

2. WINGS

Life, or all of it that was ever to matter to Noel Wien, began that May day in 1921 when he saw an airplane near enough to touch, and then actually did touch it, feeling the smoothness and the resisting springiness of the fabric, smelling the nitrate dope and the gasoline and the metal, examining the tires (disappointed to find them not etched with some mysterious pattern), and hanging on the propeller.

The landing field looked like a hayfield. At one corner were a barnlike wooden building with a strange cambered roof and a shacklike smaller building beside it. Noel walked across the narrow end of the field and, fighting shyness, stopped a few yards away from a group of men who were sitting and standing, engaged in loud talk in front of the one-room building. Noel could see the noses of airplanes poking from the barn. The bantering men were pilots, mechanics, and students in between instruction hops, charter flights, and maintenance work, practicing the eternal swapping of aerial lies that had already become a ritual at airfields.

The talk stopped and they turned and looked at the husky stranger who had walked stiffly toward them. Noel's uncertainty in this strange world brought a flush to his face and he almost turned away and retreated. Before he could do so, a man stepped from the group and Noel was face to face with something as glamorous as the flying machines themselves: a flying man, slim, erect, commanding, confident—all the things Noel knew he was not—dressed in khaki military shirt, gray twill riding breeches, and glistening cavalry boots.

"I'm Major Miller," he told Noel. "Can I help?" This was Major

Ray S. Miller, even then a famous man. He is credited with being the originator of the concept of aerial squadrons within state national guards. With another advocate he had gone to Washington and cajoled Brigadier General Billy Mitchell and other Army aviation officials into supporting their proposal. Miller organized and led the 109th Minnesota Air Squadron, the first air guard unit in the nation. He was thirty years old when Noel met him.

Noel dropped his gaze before Miller's and scuffed a shoe in the dust. "I just thought I'd look at an airplane, if that would be all right."

"It is, certainly it is," Miller replied briskly, sensing a potential customer in the sturdy, blond young man. "Look all you want," he invited. Next after looking and touching, Miller knew, often came a demonstration ride.

Noel looked all the rest of that day, diffidently keeping out of the way of the flying people, feeling the contrasting textures of the cloth covering, the rubber tires, the metal engines, the tight wires, the smooth struts.

They were doing a good business, teaching students and fellows who had bought planes. I watched them cranking up the propellers, getting in the cockpits, running the motors up and taking off, blowing dust back over everything and flying overhead. It was wonderful. All that noise! I walked back to the streetcar line that night and went to my room, but I never went back to Dunwoodie Institute to finish my course. The next day I went back to the airport and hung around all day. The day after that I went again and hung around all day sizing up things. I met the pilots. There were four of them.

I was too backward to tell them I wanted to learn to fly. They might have laughed at me. And I didn't ask any questions because I remember my dad telling us to quit cackling and let him work. At that time, anyway, I didn't have all the money from the Overland car being sold and had to wait for Ralph to get the rest of it and send it to me. I didn't want to ask questions also because I didn't want them to think I was stupid. So I just hung around and kept out of the way and watched and sized up and listened to what they talked about.

Major Miller was always pleasant to me, telling me hello and asking if there was anything he could do for me. One day I told him I had this money coming and he knew that what I wanted was to learn to fly. He said it would cost me forty dollars an hour to learn and that it would take eight hours. He could give me a demonstration hop for ten dollars. I gave him the ten and we went out to the Jenny on the line. I got in the back seat and Major Miller showed me how to put on the safety belt. It was very wide web material with a heavy buckle. He told me to keep this tight around me at all times.

They had blocks in front of the wheels and a mechanic came out of the hangar and spun the propeller and the motor started off with a big roar. That OX-5 motor had opened ports on each side and the exhaust came back and I breathed it. I gulped it in, it smelled so good! Major Miller gave her some more gas and we moved forward. Then he started off with a full roar. The tail came up and we lifted straight off the ground. I can't describe that thrill. We went straight on up and then out over the country.

I didn't know what was coming. Later I learned that the idea was to always take a new person up for his first hop and find out if he has what it takes by putting him through all the stunts—loops, wingovers, spins, stalls. If he got sick or yelled for the pilot to stop, you knew he maybe wouldn't make a pilot. We did two loops in succession, then a wingover and still had altitude enough for a short spin. He pulled up into a stall, pulled the power off, and *ffzzztt*, the Jenny would spin. After the first loop I was thrilled. It was the greatest thing that had ever happened to me.

I looked around at the country below and was amazed to see how fine everything looked. The lines, the roads, the fields, the different colors and patterns of hayfields, corn, grain coming up. I couldn't find the airfield anywhere, even though it was two twenty-acre fields long.

My heart came up and my stomach went down every time we went down for another loop and the wires began to sing. You had to dive a Jenny wide open to get speed for a loop. It was the greatest sensation I had ever had. Here I was flying and being stunted, a thing I had wished for since 1914, for seven years. It takes your breath, your heart comes up, and it is great. I wished Ralph could see me now.

For Noel, the twenty minutes of his first flight were over too soon. But they were enough to confirm his seven-year longing for wings. The farm boy had escaped the earth. Soaring free was everything that he had anticipated it would be. It was a sublime experience. He remembered his words to Ralph of years before and he knew that no matter how melodramatic they sounded, they still were true. He would rather die in an airplane than live down below and never fly. He had made no mistake. The twenty-minute flight had given him his answer to the question of what he should do with his life.

Miller also received an answer. After each maneuver he had looked back at Noel to try to read in his expression his reaction. In his work as an instructor, Miller had more than once seen terror in the back cockpit after a stall or a loop, not infrequently he had heard screams, and more than once a prospect had pleaded to be returned to earth immediately. Sometimes he had heard screams of another kind, of exultation. His passenger this day, the phlegmatic Noel Wien, had made no sound at all. He had spent the twenty minutes of zooming and plummeting, twisting and rolling, snapping and spinning, with a grin on his face. It was still there when he left the cockpit and told Miller that he wanted to learn to fly. The date was May 6, 1921.

He had six hundred dollars. The money from the Overland had come from Ralph, and now he could afford the three hundred twenty dollars for eight hours of instruction, enough to gain the proficiency to solo. He might be flat broke by the time he was ready to solo. But why worry about that? One thing at a time was Noel's unspoken attitude toward life; make the immediate decision and attend to consequences as they arise. His decision to proceed with flight instruction began a period of good fortune during which at every seeming dead-end a new road opened up. He found one job after another; he did not join the leisure class, but he ate and, above all, he flew.

There was no problem scheduling the new student. Four pilots at Curtiss Northwest were eager to fly instruction. Between teaching hops these experienced men were expected to fly charter and do anything else needing to be done, but they were paid only for instructing. To make enough to live on, from time to time they would take flying and mechanical jobs across the Mississippi at

Wold-Chamberlain Field, where Minneapolis–Saint Paul International Airport is now.

Miller liked the new student's unemotional, matter-of-fact attitude. Putting a hand on Noel's shoulder, he said, "Come back at nine in the morning. We will make one flight a day for the first few days. After we get going, we can take fifteen minutes in the forenoon and fifteen in the afternoon. But it is a waste of money to rush it.

"This is a complicated business, learning to fly. You will be using your hands and feet—and your head—to do things you have never done before. It takes time. There is much to learn and so much practice needed. It is not wise to give you too much at any one time. If you rest after a new maneuver is shown, it will come back that much easier to you next time. How will you pay?"

Listening to Major Miller talk about flying lessons had taken Noel's mind into the blue. It was a few seconds before he realized he had been asked a question. "What do you mean?" he asked.

"Well, the training is forty dollars an hour. Do you want to pay by the hour?"

Noel said he thought he would pay by the hour, forty dollars for four fifteen-minute hops in advance. With the money in hand, he was an hour early for his first lesson the next morning.

Before my first lesson, Major Miller showed me how the controls work. The ailerons do the tipping, one wing up and the other down. The four movements of the control stick, forward, back, left, right. The rudder bar for left and right. The stick was very sensitive. He told me something of the science of flight, how the wind flows over and under the wing, pushing it up and sucking it up at the same time, about lift and drag.

There were two cockpits. He showed me the oil pressure gauge and told me if the needle went down to zero that meant the motor was going to quit and the only thing to do was shut off the motor before it was ruined and land the ship no matter where you were. He showed me the other instruments, the tachometer, water temperature, and altimeter. The altimeter had one hand on a dial that was marked off in one-hundred-foot divisions. Any kind of error in it would put you a couple hundred feet off. That's all the instruments there were. There wasn't any airspeed indicator, but later I saw some Jennies with a little gadget with a needle pointer that was attached out on a strut. And some Jennies even then had a compass on the dash.

There were no brakes. The throttle was on the upper longeron on the right side of the cockpit, so you handled the stick with your left hand. I had to learn all over again when I first flew a plane with a lefthand throttle. The student sat in the back cockpit so he could see the instructor's hand signals or the instructor could yell something back to the student. There wasn't any gosport tube to talk through, and the noise of the motor and the wires was so loud that the student couldn't talk to him.

The Curtiss Jenny in its several models, especially the JN-4 series, is one of the dozen most famous aircraft ever built in the United States. A World War I trainer, it was the learning tool for the second generation of American airmen. It was the plane that bought bread and butter for the barnstormers, joyhoppers, and gypsies who swooped around the country during the decade of the twenties, popularizing aviation in every backwoods cranny.

About nine thousand Jennies in all variations were built, including a Canadian version called the Canuck that had ailerons on both the top and bottom wings. The craft weighed 1,580 pounds empty, 2,130 loaded, giving her a capacity of 550 pounds. And that included oil and gasoline, pilot, passenger, baggage, and the screwdriver and pliers tucked here and there in the cockpits. High speed at sea level was seventy-five miles an hour, produced by the equally famous Curtiss OX-5 eight-cylinder, water-cooled engine that delivered ninety horsepower at 1,400 revolutions a minute. Only the exceptionally pampered one would produce more than 1,300 r.p.m., though.

Jenny's nose was flat, her two wings were joined together and kept apart by twelve struts and a maze of wires. The outer struts poked about eighteen inches above the top wing and were called cabane struts or masts. They were guyed by wires and the handholds they presented made the Jenny the choicest vehicle for wingwalkers. Semicircular skids like half hoops hung under the outer panels of the lower wings, designed to give protection in ground loops, but giving daredevils more handholds, too. Her wheels hung snug beneath the leading edge of her lower wing, imparting a stumpy-legged appearance. Viewed from the side, the bottom of her fuselage forward of the wings slanted upward toward the slab nose, giving her a rather stylish look. There was a jaunty stagger to her wings. Some still had the old-fashioned skids forward of the wheels that looked like chair rockers and prevented noseovers.

She seemed fragile, with that model-plane aspect of early aircraft, but with patching up and, as the saying went, baling wire and chewing gum applied in cornfields and dry gulches, she was durable enough to withstand the learning throes of many of America's celebrated aviators, and then to give them livelihood.

A Jenny still in her crate for shipment could be bought for about three hundred dollars by those fortunate enough to find out where and when the government's surplus sales were held. Assembled and with some use on her. she sold for about twenty-five hundred dollars on the commercial market. She was unqualifiedly beautiful to all the young Noel Wiens of the early 1920s, and she remains unqualifiedly beautiful still to the aviation veterans and afficionados of today who see her only in drawings, old photographs, museums, and in the loving eyes of memory.

---

3. STUDENT

Miller finished his lecture to Noel and said, "All right, Wien, now I am going to take you up and we will see if you can make a flyer."

He told Noel to get into the after cockpit. Then, with one foot in the stirrup hole he hung to the plane and pointed out a few things in Noel's cockpit.

"Put your feet very lightly on the rudder bar, that horizontal board down there at the end of those planks in front of you. Put your hand very lightly on the stick, your left hand. No, not on the top of the stick. Grip it like a bottle of soda pop. Just touch very lightly with your fingers and feet, very lightly. Try to notice what the airplane does when the rudder and stick move. You do not move them. I do. You just feel. Do not touch the throttle."

Instructor and pupil were touching on a critical point. Many a plane had spun in and killed its occupants when a student froze on the controls and the instructor could not overpower him. Noel himself was to crash for this reason the next year while trying to instruct a bull-strong, mule-headed blacksmith. Miller had already tested his new student, however, had seen him respond with a satisfied grin to every sensation flying could give. He judged Noel as a no-panic personality.

The cockpit seat was not adjustable, but it was perfectly positioned for Noel's then-average height of five feet nine inches. Miller watched as Noel wrapped and buckled the webbed canvas safety belt around his middle, and then helped him put on a well-worn brown leather helmet that fit tightly around his head and over his ears and buckled under his chin, leaving only the flat of his face exposed. Most of that disappeared beneath large, padded goggles.

Miller then climbed into the front cockpit, waggled the ailerons, elevators, and rudder, and signaled to a mechanic to spin the prop. As the motor caught and blue smoke wafted through the open ports from each bank of the OX-5, Noel sniffed again the exhaust smell that to him would always mean airplane and serene, indescribable joy.

Miller ran the motor up to 800 r.p.m. and let it tick over awhile. Blocks were pulled. Two mechanics lifted the airplane's tail and turned the Jenny's nose into the wind. Miller moved the throttle forward and in seconds the Jenny was airborne.

We went fast over the telephone wires around the edge of the field and turned left, and I could see Saint Paul off to the right. We went on up to thirty-five hundred feet and over open fields north of the airfield. We did air work, handling the plane in straight and level flight, gentle banks and turns to the left and right. I kept my hand and feet very lightly on the controls. Before every maneuver Major Miller would put his hands up and I got the idea that he was showing me what his signals would mean.

Both hands held palms up with a pushing up motion meant, "Get the nose up." One palm up and hand raised higher than the other meant, "Raise that wing." Both hands palms down meant, "Lower the nose." A hand over an ear meant, "You're slipping in that direction, put in some corrective rudder." This last was very important, as you just had to make coordinated turns in a Jenny or you'd spin in at low altitudes.

Major Miller was a fine fellow and a good instructor. He wanted an instant response to his signals. He was an intelligent man and the kind of fellow you wanted to please, so you tried extra hard to do well.

The first lesson was over too soon for me. Major Miller came in and made a perfect landing. He always made a perfect three-point. Both wheels and the tail skid touched down at the exact same time without bouncing. That was the test of skill of every pilot. You tried to stall inches above the ground, stick it on and stay there and stop.

On the second hour, after I had pretty well gotten onto straight and level, banks and turns and stalls, Major Miller showed me how to do a wingover. Put the nose down a bit, pull up, twist the rudder, keep the speed up with power, and turn over on the side. The speed would keep the airplane in a curve above the stall speed.

Then we did some spins. With power, the rudder full over, and the stick full back, the Jenny would drop off into a spin immediately from stall. Then you push the nose down to get speed and put in opposite rudder at the same time and pull power half off. Gently you pull back on the stick to pull out of the dive after the spin has stopped. My third hour was a real thriller, as Major Miller let me do a loop.

Miller had found his most apt pupil. Wien's perfect coordination allowed him to perform the most precisely timed maneuver from the first attempt. Wingovers, spins and recoveries he performed by the book. Only the loop caused him trouble, and only once at that.

"Wien, when you make a loop," Miller had told him, "don't pull back too steep. Keep full power on, lower the nose until you get a lot of speed, and then pull back nice and gentle on the stick. When you reach the top, pull the stick all the way back smartly. That will keep you from hanging and will flip the plane over the top."

Noel handled the plane perfectly until he was over the top. Then he relaxed as the wonderful stomach-head sensation came. The Jenny dropped a wing and approached a stall. When a Jenny stalled, a spin was only a split second behind.

Miller kicked in rudder and the plane recovered, but dropped off the bottom of the loop to one side of the vertical plane. A bad job. Noel instantly set up another loop, and this show of initiative pleased Miller. Power on full, nose down. Gradual pull on the stick, nose pointed at heaven, stick full back, feet firmly on the rudder bar making minute, rapid, gentle corrections. Nose over the top, a swift drop, gentle back pressure, and a perfect loop executed within the vertical entry plane. Noel was to become so expert a stunt flyer that he could carry a standing wingwalker through a loop without causing enough G-force to make his knees dip.

Then Major Miller gave me another thrill. In the first two hours I had followed him through on landings also. We would set up for the field quite a ways out and start a glide. His hands were busy giving me signals, to nose down a little or to get it up and put on power if we were coming in too low over the telephone wires and the barbed wire cattle fence. Then we'd shut off the power over the lines and nose down. At that point he would take over complete control and land.

But this time, the third hour, he let me come all the way down. He put his hands up off the controls and helped me only with giving signals. I made long, gentle turns—no tight turns—at five hundred feet to set up a long, final glide to the airport. Approach speed and cruising speed were about the same in a Jenny, so you kept power on and the nose down almost to the ground. I came over the telephone wires at about sixty. I guess it was sixty—there was no airspeed indicator. The gauge was the sound of the wind in the airplane's wires. You learned that very fast.

When you were slowing up, there was a softening of the whistle, a softer, lower pitch as you reduced speed just a little. You had to keep that whistle going softly, because if it stopped, you had already stalled and were going down ready or not. There was a different kind of sing with power on than with power off, or half-power on.

Different ships made different peculiar sounds, and even one OX-5 Jenny or Standard would sound a bit different than other OX-5 Jennies and Standards.

I kept about twenty-five miles an hour above stall over the telephone wires, then shut the power. When you cut power on a Jenny, it would drop like a rock. There was little glide in them. Major Miller began signaling to keep the nose down, not to flare too soon. Then I was letting the wheels drop a bit too quick and had to pull back just a little. Major Miller gave me the exact second when to ease the nose up to a stall and make a three-point. I had to respond in a split second. The wires sang all the way down, changing sound, and when you started pulling the tail down the sing would gradually stop. You wanted it to stop a few inches above the ground when you were in a landing attitude with nose a little up.

The intent young student made a perfect three-point landing. As they rolled out toward the hangar, Miller turned around and nodded approval. They taxied the Jenny up to the dusty spot in front of the hangar, pulled the throttle back, and cut the switch. The OX-5 backfired and died. The stick in Noel's cockpit moved backward as Miller secured his safety belt around the stick in his cockpit. Pulling the stick back raised the tail flippers, to prevent the tail's lifting in the wash when the engine was again started. More than one unfortunate Jenny pilot propping his own plane without the help of a mechanic had watched the light tail rise up in the motor wash and keep on ascending until the aircraft sat on its nose trying to fly into the ground with a splintered propeller.

"Fine landing, Wien," Miller said after they had climbed from the Jenny. "You're really getting it. You have had three hours now. If this was the Army, I would be thinking about soloing you." Years later Miller explained this statement by saying the Curtiss school wanted to go by the book—eight hours before solo for all students—both because that was the general practice and because the school needed every student hour it could sell. "We needed to stay in business, so I gave Wien the full eight hours, moving on into forced landings very early."

As a schoolboy, Noel had been a poor pupil, barely moving ahead from grade to grade and being forced to repeat the eighth. His thoughts had been on wheels, automobiles, and airplanes. But now that his mind and body at last had come together in the cockpit of an airplane, he became a ready scholar. He not only learned to perform the coordinated mechanical acts necessary for putting an aircraft into flight and keeping it there, but absorbed all the nuances of the world of flight—its sounds, smells, sights, and sensations— that give the gifted aviator his total awareness of sky, ground, aircraft, and self, and their lifesaving indivisibility.

In the seat of his pants he feels and in the sing of the wires he hears a coming stall and instinctively lowers the nose, or flattens the bank, or increases the power. Piloting, he ranges a succession of visual checkpoints along the imaginary line of his course and then senses the wind drift and the correction and enters it all without deliberate thought. A higher or lower pitch in the rattle of the motor or the hum of the wires signals a change in performance or a coming danger, and instinct prepares to meet it. Suitable spots for emergency landings continually come into the consciousness, are recorded there without effort, and are then replaced by others as they come into sight ahead. From movement of leaves, bending of grain, blowing of dirt, rippling of water, he knows always the direction of the surface wind so that when the need comes he can land into it, slowly.

"Spot your field first," Miller told him during forced-landing practice. "Pick out one straight ahead so that you can get there without banking and turning. Put your nose down immediately about forty-five degrees. Go straight ahead, no matter what, unless you are going into thick timber. Then it may be best to try to turn, but never more than forty-five degrees or you will spin in, and timber is better than a hole in the ground. In a takeoff emergency, you will have to go straight ahead, for you will not have enough altitude to turn around at all without spinning."

Miller demanded expert judgment in choosing the safest available landing spots and the highest proficiency in making emergency landings. At what seemed the most embarrassing times, Miller would suddenly cut the motor and shout in the sudden silence, "All right, Wien, where would you land?"

Wien learned to distinguish a high cornfield from a high grain field and both from grass and potatoes. A potato field made a good landing field, but grass was better. Cornfields had rows to break landing gear and cause noseovers. Grain was almost impossible to distinguish from grass at altitude, unless the grain was turning brown on top. Landing in clover, despite the happy popular metaphor, was not to be desired. Jenny had an axle between her wheels and forward-sloping struts connecting the gear to the fuselage. Deep clover was tough and would grasp the axle and struts and flip a Jenny over. She was so light on the tail that often it seemed she would nose up on whim. If there was more than a foot of cover of whatever kind, prepare for a round landing.

Wien soon was able to sense a skid in a turn. If there is too much rudder on the down side, the plane will skid uphill; and if the nose is down a bit, the Jenny will immediately spin. In banks, Miller said, look out each side of the airplane rapidly to see that the craft is not skidding. Sometimes you can feel a skid in the breeze on one side of your face. There was no turn-and-bank indicator in the Jenny to show the need for more or less rudder; you had only vision, seat of the pants, the breeze, and aviator's osmosis. What instrument told a pilot he was in proper attitude for a three-point landing? Just the memory of the plane's attitude as it sat on the ground, the angle its wings made with the level earth as you sat in the cockpit on the ground.

From the rear seat of a Jenny a pilot could see ahead only in diving. When you were a few seconds from touchdown and pulled the nose up to flare, besides watching to establish the three-point attitude, you had to be certain where you were going and that a crosswind was not preparing a surprise. Look ahead from each side of the cockpit. Rapidly.

Cheap automobile gasoline would foul the OX-5's plugs. Regular auto gas of about sixty-eight octane was usable, but aviation gas of seventy-two octane was far better. Hard water used in the radiator would cause a build-up of minerals and result in overheating. Rain water was the best coolant. In cold weather, alcohol had to be mixed with the water.

The OX-5 was designed to operate with the overheads uncowled. The top of the motor was open to the weather, the two V-banks of cylinders were exposed. Rain or contaminated fuel would fill her four jet wells with water and, as the Curtiss OX-5 maintenance manual warned, the "carburetor is unusually sensitive to water and foreign matter." If one bank of cylinders went out, Jenny was going down, because she would not fly on half her horsepower. Gasoline was supplied in barrels and cans, and wise pilots strained the fluid while filling up. The handiest strainer was a felt hat, and the gasoline-soggy hat, along with goggles, puttees, white scarves and riding breeches, became insignia of aviation in the twenties.

In his fifth hour of instruction, Wien made four perfect takeoffs and landings without even hand signals from Miller. He was ready for solo but instead continued on for eight full hours, polishing up stunt flying and emergency landings and absorbing the wisdom of his instructor. He was never to make an official solo flight, but was to become a pilot in command through accident and the necessity of saving his neck.

4. SOLO

I had about two hundred dollars left when I finished up my eight hours, and I needed much more than that to solo. The Jenny was worth twenty-eight hundred dollars, and I couldn't take it up alone unless I bought a bond to cover the loss if I cracked up. That was the custom in those days. The airplane companies didn't have insurance to cover people who didn't have fifty hours of solo time already. If a student couldn't buy a bond, the only other thing he could do to solo was buy a plane, and of course that was impossible for me.

So I stayed around the airfield for about a week and then got a lucky break. One morning I heard Major Miller and a fellow I hadn't seen before talking about how the fellow had just busted up his airplane. He was stunting out west of Saint Paul and left the stick in the front cockpit with his passenger. The passenger got scared, grabbed the stick, and braced himself in a frozen position. It was always a mistake to leave the stick in the front seat with a passenger, especially if you were stunting him. The stick was the handiest thing to grab onto for a handhold when the frightened passenger thought he was going to fall out.

Major Miller said, "Come here, Wien, I want you to meet E. W. Morrill. He might have something for you." Morrill was about twenty-five years old, had been a Navy pilot, and had about two hundred fifty hours in flying. He was about my height, but slim and thin-faced, and with that commanding front like Major Miller that I guess they got in the service or maybe from being educated.

Morrill had insurance and with the money from that he had bought another OX-5 Standard J-1 and was going out barnstorming again. The Standard was a biplane that looked a lot like the Jenny. The J-1 model had been converted by Curtiss from the original old World War I trainer plane. The front cockpit was widened out to take two people side by side. The Standard flew just about like the Jenny, but a little slower and carried a little less payload. It had skid hoops under the lower wing tips like the Jenny, but the cabane struts joined together like tent poles instead of being separate. The radiator wasn't in the nose but stuck up in the air in front of the upper wing like a squared-off stovepipe. It was a good stunt plane.

We shook hands, Morrill and I, and Major Miller told him that I was a good student and he was sure I could be of use to Morrill as a grease monkey and helper. "Wien has good character," Miller told him, "and is a serious and hard worker."

I could see that Major Miller had already told Morrill about me and suggested me as a helper so I could get in some flying. I wasn't going anywhere in Saint Paul, what with no money to solo and no way to get enough money soon. Morrill told me that as soon as he got the Standard hooked up—it was in a crate—he was heading out across country barnstorming and I was free to come along.

Wien had his first flying job. A job, but no pay. Morrill proposed to swap food and lodging for Wien's assistance in cross-country flying and maintenance of the airplane, and performance of general flunky duties.

On the morning of June 15, 1921, the newly hired aviator, cardboard suitcase in hand, reported to Morrill at Curtiss Northwest and learned that he and Morrill would have company on their junket. Mrs. Morrill, a pretty and cheery brunette, twenty-two years old, was going along. She and the new mechanic would ride side by side in the front cockpit. Her job would be to advertise her husband's stunt and joyhopping in the towns where they landed and to handle ground arrangements, such as scheduling of passenger hops. Unlike the wives of many aerial gypsies of the era, she did not wingwalk, parachute jump, or perform other stunts aloft.

For flying from town to town Mrs. Morrill dressed in men's trousers, a woman's blouse, warm coat, and helmet and goggles. Wien reported that first day dressed in the typical aviator's uniform: riding breeches, laced puttees, high shoes, a dark shirt, and a leather jacket. Breeches were safer than trousers, which could catch in the rudder bar and the rudder control wires and their turnbuckles that ran aft from the bar along each side of the cockpit.

Wien had not added a white scarf, the dashing ensemble touch usually affected by the barnstormer. "To tell the truth," he said, "I always thought that was a little sissy." He got the same effect by keeping his shirt and jacket buttoned under his chin. Morrill topped off his costume with a white scarf.

The new mechanic helped his boss roll their Standard onto the field and face her into the wind. Chocks were placed before the wheels. Wien and the young woman climbed into the front cockpit, stowing their suitcases at their feet. Room had been made by removal of the forward control stick. Morrill climbed into the after cockpit. "Switch off," he responded to the call of a helper standing by the propeller, pulling it through several times. "Contact!" the mechanic called, and "Contact!" the pilot replied as he turned the switch on. After a couple of "chuf-chufs," the motor caught, gave a spurt, sputtered, smoked blue, and then settled down to a steady roar. Morrill signaled to the mechanic to remove the blocks, pushed the throttle forward, and the plane began to move. Noel Wien, reddish about the ears over the forced cuddle with the young woman and still self-conscious about his new aviator's clothing, was off on his first hop as a flying professional—a grease monkey, true, but a professional nevertheless.

It was a beautiful day, and I just sort of drank in all the country we flew over. The Standard was pretty bogged down with the three of us and our grips, but it was safely within its limits. We went first to Willmar, about ninety miles west of Minneapolis, but we found out that nobody cared about airplanes there. The place had been worked over too much by barnstormers. So Morrill decided to leave his wife in a hotel at Willmar and go to Spicer and New London, places ten and fifteen miles north, on the chance that maybe others had missed them. He put the stick back into the front cockpit and after we took off, he let me fly.

When we got to Spicer, Morrill took over the stick and dived down at the town a few times, gunning the motor and making noise to attract attention, and then headed for a landing field that he had picked out. When I saw him nose down toward this field, I couldn't believe it. It was too small, only about six hundred feet square, with a fence on one side, a cornfield on one, and high trees on the other two. But Morrill was an experienced pilot, so I didn't start worrying then.

He tried to approach over the fence, which was lower than the corn and the trees. Ordinarily that makes sense. We overshot, came in too fast, and he gave it the gun and we went up and around again. He came in from the same side again, and again we were going too fast and had to pull up. I wondered why he didn't go on back to Willmar or look for a better place to land or else try to spot where the wind was coming from.

By now I could tell that he was trying to land with a crosswind a little from the rear, crosswind and downwind. It was a matter of knowing our relative movement with the lines of perspective going down ahead of the airplane to the spot where we had to put down. The tail was over to the right and the nose a little to the left when he would reduce power. He was crabbing to reach the field, but he didn't seem to know it and it wasn't slowing us down any. There was a quartering breeze maybe five miles an hour.

We were pulling up again and I saw that Morrill was going to try to land a third time from the same approach. His training in the Navy on larger fields had driven into him the thought that you should never start to stall before reaching your field. If he had shut off the power before we got to the fence, we would have been able to stall just over the fence and get down, even though we weren't going into the wind and getting its help to slow us down.

Morrill came around again. He banked and nosed down and set up for the fence again, flying the same way he had the first two times. He was still too fast, but over the fence I could feel him jiggling the stick and I knew he was feeling for a flare and was going to set us down. He wasn't pulling power off soon enough, but was trying to push the ship down, feeling for the ground. I knew that if we landed, we would already be halfway across that six-hundred-foot field and would roll across the field and crash into that corn. Even if we weren't hurt, we would crack the propeller and tear up the wings.

Instinctively I did something that a pilot should never do and maybe can get away with only once in his life. I took over. An unsoloed pilot with only eight hours of instruction, I took over from an experienced pilot in command who also owned the ship.

I reached down with my right hand and jammed the throttle forward. I took the joystick° in my left hand and put the nose down a bit to gain speed and then pulled up. We went across the field and just clipped the corn with our gear. As I pulled up over the cornfield and banked, I looked back at Morrill sort of expecting him to be yelling at me or maybe to whack me. But he stuck his arms straight up into the air to show me that I had the controls.

I had never flown a Standard before except for the straight and level in cross-country. I pulled on up to about five hundred feet, banked, and came into the field from the only direction I thought possible—from over the high trees instead of from over the low fence. That was the way some people would have thought was the hardest.

About fifty feet in the air, just over the maples and oaks, I cut power. We were about two hundred feet from the edge of the field. I put the nose down and down we went. At the last second I nosed up and we dumped into the field. I knew it was going to be a good landing even before we hit. I knew we weren't going to bounce. If we bounced, we might crash into the trees at the other end, because a plane flies a little between bounces and takes longer to stop. It was a good three-point landing. We rolled on, and with the rudder taking the wind—a Standard is so light on its tail—I was able to turn a little and stopped with one wing a few feet from the corn tassels.

° Aviators' slang for the stick by which the aircraft's attitude was controlled.

Wien cut the switch and looked back at the aircraft's owner, embarrassed at his audacity and apprehensive, expecting at least a verbal rebuke. But Morrill was even more man than he had shown before.

"Whew!" he exclaimed. "How in the devil did you know where the wind was coming from?"

"Well, I could feel it," Wien answered.

"I couldn't," Morrill was honest enough to admit. "That was a fine job."

It was. Wien had been in command; he had soloed. His quiet confidence in himself and his instinctive response to danger had led him to take over from the experienced pilot and land in a field where the older man could not. Equally important, after demonstrating his competence in the emergency, the new pilot still showed his employer his characteristic unassuming deference. Morrill, although chagrined, could not take offense.

"Get her out of here," Morrill ordered Wien, "and let's go back to Willmar. This field is too small for passenger hops."

Wien made a catercorner takeoff, neutralizing the breeze and having only the low fence to clear. Full power to three hundred feet, throttle back to 1,250, just above cruise revs for the gradual climb out, set cruise to Willmar. Solo! If there was exultation in the heart of the new pilot-in-command, there were no signs of it in his face and manner when he and Morrill deplaned at Willmar.

5. BARNSTORMER

"Hi, mister! You the aviator, ain't ya? Take me up in your airplane, please mister, will ya?"

Children followed him on the street, skipping alongside, pulling at his jacket sleeves, begging. No longer only a grease monkey in a one-plane gypsy outfit, the former Minnesota farm boy was now a pilot. After the expert landing in the field north of Willmar, Morrill "took a chance" and decided to allow Wien to fly half of their joyhops. By accident, Noel had become a barnstormer. Because he could not yet be covered by insurance until he had fifty hours solo, his boss was staking his three-thousand-dollar airplane on Noel's skill.

Neither pilots nor aircraft were licensed in those days, although some states soon began the practice of licensing ships. Anyone could stroll out to an airplane, climb in, and try to take off. Legally. There are such cases on record, and not just a few. The practical and sometimes unsolvable problem for serious would-be professional flyers was to find an owner who would let them fly his ship until enough hours had been accumulated to qualify for insurance. Because of his brilliant performance in the short field, Wien had found such an owner.

The Morrills and Noel worked their way westward across Minnesota and into South Dakota, following the rudimentary road maps of those days to such population centers as Clara City, Marshall, Verdi, Watertown, Clear Lake, Red Field, Stockholm. Morrill had not barnstormed before, but he knew that in order to make eating money they had to discover towns that had not been too well worked over by other flying wanderers. There were not many such towns, and those that remained were usually of less than three thousand population.

Arriving over a new town picked from the map, the flyers would dive the Standard at the town square, pull up into a slow roll, and fly over the area, gunning the motor. When they thought that their noise had stirred enough people, they would make a low pass and nose down for landing in a field already picked out.

"This was always the race track," Wien said, "if there was a race track. A half-mile track had a clear infield twelve hundred feet long, and that was the best of all landing spots. If there wasn't a race track in town, next best would be a field close to town that seemed to be clear of crops and cattle." A race track, being public property, had another advantage over a private field. On it there was no welcoming committee consisting of a farmer with his hand out for a landing fee.

Before touching down, they would drag the field, one looking to the left, the other to the right, alert for gopher holes and anthills. Gopher holes broke landing gear. They showed as darker spots in a field. Anthills caused ground loops. They usually could be detected by the shadows they threw on a field.

At towns where the airplane was still a novelty, people came running toward the place where the Standard had landed. In the rare community that had been bypassed somehow by the flying nomads, everybody came for a hop or to see the fantastic flying machine. Alternating with Morrill, Wien flew off with old, young, male, female, hale, hearty, and infirm.

After securing his two passengers into the front cockpit, Noel would ask, "Do you want to do any stunting? You might not like it." If they answered no, or if Noel sensed that they did not understand what stunting was when they answered yes, he would give them only a very level, sedate ride over the countryside and then land to take the next two passengers aboard. Frightening customers was bad for business.

Often a girl was reluctant to stunt, but her boyfriend, feeling the need for manly bluster, would demand that they be given the full treatment. Noel then would try a wingover. If the girl did not respond with hysterics, he would follow this with a loop. If there were no screams during the loop, and if the couple was not too heavy, he would come out of the loop into a spin. For a straight stunt ride, he would take only one passenger and the flight would be shorter than the sightseeing hop. More than one loud hero returned to earth a nauseated mouse.

Sundays were the best days. "People seemed more willing to spend then," Wien said. His log for the two-month tour shows that his best day brought fourteen hops, his worst six. Passengers paid $3.00 each. Under his new agreement with Morrill, Noel was to get half the fare paid by those he took up. Accounts were to be settled after the tour. Expenses for each of the three troupe members were about $1.50 a day for room and $4.00 for meals. Wien kept no record of his take. His only concern was with flying.

When he was not joyhopping, Noel would sometimes go up and stunt over town to try to draw more prospects out of the stores and wheatfields. Unlike many barnstormers, Morrill did not pass the hat after these stunts. He limited his business to passenger hops. He would not take small children or obvious drunks, and the authority evident in his personality allowed him to enforce these prohibitions.

The heat of the summer enveloped the land. It was dusty, grimy work, with the sting of gasoline on skin and the stain of oil and grease under fingernails. But there was also the smell of exhaust, the sing of the flying wires, the thrill of flight. Noel loved it, every second of it, and could joyfully have spent the rest of his life doing nothing else.

His flights were joyhops to his passengers and stunts to the spectators below, but to Wien they were duties to be done as meticulously as a man could perform them. Each flight was a lesson, a practice for the future. As he had done with his bicycle when he was a small boy and later with the county truck and his first automobile, Wien made every move deliberately, precisely, striving for perfection. No thought but of flying entered his consciousness while he was aloft.

Noel would get up about seven in the morning; have a breakfast of fruit, oatmeal, eggs, toast, and milk; and walk to the field where the Standard was waiting. Morrill and Noel would take turns flying. Mrs. Morrill would line up customers, collect money, jolly the reluctant, and talk up the wonders of flight. Noel was expected to join this pitch during his ground periods. "I wasn't nervy enough, though, so what I did was a lot of smiling mostly." Often that was enough. Noel Wien smiling was a handsome sight, and girls thought his mixture of hero and small boy charming.

Noel was at the controls leaving Mobridge, South Dakota—he did all the cross-country flying now—and the Morrills were in the front cockpit as Noel began his takeoff roll from the race track. There was the usual low fence around the track, the grandstand to the right and tents and booths scattered here and there, the whole encircled by a twelve-foot board fence.

A breeze blew over a hill to the right and down over the track infield, which sloped gently downhill. "Because we were going downhill," Noel recalled, "I thought we would have good perform-ance even though the wind was on our quarter. We took off with a very short roll and I thought that was that. But then the airplane for some reason didn't want to climb. We were about five feet off the ground and that high fence was coming up fast. I couldn't stall out because we were too close and would roll into the fence. The OX-5 was wide open, straining with the load of us three and a full tank."

Noel was in a trap that many aviators have found themselves in at least once. He was committed to flight; his craft did not want to climb; remaining in the air was safer than attempting to return to earth, but remaining in the air probably meant only delaying, not preventing, the crash. Most flyers want to take their chances in the air, for there always seems to be a hope that the craft suddenly will soar free, while landing makes a crash certain. Perhaps, also, any flyer would rather do his crashing from the air than roll into an obstacle like some rube behind a runaway team.

The fence that once was a half mile away now was only two hundred yards off. Flying at five feet, they barely cleared the track rail and racketed toward the high boards. "The only thing to do," Noel said, "was to hold the nose down and hope we got up enough speed to pull up and clear the fence."

They cleared it. By maybe two inches. The OX-5 clattered out of the fairgrounds, hoisting the Standard's wheels barely clear of the fence. Relief washed over Noel, but in another second he saw that the thrill was not yet over. The Standard simply would not climb. It went winging out low, following the downslope of the treeless hill toward the town and the river, two hundred feet below the race track. At full speed, with her pilot tugging back on the stick as far as he dared, the Standard flew twelve feet above the downward slope, curving with it toward the town, held by a force Noel knew nothing about.

"I couldn't land," Noel said, "although the hillside was clear except for sagebrush. We were going full out, about seventy miles an hour, maybe eighty ground speed, and I didn't even want to touch wheels at that speed. I couldn't turn right into the wind, because the hill was there."

And the town was dead ahead, a half mile off now, with steeples and telephone poles poking into Noel's airspace.

"I thought that if I turned left I would get even more tailwind and that wouldn't help us to climb."

But there was no other choice. Gently Noel put the stick over to the left and pressed the rudder bar on the left. Like a dragonfly suddenly released from the hands of a small boy, the Standard sprang into the air. Noel banked more to skin by the steeples and poles, flashed over the edge of town, and turned downriver over the water. The Standard climbed out and her three riders relaxed. Morrill blamed their near miss on a downdraft created by the wind blowing down over the hills behind the fairgrounds. If the draft had not ended just at the edge of the town, he told Noel, they certainly would have bored into the buildings at full speed.

That would have been a more dramatic ending to their tour than was the actual final curtain. After two days of flying at a fair, they pointed the Standard's flat nose toward Aberdeen, which had been so picked over by flyers that not a single customer bought a ride. After this failure, Morrill reported that he had fifteen dollars left in his pocket, that their expenses had eaten up all the rest of their income. Noel would gladly have continued forever, but just getting by was not enough for the Morrills. They flew back home to Curtiss Northwest at Saint Paul.

I remember changing seats at Howard, Minnesota, and Morrill got in the back cockpit to fly us on to Saint Paul. Coming into the Twin Cities where his insurance policy had been bought, he didn't think I should be pilot in command. Maybe it was a good thing, because when we got there it was black dark and I'd never done a night landing.

There weren't any lights at Curtiss Field and all he had to go by was some reflected lights from the city and some little lights along Snelling Avenue. The airport was a big black hole and as Morrill nosed the Standard down, I thought about the high telephone wires at both ends. I was plenty worried, my first night landing. But Morrill came in high, he could do that because we knew we had two thousand feet to land on, and made a fine landing. Landing in the dark would have been illegal a few years later after the regulations came in. All three of us were so relieved when we got down all right. We were fortunate.

I was forever indebted to Morrill for giving me the job. He gave me seventy hours and fifteen minutes of pilot-in-command time when there was no other way I could get even one minute of time. He and his wife were two of the finest people I have met and they were instrumental in getting me started in flying. I am sure that no one else would have hired me to fly their plane. Morrill went back into the Navy, I think, and later lived in Florida. I sure would like to meet them again.°

We said good-bye that night. I was more interested in flying than ever. I just didn't care to do anything else. I didn't want a regular job, even if I went hungry. If I couldn't fly, then I just wanted to hang around airplanes on the ground.

And that is what he did. For the next two weeks he scuffed the dust in front of the Curtiss Northwest hangar, listened to the flying talk, looked at the airplanes, lived on hot dogs bought at an old man's stand at the end of the streetcar line. He knew irrationally that something would turn up.

6. BONDAGE

The something that turned up was George Schermerhorn, a fifty-four-year-old blacksmith turned farmer. He was a huge, gruff, weather-beaten, bulldog-faced man with meaty shoulders, a bulging chest, a loud voice, a mean temper, an expanded ego, a young wife, and the incongruous desire to take to the skies and fly like a bird.

Schermerhorn came to Curtiss Northwest one day in late August 1921 and bought the old JN-4D Jenny in which Noel had learned to fly earlier in the year. By now the craft was in need of overhaul. In particular, her skin had loosened so that it flapped in several spots, and there were rips and holes in it here and there. Because of these Schermerhorn was able to buy the craft cheap. He took it to his

---

° But he will not. Navy records show that Edgar William Morrill was born September 7, 1897, at Miller, S.D. He completed flight training at Pensacola in 1919. He did return to the Navy, was retired in 1935, and was recalled at the start of World War II. He died of undulant fever on May 13, 1942.

farm at Eyota, a village about twelve miles from Rochester in the southeast corner of Minnesota. There he proposed to re-cover it and put it in shape for flying, although he knew absolutely nothing about such a project. His ego was equal to the attempt, however.

Along with the Jenny, Schermerhorn took with him the young, unemployed pilot, Noel Wien, who had been waiting around Curtiss Northwest since August 8. Schermerhorn's grand plan was for Noel to overhaul and re-cover the Jenny during the winter and then teach Schermerhorn how to fly in her in the spring. In the summer, he, Noel, and young Mrs. Schermerhorn would set off barnstorming to fame and fortune. Noel's pay during the winter would be room and board at the Schermerhorn farm. Flying pay for the next year would be negotiated later.

Once again Major Miller had cadged a job for his favorite student. It seemed strange that the quiet and proper young flyer would bond himself, as it were, to this loud, grubby, profane farmer. Perhaps to Noel, no man who wanted to fly could be all bad. Undoubtedly, the main element in Wien's decision was the Jenny. "If I couldn't fly," Noel had said, "then I just wanted to hang around airplanes on the ground." This was better than that. He was going to spend the winter with his old Jenny and the following year he would be back in the air with her again.

I worked all that winter on the Jenny in Schermerhorn's carpenter shop and lived in his farmhouse. His place was right in the middle of Eyota, which was just a few buildings and a store. He owned a big steam tractor and a threshing rig and went around the country threshing for other farmers. His son drove the tractor. He was about twenty-eight, the same age as the young wife, and really was a nutty, lazy guy, and the old man was very harsh on him.

Schermerhorn never told me anything, but I did learn that he'd been a carnival balloon jumper for a while years before and always wanted to own an airplane. Maybe it took him this long to save enough money to buy a ship.

Before I left Saint Paul I asked the mechanics about re-covering and overhauling and they told me as much as they could. That was all I knew. In those days, just like there was no licensing for pilots, mechanics didn't have to be licensed either. Anybody could fly and anybody could do any kind of work on an airplane, even build one from start and fly it. A lot of pilots with almost no time at all hauled passengers and told people they were war aces.

Schermerhorn bought some fabric at Curtiss, the cheapest kind. It was cotton, not linen. Linen was too expensive for him. He wouldn't let me put enough dope on it and it was floppy when we finished. He bought acetate dope, not nitrate dope. Nitrate is clear and thick and costs more. Acetate is yellow and thin. Nitrate would shrink much faster and better. But acetate wasn't being used on good jobs anymore, so there was plenty of it and it was cheap. Everything was second-class with Schermerhorn.

We took the wings off the Jenny outside and moved the fuselage into the shop and worked on it, stripped it and started covering again. Then we brought the wings in and re-covered them, sewed them up, doped them. While I was taking the old fabric off, I watched how it had been put on and tried to put the new fabric on the same way. It took almost all winter to do this because we had no experience. After we got finished, he put me to work in the carpenter shop repairing equipment and furniture and buildings. I did the son's work most of the time. He was the laziest person I ever met, except for one. Schermerhorn didn't pay me for this work, although he hadn't told me I would have to do anything but put the Jenny in shape. I didn't ask him to pay me. I should have, but that wasn't the way I ever did and I knew it would lead to trouble.

The man's crudity was repulsive to Noel, but he stayed on because he had said he would and because of the prospect of flying again. There was nowhere else to go in the frigid dead of a Minnesota winter.

Schermerhorn played checkers every night. He liked to beat people and thought he was really good. He would make me play with him. I'd get wiped out in just a few moves. I didn't play checkers and Schermerhorn didn't offer to teach me. He beat me continually for two, three months.

He enjoyed it. He never let up. He never felt sorry for me. Then, with all the practice I was getting, I began to beat him. When I did, he would turn red and curse. Sometimes he'd throw the board to the side and the checkers would fly around the room. He hated to lose, and after a while I beat him every time and he stopped playing.

Schermerhorn was pretty mean to his wife Lottie, always yelling at her, like he did to everybody, when she did anything wrong, and bawling her out when she didn't jump fast enough. Lottie was a country gal, quite a gal, good-looking, young and playful when he wasn't around, and a good cook.

The unhappy winter came to an end. On May 10, 1922, Noel and Schermerhorn rolled the Jenny from the barn where it had been waiting for the snow to vanish. They attached the wings and Noel began to preflight the plane, his fingers gentle like those of a horseman examining a thoroughbred foal. But Schermerhorn, impatient and demanding, ordered him to get into the cockpit and fly, now. It was the last time Noel was to be blustered by a superior into an unsafe flight.

Pulling on his helmet, Noel entered the plane. Surprisingly, after the winter of nonuse, the OX-5 caught up with a roar after the third pull by the bull-like Schermerhorn, and there it was again, that wonderful smell of exhaust whipping around the windshield into Noel's face. He had missed it. He tested the ailerons, elevator, and rudder, adjusted the choke, pushed the throttle slowly forward. The Jenny rolled. She picked up her tail in a few yards and then her wheels. Wien was flying again.

I got up only about one hundred feet, and one bank started sputtering and then cut out completely. When one bank of the OX-5 goes out, you're going down. You have maybe thirty horsepower, instead of the full ninety, and your thrust is almost zero. If Schermerhorn had decided to go along on this hop, it would have been a bad story. He was six foot and 220 pounds. As it was, with just me in the ship, I put the nose down immediately and could barely half fly and half glide to a little pasture ahead. It's lucky there were no trees. The ground was hard and not mushy from thawing and I plunked her down in a good landing and saved the airplane.

I spent all the rest of the day cleaning the engine with Schermerhorn standing over me yelling, cursing and berating me.

He didn't credit me at all with saving his airplane. He hadn't let me screw the cap off under the carburetor and drain the water before the flight, but insisted that I take the Jenny up immediately, he couldn't wait. The tanks were aluminum, and during the winter the condensation had put water into the gas, and the water had collected in those little caps under each jet. There was no sump or quick drain, but I could have checked. Schermerhorn, though, was very stubborn and you couldn't tell him anything. If he said it was good, that was it and everybody around him jumped. He bawled me out like his own kid.

I drained the tank and all the jets, picking up the ship's tail and shaking the airplane to rock the water down through the gas line and into the carburetor, where it could be cleaned out. I really learned something from this experience: to check for fuel contamination no matter how much time and trouble it took, and not to be bullied or rushed into any flight.

Wien tells about this without rancor. He flew the Jenny from her pasture haven the next day and put her through an hour's test flight over Eyota and Rochester. The following day he spent tinkering and touching up, trying to do something about the luffing spots in the fabric. Schermerhorn intended to begin stunting and parachute jumping without delay. His big surprise for all was that Lottie would be the jumper.

The young woman was terrified. She had never been up in an airplane, had never had any desire to leave the ground, certainly had never thought that one day she would be forced to leap from an aircraft. So afraid was she of her domineering husband, however, that she found the courage to obey him. Two days after the emergency landing, Wien took off on an indoctrination flight with Lottie in the front cockpit. He flew sedately for a bit over Rochester and then, because he knew that much worse was in store for her and wanted to prepare her for it, finished off with several loops, spins, rolls, and stalls.

At the end Lottie was white-faced and grim, but she kept her courage. The next day Schermerhorn tied her onto a pack chute, an Irving that he had used in the carnivals, attached a rip cord inside the cockpit, and sent her aloft again.

"We went up to about thirty-five hundred feet," Wien said. "The old man had spent the last few days advertising the jump all over Rochester. I figured wind for Lottie and gave her the signal to jump when we reached the right spot for her to land in the Rochester race track.

"She was brave. It was only her second time in the air, but she came out of her seat and jumped. The cord, about twelve feet long, opened the chute and she went down and into the race track infield. That was my first parachute drop, a thing I was to do hundreds of times later with flying circuses. Lottie was more afraid of her husband than of jumping."

Wien circled and descended with Lottie, thinking that escorting her would ease her fear. She made a hard landing, injuring her ankle and enraging her husband as if she had landed on his head. He had advertised over the territory that airplane stunting and parachute jumping were coming, and he did not want to lose a dollar by postponing the great events. While Lottie recuperated, Schermerhorn ordered Wien to give him instructions as they flew to Saint Charles, Predmore, Winona, and other towns seeking joyhoppers. Noel gave him several hours of air time under instruction, but in eight days of barnstorming found only thirty-six passengers for hops in the Jenny.

Then came Schermerhorn's first attempted takeoff while following through on the controls.

I told him to hold the stick very lightly and not to grab it in his big grip. We took off all right but we hit an air bump when we were about ten feet up. That tipped the right wing up a bit and I started to ease the stick over and straighten the airplane up, but it wouldn't budge. I was surprised when I found I couldn't move it.

Schermerhorn was scared stiff. He thought the plane was turning over, so he grabbed ahold of the stick and froze solid. It seemed like a long time that we went sailing back down, the right wing up, the nose down, right on into the ground. We didn't hit too hard, just went on in slowly, but we wiped the landing gear clean off.

It didn't damage the wing bad or hurt anybody. But do you know what Schermerhorn did? He got out and stood over me yelling and cursing because I didn't fly the airplane right and had wrecked it. It didn't do any good to tell him what had happened. He knew anyway, but he would never admit it for a second. He didn't take my warning about not grabbing the stick, he wasn't going to take any warning from anybody about anything. He would never have been a flyer and I wasn't going to solo him. He wouldn't listen and I couldn't instruct him because he knew more than I did.

That was June 1, 1922. Wien had been with Schermerhorn for eight long months and had been able to fly only 23:45 during that time. He realized now that, despite his earlier belief, something more than proximity to a flying machine was needed to make life bearable. Even though Schermerhorn sent to Curtiss Northwest for new landing gear and struts and the Jenny could soon be airworthy again, Wien knew he had arrived at the end of another experience. He would have to leave Eyota, but how? He had no money, no other job, and no prospect of one. He was physically afraid of Schermerhorn and would not ask him for money. And then serendipity again.

Two days after the crash, Wien was at the Schermerhorn home alone when a motorcycle came dusting into the farmhouse yard. Aboard was Bert Kogle, about nineteen years of age, whom Noel had met in Minneapolis. Bert was an airplane enthusiast, a real flying nut, whose flying was now confined by short finances to the sidecar machine he wheeled to a stop as Noel came out of the house.

Loud greetings from Bert, quiet ones from Wien.

"What are you doing here, Bert?" Wien asked.

"Why, I came to see you."

"All the way out here, 140 miles, just to see me?"

"Yep. And to show you the cycle." Kogle patted the sidecar. "Would you like to take a ride?"

"I sure would," Noel shouted, in a rare show of emotion. "All the way to Minneapolis. Let's go!" He got into the sidecar.

Kogle thought his friend was joking about taking a 140-mile ride, but he soon found that Noel had decided now was the time to leave Schermerhorn and Kogle was his deliverance. Noel was not even going to wait to pack his few belongings into his cardboard grip. "Schermerhorn had gone to town," he said. "I didn't want to give him even a minute to get back. He might have beaten me."

With only the work shirt on his back and the overalls covering the rest of him, Wien departed his bondage. Many years later Wien learned that poor Lottie had also managed to escape from Schermerhorn and had obtained a divorce.

The unexpected arrival of Bert Kogle was not the only providential happening of that day. Wien and Kogle had got no farther than Northfield, about sixty-five miles south of Minneapolis, when, lo, there in a pasture beside the road sat an OX-5 Standard, pilotless, passengerless, and seemingly abandoned. Children were playing on the other side of the road.

"Stop, Bert, stop!" Noel yelled above the wind. The motorcycle slued around in the dust as Kogle applied the brakes. Noel walked over to the pasture fence and looked longingly at the Standard. It was like a miracle that, out here, an airplane should suddenly sprout in a field like a mushroom. The children told the stocky blond stranger that the airplane's owner was Mr. Dawson and that he lived in the next house down the road.

Byron Dawson was the same age as Noel, twenty-three. He wanted to learn to fly and had talked his mother and a brother into helping him buy the Standard. Dawson hoped to make his instruction period a paying proposition by hiring a pilot-instructor and having him joyhop and stunt fly to bring in money between flying lessons. Unfortunately, the pilot he had hired was a lazy type who had not made the airplane pay. Dawson had fired him that day. But Dawson's own serendipity was working, for here out of the dust came a pilot in a sidecar. Noel was hired for ten dollars a day. But pay was not to begin until Dawson could evaluate Wien's performance and "see how well we can do in the barnstorming." Until he decided that the scheme could be a paying one, Wien would receive only room and board. This was no better than Schermerhorn had done for Noel, but Dawson as an employer was a vast improvement. "Dawson wanted to make money," Noel said, "and I wanted the experience. It was a good deal."

It lasted about six weeks. Noel taught Dawson to fly as they barnstormed around the Twin Cities and into Wisconsin to Eau Claire and Chippewa Falls, taking up as many as twenty-one passengers a day. Noel's probationary period was over in a few days and he began to receive the promised ten dollars a day. He might have been better off on room and board, because ten dollars did not go very far beyond paying for three restaurant meals and a hotel room. Dawson received flight instruction and took in three dollars a passenger, five dollars for two.

He left Dawson in mid-July to go barnstorming with Bill Yunker of Rochester, owner of an OX-5 Standard, and his friend of the motorcycle, Bert Kogle, who became the parachute jumper for the gypsy trio. When there was time, Wien gave both of them flying lessons. Yunker, a master mechanic, departed the group at the end of August, leaving Wien and Kogle without a plane. Two years later Yunker got Wien his first job in Alaska and was his mechanic on the historic Anchorage-Fairbanks flight.

7. HOMECOMING

On September 2, 1922, Wien fell in love. She was pert, pug-nosed, spirited—and fast. After all, ninety-five miles an hour in those days *was* fast, and ninety-five was the high speed of the Thomas-Morse Scout, a single-seat biplane built originally as a World War I fighter trainer. It had been used only as a trainer, however, and some six hundred in several modifications were built. The one that captured Noel was an older S-4C powered by a Le Rhone eighty-horsepower rotary motor. When Wien saw her standing saucily on the Robbinsdale airfield northwest of Minneapolis, he knew he had to fly her.

"I had never seen a radial motor," he said, "much less a rotary. It was some beautiful little ship."

Among other pilots admiring the Scout were Charles (Speed) Holman, even then a widely known aviator who was to spend a day in 1928 looping-the-loop 1,443 times before letting the blood settle; Walt Halgren; and Ed Belleau, a fighter ace who had flown for

Canada in the war. The owner of the Scout, looking for a sale, sent Halgren up to demonstrate the little ship. Her span was only twenty-six and a half feet, clipped when compared with the Jenny's and Standard's almost forty-four. Her speed was blinding compared with the Jenny's seventy-five and the Standard's seventy.

It was the hottest airplane I'd flown. I'd never had any trouble with torque before, didn't even know what it was. The Standard and Jenny are so long that torque isn't a problem. But when I gave the Scout the gun, she seemed to want to spin like a pinwheel, and we shot off to the edge of the field until I smacked in enough right rudder. After that it was the most fun I ever had. That rotary engine seemed to fire continually with one loud, high-pitched sound like paper ripping, about like a jet sounds today.

Noel bought it. The price was four hundred fifty dollars, and he paid two hundred down, every dollar he had. He needed it like he needed a trombone. The Scout was not a working craft, it was only a toy, but four hundred fifty dollars seemed within Noel's reach and how else was he ever to become owner of a flying machine? It was a dream fulfillment, and the farm boy succumbed.

Because Kogle was small, Wien found that by making certain rearrangements in the cockpit he could stuff his friend in beside him. Jammed together like two olives in a bottleneck, Wien and Kogle flew off, the Le Rhone buzzing like a thousand hornets, down to Kogle's home town, Mason City, Iowa, just showing off and flying. Head winds on the way south caused two forced landings for fuel. The wind reversed for the return trip, as some aviators swear it does always, and the Scout's two-hour supply of castor oil ran out coming back.

As oil pressure diminished, Wien spotted a farmer plowing aboard a tractor and landed beside the startled man. He bought some tractor oil, fed it to the Le Rhone, and listened to its coughs and sputters all the way back to Robbinsdale. The rotary had been designed as a solution to the problem of how best to cool an air-cooled motor. By whirling instead of remaining stationary, it created its own breeze. But the Le Rhone, although it was used by the thousands for years, had its own doom built in—the terrible torque and the necessity for using castor oil as a lubricant. Many a pilot flew gagging behind the motor, nauseated by the aroma of castor oil. Not so Noel Wien. He could stand any mere odor in order to be at the throttle behind a motor that he had read of and dreamed of since he was a boy.

At the end of two weeks, the final payment of two hundred fifty dollars was due on the Scout. Wien became a former aircraft owner. Once again he was broke. He told Kogle good-bye, never to see him again. The slim, young man became a pilot and disappeared on a flight over Lake Michigan in the early 1930s.

In two days Wien was back in the air. An OX-5 Standard owned by Clarence W. Hinck, a Minneapolis aviation promoter, became available, and Wien and a mechanic named Harry Anderson took her off barnstorming on shares. The arrangement lasted three months, during which time Noel taught Anderson to fly, spent two weeks in bed with measles, and made a triumphant return to the home farm, landing the Standard on a field he himself had helped to clear.

Pilots were not required to keep logbooks in those days. Wien's early log, reconstructed years later to satisfy the government's retroactive curiosity, shows the following entry for October 14, 1922: TYPE PLANE—Standard; LICENSE NO.—None; TYPE ENGINE—OX5; FROM—Ely Lake; TO—Home; REMARKS—landed home first time since learning to fly; DURATION—1 hr. 15 mins.

In just this dispassionate manner does he recall the second most memorable event of his life up to that time, the homecoming being outranked only by the thrill of first flight. Against formidable odds imposed by lack of education, lack of money, and a rigidly disapproving father, the Scandinavian farm boy had made his dream come true. Now he was going home, not by scow as on his first arrival, and not by truck or on foot, but in an airplane, the material of the dream itself.

I ran low on fuel on the way up, so I landed in a field near a town and walked to a filling station. I had to buy the cheapest gas they had. They didn't have octane ratings then, but I guess this would be about fifty-five octane. The trouble was, it fouled the spark plugs plenty and I had three forced landings. I would go about fifteen miles and the motor would start missing, running rough and vibrating. I knew it would get worse. I would pick out a field and go down before more cylinders would go out. Then I'd take the plugs out and clean them, scraping the goo off with a knife, digging in on the side of the electrode and scraping the ends. I'd put them back and take off again. I sure did watch for every bit of smoke on the ground, the water ripples, trees swaying, even grass swaying, to keep track of the surface wind direction. I knew in a few minutes I'd have to be landing again, as soon as the knocking and vibrating started up. I'd fly full open, about 1,300 r.p.m., to try to keep ahead of the build-up by burning it out, but it wasn't any use.

I was anxious to get home, because I had been away two years. I'd left home knowing nothing about flying, just wanting to fly, and feeling sometimes that maybe I'd never get to be a flyer. Now here I was coming back home in an airplane, flying over the country where all my family and friends were.

About six miles west of Cook, there sat the old home. I buzzed down and did a few wingovers and a split-S, performing pretty good, and then sailed on down into a field on the east forty, some twenty acres long, about twelve hundred by sixteen hundred feet, that I had helped stump. The hay had been cut and it was fairly solid ground. I rolled up to the fence, cut the ignition, and swung my legs over the side of the cockpit and sat up there and waited.

The six Wiens at the farm (Ralph, age twenty-four, had left home and was struggling to establish an auto repair business in Cook) heard Noel's airplane and rushed from the house to watch it twist and dip in the sky above. Noel had telegraphed that he was coming, and impatience had made the wait long for his brothers and sister. Pa Wien already was cranking the Model T when the Standard glided down out of sight. Mother climbed in and then Enid, twenty-two, Fritz, twenty, Sigurd, eighteen, and baby Harold, twelve, clambered aboard.

Fritz and the others tried to maintain the Wienlike reserve so as not to displease their father, but the moment was too much. Soon they were leaping around their pilot brother and his airplane, touching the craft and getting into the cockpit and waggling the joystick. Pa Wien greeted his son with a somber handshake, but Ma Wien gave him a quick hug, for her an unusual show of affection.

Neither parent believed in showing emotion, including even love, and taught their children a taut reticence. Talking was to be done sparingly. A voluble person was just a *snakkesalig*, a chatterbox. But Enid, gentle sister, bubbled around the homecoming brother she adored, exclaiming over his dashing breeches and puttees, embarrassing Noel. Fritz went off in the Model T to get some better-grade fuel, while Noel drained the last of the low-grade fluid from the OX-5.

Noel took each member of the family for a hop, stunting wildly with Fritz and Sig, who loved it, less so with Harold and Enid, and not at all with his mother. In the next ten years all of the brothers, including Ralph, were to go to Alaska, and all but Harold would remain and work in Wien aviation.

Pa Wien watched in silence as the Standard took off and landed, as if studying the strength of the machine and the skill of its operator. He looked upon his son's occupation as a mere game unworthy of a man's labor, and one at which he could never hope to earn a decent living. He could hardly have been more disapproving had his son taken up acting or poetry. But after all the others had flown in the Standard, he got into the front cockpit and rode through one flat turn around the fields, over the farmhouse, and back to a landing. This pleased Noel more than any other part of his homecoming, for it at least hinted at a kind of paternal approval.

For the next six months Noel was in and out of the home field, between barnstorming forays. During his stops at home, Noel's sister and brothers pestered him with questions about his flying adventures, never tiring of hearing the same stories over and over. They wanted the far-away derring-do, the glamour so in contrast to their humdrum life on the farm. With them Noel was relaxed and even garrulous, so unlike his "outside" personality.

Pa Wien was interested only in the machinery that made the airplane go, not in the "fooling around" done by his son. He peered into the OX-5 to examine and touch it, and Noel knew that he would like to take it down. When Pa learned of the cups beneath the carburetor for trapping fuel contaminants and how frequently they filled and stopped the motor, he offered a simple solution: make the cups deeper. Someone in aviation engineering thought of this later, and the new engine with $1\frac{1}{2}$-inch cups was a splendid improvement over the original OX-5 with $\frac{1}{2}$-inch wells.

Noel worked the Iron Range, flying out of fields near Chisholm, Virginia, and Evelyth. The northern Minnesota winter allowed him to take to the air only three times in November and December and twice in January and February. In April he returned to the Twin Cities. In the entire six months of barnstorming, he had carried only one hundred fifty paying passengers on joyhops and had made three short charter flights. The return was not sufficient for the owner and Wien had to relinquish the plane. Once again he was grounded and spent his days listening to pilot talk and scuffing the dust, his nights at the Saint Paul YMCA.

8. CIRCUS

Clarence W. Hinck, the Robbinsdale airport operator whose plane Noel had flown in the fall, was a large, robust man of about thirty-five years, a showman with a big voice, a hustler, a spieler with an uncommon ability to talk crowds into forming and exchanging money for airplane rides. A war veteran, Hinck had owned airplanes and now was branching out as an impresario. He was organizing a troupe to be known as the Federated Flyers Flying Circus, and he proposed to tour the United States.

Hinck's flying stock included two Standards and two Jennies, all powered by OX-5s. He needed three stunt flyers. From the Twin Cities dust kickers he picked Glenn Soden, Joe Westover, and Noel Wien. Pay was three hundred dollars a month, an attractive sum in a day when college-educated professional men of Noel's age worked for far less.

Soden and Westover were more experienced in every way than was Wien. Then in their early thirties, they had been trained in the military and were elegant figures in their breeches, boots, and scarves. Both were ladies' men. Soden, the smaller of the two, was usually surrounded by admiring females. But he wrote his wife every day. Westover, tall and suave, was inhibited somewhat in his contacts by his wife, who drove a Model T from stop to stop along much of the circus's itinerary. Westover had worked at Curtiss Northwest as a mechanic; he was a master. He smoked one cigarette after another. When the ash grew long enough to droop, he blew it away with a sudden explosive "puhh" from the other side of his mouth. This had an intimidating effect on Wien, a nonsmoker. Westover was tough, but he smiled a lot above a square jaw and around his glowing cigarette.

Hinck's operation, at least in the beginning, was well organized, the first such aviation enterprise Wien had seen. There was an advance man, Delmar Snyder, a former Army lieutenant who flew one of the Jennies along the route about a week ahead, booking the troupe at county fairs, state fairs, American Legion shows, posting bills and ballyhooing the coming event. Snyder was a "nice-looking, presentable fellow," Wien said, and, like Hinck, a talker. Snyder, Hinck, and a Hinck brother, who was a Minneapolis lawyer, were members of the young American Legion, and this connection gave them a special entree in some cities. Hinck envisioned a grand tour, across Minnesota, the Dakotas, Montana, Idaho, Utah, Nevada, down the depth of California, and back to the Midwest by the southern route. It was a first-class effort, and money would roll in for all. The jolly Mr. Hinck promised it.

Star of the show and the highest paid was George Babcock, a YMCA physical education instructor and tumbler who in the short time before he was killed became one of the best-known barnstorming daredevils of the Jenny era. He was the wingwalker, the parachute jumper, the crowd scarer. His pay was three hundred dollars a month, but he received an extra fifty dollars for each parachute drop. During the tour he was to make fifty-four drops and build up a stake unattainable at the YMCA. He never returned to the gym.

The Flyers entourage also included four hell-for-throttle motorcycle riders and auto polo players and a mechanic whose charges were the planes, the cycles, the truck that carried the cycles from town to town, the autos, and the personal rolling stock of the caravan. On May 10, 1923, Federated Flyers took off and rolled away from Robbinsdale.

Wien's reserve—often taken as an expression of aloof superiority

—his straight habits, and boyish good looks made him a target for the low wit of his roistering colleagues. They tapped the bottle a bit, rarely to the staggering point, but often enough to maintain a rather high elation level. "Lambie Pie," "Bashful Boy," and "Goodie-Goodie" were some of the names applied to Wien. Of course, they tried to trick him into sampling their bootleg goods. Once he took a sip of brandy and nearly choked. But he took their sallies with a grin, even when he sensed a touch of scorn. Their very loudness made him uneasy, as when Hinck would roar at him from a block away down the main street of some little town, "Hi there, Wienie, how's a boy?" Wien would give a half-wave and duck into a doorway or around a corner to escape the stares of people attracted by the noisy greeting.

Another thing. Hinck and Babcock had studied the three aviators and decided that the one who would fly the exacting flights that carried the wingwalker would be not the hot shots but Wien. This was both a blow and a relief to the other flyers: they were not eager to fly under the restrictions necessary to execute the walking stunts safely, but they did not like any suggestion that perhaps they *could* not perform them. After Wien was designated as Babcock's pilot, the kidding sometimes took on an edge. The laconic farm boy moved with but apart from the pack. Before the tour ended, however, his skill as a pilot, his quiet courage, his decency and generosity had earned the admiration of nearly everyone. The hazing gradually stopped, for what sport is there in riding a man who responds only with a grin? They came to regard him somewhat uncomfortably. Here was a flying machine flying a flying machine, and they did not understand it.

Even though I was bashful and backward and didn't fit in too good, Hinck picked me for the wingwalking job. It was probably because I didn't drink and didn't smoke and was the most conservative. Soden and Westover didn't like it too much, but they weren't really mean. They just liked to kid. They both called me "Wienie" and that's the only nickname I ever had, except for Ralph's "Nonie"—when I was born, he couldn't say "Noel."

George Babcock was about my age, twenty-three or twenty-four. He was a little fellow, five-two and 120 pounds. Very wiry, with bunched muscles. He was very strong and a fine tumbler. He could do a forward or backward somersault without touching his hands, from a stand. He was always bawling the other fellows out. "Drinking, tearing around, smoking, looking for women," he would tell them, "should be no part of a man's life." They kidded him some, but he gave it right back to them. Wine, women, and song were not for him. He and I became good friends.

Babcock flew with me in my Standard on cross-country. We both had old cardboard suitcases with a change of underwear and a couple of shirts. The pilots all wore khaki breeches, as those were the cheapest kind. Soden and Westover wore high-laced boots and the white scarf. I never wore a scarf, and I used puttees and then got some boots.

The show we did lasted two and a half hours. It would start with the motorcycle races, a lot of noise and spills and dust and excitement. Then the auto polo matches would come. We had four stripped-down Model Ts, with the bodies removed and just a board for a seat behind the wheel. The malletman, who used a long-handled croquet mallet, had a short running board for his right foot and a handle on the driver's bench for his left hand. He stood with his left foot on the auto frame.

The idea was a scrap between the two cars with the drivers and malletmen trying to see who could knock a soccer ball through a goal first. The game would last about a half hour. It was exciting for the spectators because there were always a few spills. One of the cars would be deliberately rolled over with its driver and malletman just barely escaping. When one of the malletmen was hurt, the pilots had to be malletmen. I hated it, but I was athletic and always was able to time my jump just right and not get hurt.

Then three airplanes would come flying over the grandstand in tight formation, two Standards and a Jenny. We'd come back again a little lower, maybe four hundred feet, and the two outside ships would pull up and turn outside with wingovers. I would fly Babcock in the front cockpit of the middle ship and we would fly off and land while Soden and Westover stunted. They would do the whole thing—wingovers, barrel rolls, stalls, spins and loops, almost down to the ground.

Joe Westover was the best pilot, a little more daring. Soden was a good pilot, but more conservative and was the best man for some kinds of flying. Neither one of them did a specialty, a stunt that other flyers weren't doing at the time. The famous names did the real daring things. I read that Lincoln Beachey, who was one of my boyhood idols, did loops at three hundred feet. He got killed in 1915 when his wings came off at San Francisco.

Just before Soden and Westover were through, I would take off again with Babcock and be ready to make a first flyover when the stunters flew away. Our show would be five or six runs in front of the grandstand at three hundred to four hundred feet, slowed down to about fifty miles an hour so the crowd could see better and Babcock didn't have too much wind to work against. On the first flyover George would just be out on the leading edge of the lower wing in the outer bay, leaning forward with one arm and one leg stretched forward like in greeting. Between flybys he'd run back to the cockpit through the struts and wires.

Next time, George would be on top of the upper wing standing on his head. He would never tie himself on as some others did, and he was proud that he was up there on his head holding on with just his own strength and balance. The cabanes were far out on the wing, and when Babcock was out that far, I had a tough job keeping the airplane level. I had to use full aileron and I had to ease it in at just the right second when he reached the cabane and then ease it out at exactly the right time to keep level all the way as he ran back to the cockpit. I had to fly straight and level so the spectators could see the whole show and every split second I was changing aileron, rudder, and power to keep up with where George was and what he was doing.

Next flyover George would be hanging from a lower wing by one hand, grabbing a strut. I would fly a little faster for this so he would sort of stream out behind the wing.

Then he would climb down the leading edge of the lower wing and hang by his feet from the landing gear. This was a real thriller. He would sit on the axle facing forward and then drop back suddenly and the crowd would gasp. As he fell he would slip his feet forward of the axle and hook his toes behind the gear struts. He would hang there, arch his back, and wave both arms at the crowd. Each stunt got a little harder and more exciting.

The next was hanging by his teeth from the middle of the axle. He had a strap with a mouthpiece and a loop on the end. The loop went around the back of his neck, so he was supported by this although it seemed to the crowd that he was hanging just by his teeth. This was the only stunt he did that had a little trick in it.

That would be the last regular stunt, except for the days when a loop or parachute drop was scheduled. But toward the end of the tour Babcock cooked up a trick that sure had the crowd screaming. He attached a one-inch rope to the outer bay struts and ran it back along the leading edge and attached it to the middle bay struts. His running back and forth between the wing tips and the cockpit was like a monkey—so quick. On the fifth or sixth time over the stands he'd pick up the inboard end of the rope and snap it onto a ring he had on his ankle. Then he'd run along the leading edge and trip over a flying wire and fall over the edge. Down he would go while the crowd jumped up screaming and fainting. After about a ten-foot drop, he would jerk to a stop when he reached the end of the rope. He would wave and then twist himself up and crawl up his rope to the wing.

This last stunt put a great strain on Babcock, the rope, the strut, the wing, the aircraft, and Wien, who had to maintain straight and level flight despite the continual changes in balance and stress on his plane. When Babcock fell from the craft, Wien had to prevent the wing's sudden sweep upward. He had to anticipate and compensate for the sudden great downward pull when Babcock hit bottom and the wing again took his weight in the slipstream. Gradually put in aileron and rudder as Babcock ran outboard; neutralize at the instant he fell; count three and instantly put in nearly full aileron and rudder. This stunt was Babcock's invention and it became his trademark throughout the country. It was a most difficult timing trick for the busy pilot.

The hardest stunt to fly was a loop-the-loop with the wingwalker standing on the top wing. After a flyover, Babcock would run back to the cockpit and put on a belt that he had made special with cables hanging from it in front and back. He'd climb up through the upper wing cutout and on top of the wing. He'd hook the cables to four snaps bolted to the wing and stand with his feet apart facing forward and I would do a loop. This was very ticklish, and I had to fly this loop perfect or the stunt would be ruined.

As easy as possible, as slow as possible, I had to almost stall upside down. If I went too fast, the G-force when I pulled the nose up would force Babcock to his knees. This wasn't graceful, he said, and he wanted to stand straight up through the whole loop. The slow entrance would put us slow at the top, and I'd try to snap it over just at the stall.

A smooth, slow, gentle pull was needed. We were so slow that if we stalled we wouldn't go over, so I'd have to snap it over and then work to keep from dropping off and spinning. Everything had to be perfectly coordinated in a Standard or Jenny, even ordinary banks and turns when making routine landings. They were critical planes. They didn't forgive a mistake. They'd spin in. Later, when we got Hisso motors in the plane, with their extra power, I could put the Standard up over the top without the near stall and still let Babcock stay upright.

9. WESTWARD

As brother Fritz said, "Noel was patient. He was almost completely different than myself and Ralph and Sig when we were boys. He was patient. We always used him to untangle our fish lines, to get them out of the brush or thorns. Noel had the patience to sit down and completely untangle a fish line. If you've ever tried it, you know what that means. He would work away calmly, without saying a word, even if it took half an hour."

The patience and perfectionism that Noel exhibited as a boy were now applied to his job of flying the wingwalker through a loop. He felt compelled to edge closer and closer to the speed at which Babcock would fall to his knees in pullout, to try to discover the precisely correct speed of entrance that would give him a perfect loop and allow Babcock perfection also in his part of the stunt. He consulted Babcock after each show. One day, Noel's feeling of having achieved perfection coincided with Babcock's. He had it "grooved," as he was later to groove every precision flying skill that the perilous Alaska weather and terrain were to demand of him.

We would do just the one loop at a show. Then we'd finish with the parachute drop if it had been scheduled. Babcock never did use a backpack or breastpack. They cost much more. He used a sack chute, the oldest type. He would spend an hour packing the chute. He would fold the panels and loop the shrouds just so, and put pieces of newspaper between each level, to separate the shroud coils. It was very important to keep them apart, he said, so they wouldn't tangle up. When he jumped and the sheets flew out, that added something to the show. "He's lost something!" the crowd would shout.

The chute would be carefully packed in a bag and attached to a strut on the outer panel of the lower wing. George would attach himself to the parachute with two big buckles on his belt. He'd be giving me signals, directing me right or left. He knew the winds expertly. While hanging on a strut, Babcock would pull a string that would open the bag and the chute would pop out and fly back and pull him off the wing.

I worried all the time about flying with Babcock out on the wings. If the motor had quit while he was out on a top wing tip, and the ailerons were at full travel, or even if the motor just sputtered, I'd have had to dive to keep up speed and Babcock would have been in real trouble. We talked it over and he knew he'd have to get back to the cockpit in the fastest time. He was the quickest man I've seen, like a cat, and I thought maybe he could make it.

He wanted me to fly as low as possible all the time, from three hundred to six hundred feet, depending on the wind and the turbulence. If a motor bank had gone out at three hundred feet, we wouldn't have had enough altitude to recover. That could mean crashing into the grandstand. Some fairgrounds were right in the town and houses were at both ends. That was a terrific worry, flying that low, but Babcock wanted to be at three hundred feet to give the crowd a thrill.

When we got to the mountain country where the landing fields were four and five thousand feet up, we found we didn't have enough power for stunting and wingwalking. From western Dakota on, the old OX-5 just wasn't going to make it. Hinck was a big operator, so he sent the stunting planes back to Robbinsdale to have Hissos installed in them.° After that, my Standard and Soden's Standard and Westover's Jenny could do the same stunts at seven thousand and eight thousand feet above sea level that the old ninety-horsepower OX-5 did at three thousand feet. The Hisso was a more reliable motor than the OX-5, because it didn't have that balkiness over a drop of water. The Hisso performed well at even twelve thousand.

Before the show crossed the continental divide it suffered twin blows of bad luck that nearly put it out of the flying business. At Stanley in northwest North Dakota, Soden's and Westover's planes were totaled by a tornado during the night. Hinck sent back to Minneapolis for one new plane, but in the meantime only Wien's Standard was left to carry the load. Delmar Snyder was off ahead in the second Jenny, promoting for a show that now might not be able to produce as advertised.

Shows must fly on, it has been said, so what was left by the tornado went on to Williston, where Noel and the only remaining plane were to joyhop for a day before the scheduled show by the Federated Flyers. On the first hop of the bright dawn the next day, Noel's plane rose about two hundred feet, pointing toward the houses of Williston, and the engine quit cold. There was no warning, no sputtering, no sighing. Just sudden and complete absence of sound.

Major Miller had drilled into Wien the fundamental rule for coping with takeoff loss of power: if you do not have altitude, put the nose down and land straight ahead, no matter what impediments may be there; if you try to turn back to the field, you will stall in the turn and spin in and kill yourself. "No matter what Major Miller taught me," Noel said, "I couldn't fly on into those houses. People in them would get hurt and so would my passenger in the front cockpit."

° Known to pioneer pilots always as the Hisso, this engine was a 150-horsepower, water-cooled Hispano-Suiza manufactured in the U.S. by Wright under license from its French owners. Larger models were built. It cost about 40 percent more than the OX-5. As an instrument in the development of American aviation, the Hisso was as important as the OX-5, although no sentimental cult has been formed to worship it, no Hisso Club to correspond to the OX-5 Club.

So he tried a turn. He went in but he did not hurt either his passenger or himself. The plane was badly sprung. The nose was bashed in, the wing tip crushed, the radiator punctured, an outer rib was fractured, and the fuselage bracing wires on one side snapped where they crossed through the after cockpit. All three performing airplanes were now out of commission, a show was advertised for tomorrow, and the only props in working order were some motorcycles and auto polo Model Ts. What now?

Well, we had to repair my Standard. We plugged up the radiator, patched the wing tip, and straightened out the nose. Luckily, the propeller hadn't been split or cracked. But the worst thing was the fuselage cross wires. These were bracing wires fore and aft that helped keep the fuselage in shape. Without them the fuselage would fold up. We heated and bent the wires—we couldn't join them back—and wrapped the ends around bolts and fittings in the cockpit. We should have taken some haywire and spliced it. It would have been stronger.

The next day at the show it was settled that there wouldn't be any stunting—just motorcycles, auto polo, and Babcock's wingwalking. The Standard did fine until we were coming out of the loop with Babcock on top, and a wire snapped. It was such a snap it jarred the whole ship and shook me. I was scared stiff the fuselage would buckle in the center. I shut off the power and started a shallow glide. Babcock reacted just as he planned for an emergency like this. Like a monkey, he zipped back to the front cockpit.

We landed all right but the show was off. We stayed at Williston until the new plane came in from Minneapolis, and we repaired mine, but this time with good piano wire. Hinck must have had insurance on the planes wrecked by the tornado, because the new plane came right away and it was a new Standard. We couldn't afford four planes now, so Snyder's Jenny was put into the show and he went by train for his advance work.

My motor had quit on takeoff probably because a joyhopper from the day before turned off the gas. The gas shutoff was a long rod that went into both cockpits, with a round handle in each. It made a right handy brace for a nervous passenger. You turned off the gas supply by turning this handle a quarter turn. The last passenger the night before must have turned it. Pilots weren't so careful about preflight checks in those days. They checked outside, but not in the cockpit. Every time after that I checked that cutoff before I started up and told the joyhoppers not to touch it. We spread the story to other barnstormers so they could watch the cutoff too.

As 1923 waned, the Federated Flyers continued their barnstorming across Montana, Idaho, Utah, and into Nevada. Wien's remarks column in his log contains such terse entries as, at Roundup, Montana, "electric storm Babcock landed chute in tree 4 hops"; at Burley, Idaho, "had bad blowing valve leaking radiator 1 pass"; at Ogden, Utah, "lost spark plug forced down at Ogden"; at Salt Lake City, "Air Mail pilot flew Oriole in formation flight with us"; at Elko, Nevada, "boys got drunk rain bad weather."

At Reno Wien fought a battle and a rematch, losing both, with a mountain wave. Assigned to fly Delmar Snyder across the Sierra Nevada to promote the circus at Placerville, California, Noel headed the Standard into the wind which poured down from the west over 11,000-foot Mount Rose. He should have been off the ground like a rocket, into a stiff wind such as that. Instead, the Standard just barely cleared the fence and headed toward rising ground. Memories of Mobridge jarred the pilot. He banked gently to the left and sailed on southward, almost clipping jackrabbits with his landing gear. He caught a sudden glimpse of wagon tracks ahead in the sagebrush and in the split second cut power, stalled in, and went "Whew!" while Snyder turned to look at him questioningly. Wien told him he could not gain altitude and they had best walk back to the airfield. They did.

In the cool of the evening, when the afterglow of the sun that had slipped beyond the Sierra radiated an eerie whiteness through the sky over Reno, Noel returned to the plane for a second try. The breeze was light, still from the west. There should be no strain. But again, after he took off, no matter how he tried, full power would not take him more than a few feet into the air. A gully was coming up ahead. A farmhouse sat on its far rim. From his flat angle Wien could not judge how wide the gully was. But there was only one thing to do to keep from crashing into its far side or into the house. He had gone beyond stopping. When he reached the near rim, he jammed the stick forward and dove toward the bottom of the gully, picking up a few extra notches of speed. At the bottom he came full back with the stick and the screaming Hisso pulled him up over the far rim.

He was higher now, but he could sense that he was not going to gain another inch. On the edge of the rim, east of the house, he spotted a beautiful green field. The instant of spotting was the instant of deciding. He cut power, pulled the nose up, and plunked down in a full-stall three-pointer. Luck gave him a smooth field and the Standard was undamaged. This was flying: observing, judging, choosing, acting all in a flash and all correctly. This was not the unimaginative man that Wien seemed to be on the ground.

Before Noel could dismount, a rancher came clopping up on his horse. "Mister," he gasped, "you gave me a fright. I seen you take off down there and then you went out of sight and I knew that gulch had grabbed another one. I been in there before picking up pieces of you fellows. Then you shot up out of there like nothing I ever seen before. You all right?"

Noel was all right, and a lot wiser. He knew that as long as wind was pouring down that slope from the west, he was not going to get the Standard up to a workable altitude. Much has been learned about downdrafts near high mountains in the decades since Wien began making an acquaintance.

Wien and Snyder made their Sierra flight the next day when the wind had shifted. In Placerville, old Hangtown of the Mother Lode country, Noel helped Snyder put up circus posters. Noel carried a camera with him through his barnstorming and Alaska days and amassed a treasure of photographs tracing fifty years of aviation history; but he did not take a photo of any of these posters nor did he save a poster itself. He was uncomfortable about the "daring" and "death-defying" and other adjectival excesses committed on the bills. He was red-faced and stammering when accosted on the streets by people who recognized him from his picture on the signs.

10. HUNGRY

California had been worked to the bottom of its pocketbook by aerial artists. By 1923 there were very few rubes left who could be enticed into joyhops and to watch stunting. An ominous note emerged from Wien's log entry at Stockton: "No dates ahead for one week."

Federated Flyers put on shows at Chowchilla, Visalia, and Bakersfield, but blasé Californians did not come in droves to watch. And then Hinck missed a payroll. This was a signal to Babcock, the star of the circus, that it was time to sell his skills to another employer. He was marketable. He moved on, and Noel discovered how much he had come to admire the clean-living little man and how close they had become. Wien was to work for two months in 1926 with Babcock, who designed a truly "death-defying" stunt of hanging from a ten-foot rope ladder attached to the landing gear of an airplane and dropping into a lake without a parachute.

Babcock died a few years later executing a parachute jump into Lake Minnetonka. It was his four hundredth drop. He was attempting a stunt the news accounts said had not been done before. From thirty-five hundred feet, he tried to use five parachutes in succession on the way down, cutting free from one, opening the next. George opened the first chute, cut it away, opened the second, cut it away. The third streamed out but did not open. He cut it away. The fourth chute also failed. A fifth chute opened ten feet above the surface and Babcock's small body hit the water and threw a spout twenty-five feet into the air. As spectators shoved off in boats trying to help, the two chutes that had opened floated silently down and folded over the still foaming spot where

59

Babcock had hit. "Every bone in his body was broken," read a newspaper account.°

Meanwhile, it was autumn 1923 in California and Snyder was beating the arroyos and beaches trying to find spots where the Federated Flyers could attract some customers. One day Hinck had Noel pilot him down to San Diego in the Standard. They landed at Claude Ryan's field and from what he could hear of Hinck's conversation with Ryan Wien decided that his boss was trying to sell his airplanes. The only other planes on Ryan's field were OX-5 Jennies and T-M Scouts. They flew back to Hollywood that day. Then word came that Snyder had lined up a show at Phoenix. The three planes set out.

"I'll never forget Phoenix," Noel said. "Such a small town with a landing field right close in. It was warm, even in December. This was our last show and it wasn't much. We didn't have many passengers. Soden and Westover got disgusted and left the circus and went back to Los Angeles.† Snyder came to Phoenix to fly the Jenny and brought with him another pilot named Otto Enderton."

Wien did not know it at the time, but something was up besides the death rattle of Federated Flyers. The three planes, with Hinck riding forward in Wien's Standard, hopped to Tucson, Douglas, and then Columbus, New Mexico, the village that Pancho Villa had raided in 1916. Noel saw Hinck and Enderton in earnest conversation with several "Mexican-looking" men. Then the Jenny and two Standards hopped to El Paso. Christmas there was anything but merry for the three pilots. Hinck disappeared.

He returned on January 4, 1924, assembled Wien, Snyder, and Enderton, and announced in ringmaster tones: "Great news, boys! I've fixed you up with good jobs in Mexico. Here's train tickets to New Orleans." He handed tickets to Wien and Snyder, but not to Enderton. "Wait here in El Paso until you get the word from Otto to go to New Orleans. When you get there Enderton will let you know when to go on down to Vera Cruz. It won't be long."

Questions by Snyder elicited the fact that the "good jobs" would be flying for a Mexican revolutionary general. "We would be throwing bombs out over the top of the cockpit," Noel said. Pay was

---

° Unidentified clipping in Noel Wien's scrapbook.

† Wien thinks both later worked for airlines. Soden did work at one time for Lockheed, where Wien saw him in 1957.

to be five hundred dollars a month, a handsome increase over the three hundred dollars circus pay and an infinite increase over the nothing a month the flyers had drawn for the past eight weeks. The nature of the job came as no shock to Wien. He accepted the assignment, bizarre as it was. The job was flying, it was the only flying job in town, and Wien would have done it for board and room, a tent and frijoles. Besides, it was presented to him in such a take-it-for-granted manner by Hinck, and there were no objections from either older man, Snyder or Enderton. There were none from the trusting Wien.

Hinck did not go so far as to hand over eating money along with the tickets, although it is to be assumed that he had collected something from the Mexicans. He had sold them the three airplanes. Hinck merely waved good-bye and boarded the cars for Minneapolis. During the next ten days the three aviators took the airplanes apart, crated them, and had them hauled to the railroad station. Wien had about three hundred dollars, having tried to keep on hand the equivalent of a month's pay during the tour; but he was frugal with it, as if he did not have the splendid war job coming up. He lived in a small hotel near the depot and ate only a bowl of chili a day, packed with crackers and doused with whatever accessories he found on the cafe counter.

After ten days of this, Snyder and Wien watched their crated airplanes loaded aboard a train, received the good-byes and assurances of soonest notice from Enderton, who headed south into Mexico to activate the great adventure. The other two got aboard the Southern Pacific train that hauled their planes and started the journey across endless Texas to New Orleans. In his innocence, Wien did not wonder if perhaps Hinck was gone for good with the six hundred dollars in unpaid salary owed him, plus sale money for the airplanes and maybe even a commission for signing up the warriors. If you are going to Minneapolis, New Orleans is a pretty good spot to send your creditors to. Snyder, however, appeared to be in the same fix with Wien, and it was hardly likely that this pitchman, wise to carnival ways, would allow himself to be shunted down the river so easily. What happened in New Orleans, however, makes Snyder's motivations difficult to infer.

The two men arrived in day-coach grime at New Orleans, took a cockroach-decorated room on the fourth floor of an establishment on St. Charles Street, and waited for a message from Garcia or whomever. They waited for two months. They started with nearly three hundred dollars, mostly Wien's, between them, and for a while they ate well in a hotel and at a Greek's cafe up St. Charles. They even went to a movie, walking down to a glittering movie house on Canal.

No message came from Mexico, and 1924 grew older. Snyder was broke, or at least he said he was. Wien's evaporating funds went to pay their rent and for daily plates of red beans and rice at ten cents a serving. On occasion, Noel walked six blocks to the wharves on the river and bought a meal of small, mushy bananas for three cents a dozen. Toward the end, bananas became their staple. Nothing else was so filling for three cents.

Wien could not find a job. He tried at garages and woodworking shops, at cafes and on the docks. Snyder did not seek work, did not accompany his roommate on his rounds; it was as if he counted on the strong-backed, naïve country boy to provide. Silently, Noel did. Having no money for the streetcars, Noel walked. He got to know every square, street, avenue, and alley in the Canal Street and river area of New Orleans. He enjoyed the exercise and the curious fact that when he walked, time seemed to pass more rapidly. Walking, and later running, were to become favorite recreations. During Mardi Gras he walked among the masked, frolicking throngs in the streets, enjoying the novelty of several hundred thousand lunatics moiling so after pleasure.

It seems strange that he did not try to find a job in aviation, did not even go out to the airport, even though with 486 hours of command time he was among the country's more experienced pilots. But he had been told to wait for word from Enderton in Mexico. He was not going to stir far from the place to which that word would come.

No word came.

When his capital reached the purchasing level of only a few more banana stalks, he wrote home for help. During the nine months of barnstorming, Noel had sent about four hundred dollars to his mother. He hoped she had some of this left and could spare enough to get him home. And Snyder. Mama Wien sent seventy-five dollars, and Noel bought two day-coach tickets to Minneapolis. He and Snyder got aboard the Illinois Central for their first leg to Chicago.

Between trains there they visited a brother of Snyder, and Wien was surprised to discover that the man was a physician living in comfort. "I guess Snyder would have been lowering himself to ask his brother for money," Wien said. "When we talked with his brother, Delmar didn't even mention that we were broke and had been for two months or so."

Impresario Hinck pleaded poverty when Wien went to see him at Robbinsdale on April 10, 1924, the day he arrived from New Orleans.° "But I'll tell you what I'll do," Hinck told Wien. "I have a Hisso Jenny over at Curtiss Northwest that I'll let you take out on a fifty-fifty basis. I won't be able to pay you the six hundred dollars until next year, after I've had a chance to get started again." It was flying, so Noel took the offer and flew the Jenny north toward home. He had blown two months and all his money waiting in New Orleans, but he gave no thought to recriminations.

Noel had not been in a cockpit for more than three months, since he had deplaned January 4 at El Paso. On the way to Cook there was, of course, a forced landing, which was as normal in those days as a planned landing and far more frequent. Lieutenant General Lester Maitland, who piloted the first flight from the mainland to Hawaii as a young lieutenant in 1927, said he had made as many as one dozen forced landings in a day of flying.†

"A snowstorm so thick I couldn't see anything came up," Wien said, "and I landed in a field where there were three inches of snow. I don't know why I didn't nose over. Lucky, I guess." He has a photograph of himself and a young schoolteacher who boarded at the farm where he put down and spent the night. Next day at the home farm, there was the usual restrained Wien greeting from his parents, and a more exuberant one from his sister and brothers. During the next month, flying from his home field, Noel joyhopped 102 passengers before a different kind of job appeared.

Curtiss Northwest Airplane Company, headed by William A. ("Bill") Kidder, had obtained a contract to make mapping photographs of northern Minnesota for a power company. Kidder had always admired Noel Wien's sure and conservative hand on the

---

° Clarence Hinck remained in Minnesota, selling airplanes, running a flying school and a glider school. He died in the 1960s. His brother Elmer was killed in a plane crash in 1942, the only crash he had in twenty years of flying.

† Conversation with author at Red Bluff, Calif., in 1965.

stick; he was a natural for the exacting job of flying a photographer. Pay was three hundred dollars a month, the standard for daredevil stunting, instructing, charter work—everything but Mexican bombing. Paul Hamilton, in his early thirties, handsome and tall, chief photographer for the Minneapolis *Tribune*, was to handle the cameras. He and Noel flew their sorties in a K6 Standard—a Standard with a Curtiss K6 six-cylinder, water-cooled, in-line engine of 150 horsepower. Piloting required the flying of exact tracks at precisely maintained altitudes. Noel found it interesting to estimate and sense drift and to compensate for it, flying imaginary lines through the winds as straight as those he had laid into the earth with his auto tires.

The job lasted only a month, and then Noel Wien was on his way to Alaska.

The Mexican general? Wien said the name sounded something like Huera or Fuera. It probably was Adolfo de la Huerta, one of the many generals intriguing for power in the long turmoil that followed the unseating of Porfirio Diaz. Huerta had been an interim president and in 1923 was vying with Plutarco Elías Calles to be chosen number two man behind Álvaro Obregón. Huerta evidently was preparing for the showdown when he bought the Hinck planes and put Wien and Snyder on stand-by. Failure to call them up may have saved their lives. In the showdown, Huerta's forces were crushed by Obregón and Calles, and many Huerta people met the firing squad.

PART II

11. ALASKA

There'd only been two working pilots in Alaska's Interior when I went up there. And only one of them, Ben Eielson, thought that Alaska was flying country and that a man could make a living flying there. Ben Eielson later flew Sir Hubert Wilkins from Barrow to Spitsbergen, in 1928. That was called the first airplane flight across the top of the world. Ben had been teaching school in Fairbanks in 1923 when some local businessmen put up money for a Jenny and Ben flew it around Fairbanks.

A few months before I got to Alaska, he got a mail contract and a De Havilland D.H. 4 from the post office department. It was a trial contract. Ben flew eight trips from Fairbanks to McGrath, about 280 miles, for two dollars a pound. That was half the four dollars a pound the men running the dog team star routes were getting. Ben cracked up three times and the post office thought his idea was no good. They canceled his contract and told him to send the airplane back Outside.

I met Ben Eielson in Anchorage in June of 1924 when I was going in and he was going out. He was about twenty-seven, a slim, fine-looking Scandinavian fellow from North Dakota who really believed in Alaska flying, the need for it. He was soft-spoken and intelligent and he was nice to me. "You'll like it up here," he told me, "and you'll do well." Ben came back two years later to fly for Captain Wilkins, which he did for nearly three years, and I got to know him well before he was killed in 1929.

Then there was Art Sampson at Fairbanks. When I got there, I found out that Art, who had been in Fairbanks a month or so, was just waiting for me to come in so he could leave. He and I had been hired at the same time down in Minnesota to go to Alaska and fly for Jimmy Rodebaugh. Rodebaugh was from Rochester and was senior conductor on the Alaska Railroad. He had this idea about airplanes in Alaska and asked Marvin Northrup at Robbinsdale to send him two pilots and a mechanic. Northrup was an airplane dealer and wasn't any relation to the airplane builder Northrop.

He got Bill Yunker as mechanic, the same fellow I'd barnstormed a little with, and Bill hired Sampson and me. Rodebaugh had just bought two Standards from Northrup and they were at Robbinsdale having the OX-5s exchanged for Hissos. These were J-1 Standards, the ones converted by Curtiss, with the bigger front cockpit. They had a nose radiator instead of the vertical radiator. As soon as one of them was ready, Yunker and Sampson crated it up and started up to Alaska with it. I took the mapping job while the other airplane was being converted and when it was ready I quit the mapping job. My last flight on that job was May 16, 1924.

Noel went home to the farm to tell his family good-bye. He knew nothing of Alaska, other than the names of a few gold towns that had bloomed and died, and the memory of having read about the 1913 tidal wave that swept Nome. He had never heard the name "Fairbanks." His pay was to be the standard pilot wage of three hundred dollars a month. In the mail he received a coach railroad ticket from Minneapolis to Seattle, a boat ticket from Seattle to Seward, and a twenty-dollar bill for expenses. Was Rodebaugh perhaps another Hinck who might leave him stranded, this time at the end of the northernmost road on the continent? Wien did not consider this for a second. "I wanted to fly," he said. "I had nothing in Minnesota to look forward to, and this looked like a steady job in an interesting place. Flying was just about dead in the States."

At the farm, his mother brought out her atlas and together they ran fingers over the map of Alaska, not grasping the gigantic size of it or its terrible remoteness. In its center was a little name, "Fairbanks," at the end of a proposed railroad line from Seward. The road had been completed since Mrs. Wien's atlas had been published. Noel did not go to a library for other information on his home-to-be. He was going to Alaska to fly, not to explore or to sell goods, and what he would need to know was not yet in books. His mother and the younger Wiens were interested. Papa Wien was pessimistic as usual, believing still that a man should engage himself in a trade with some history, some lineage. Noel did not seek his father's approval, knowing he would not receive it. Brother Ralph, by now twenty-six years old and married, was excited by the thought of Alaska. A much larger man, at six-one and 200 pounds, than any of the other Wiens, Ralph yet closely resembled his brothers, having the same open countenance, blue-eyed and fair. At his auto garage in Cook he was working to the limit of his time and strength but slowly going broke. He could not collect his accounts.

"Nonie," Ralph told his brother, "let me know as soon as you can if there's something up there for me. Maybe they need mechanics up there."

The train took three days to reach Seattle, from which point the Alaska Steamship Company dispatched a boat to Seward weekly. Noel boarded the 300-foot, single-screw *Northwestern* for its ten-day voyage through the Inside Passage, coming close to seasickness when the ship struck open water for a time north of Vancouver Island. His fellow passengers learned that he was a flyer and pestered him with questions, but he returned only name, rank, and serial number. They had heard of Eielson's efforts and they prophesied that aviation would not be adaptable to Alaska weather and space. Rodebaugh, they said, was a jolly fellow, well liked by all.

With maturity, Noel's aura of innocence was altering to a protective dignity, so no one attempted to shock him with tall tales of Alaska, although its weather, bears, and mosquitoes, among other items, offered prime material. Noel was interested in the glaciers that he saw from the ship, but his attention was mainly focused on the 'hundreds of miles of steep, spruce-covered mountains that plunged straight into the deep sea. Flying here could be only by seaplane, he thought. But airplanes of any kind then being built were too slow, too short-ranged. Would anyone ever fly back and forth over these waters to Alaska? Eddie Hubbard, he knew, was flying the mail between Seattle and Victoria for the Boeing Company, but Victoria was far south of Alaska proper. Roy Jones had flown a Curtiss/MF Seagull to Ketchikan on the southern tip of

Alaska, but crashes had put an end to his dream of establishing a flying service.°

Aboard ship, Noel learned that he was a *cheechako* (chee-CHOCK-koh), a newcomer. He ate four meals a day—breakfast, lunch, dinner, and an extra lunch at 11:00 P.M., remembering thin chili in El Paso and old bananas in New Orleans. Between meals he spent much of his time forward on deck beside the two crates in which his Standard was making the voyage. He needed to be with airplanes, even if they were disassembled and encased in wood. He was eager to get to Seward, to Anchorage, to Fairbanks, to . . . where?

To the Great Land. Granite peaks scrape the sky. Muskeg, a trackless ocean of rotting vegetation, fills the undrainable remains of Ice Age glaciers. Uncharted tundra hardens to marble in winter, changes to sucking glue in summer. Thousands of rivers crash through mountains and fatten to writhing sameness where they meet the muskeg and tundra. Glaciers creep as slowly as the ages down to the sea to calve.in splashing thunder. Ten thousand years of snow are piled into mile-deep ice fields that run for hundreds of miles. Bays, sounds, coves, bights, and seas outline a coast longer than that of all the lower states together.

Terrible winds are compressed through mountain passes into the irresistible fury of 400 miles an hour. Haze, mirage, reflection, or blowing snow sometimes produces a total whiteness in which the horizon and sky blend to create the aviator's dreaded whiteout. Cold in the Interior can reach seventy below zero, at which temperature gasoline has frozen, human and animal breath is visible not as vanishing steam but as ice fog that remains suspended where it is formed. Dryness matches that of the Sahara, creating bolts of static discharge between human bodies and causing dogs to flinch from affection. Snow is so dry that a yard of it yields only drops of moisture and mukluks shriek, not squeak, as men walk in it. Coastal rains fall in sheets like waterfalls, soft fogs drape spruce forests. The stepping-stone Aleutian Islands are beaten by winds born there in the nest of storms where frigid air masses departing Siberia mate with waters warmed by currents from the lower Pacific.

The aurora borealis—the northern lights—dance, flicker, pulse,

° Roy Jones died at the age of eighty in February 1974 at Vancouver, Washington. He was a retired customs service officer.

and glow in sheets, rays, and curtains of white, green, yellow, and red. Volcanoes simmer. Earthquakes rumble in waves across the land, as many as three hundred recorded in a month, some of an intensity that would flatten cities, were cities there. Mountains change shape in mirage before one's eyes. Permafrost, glacéed earth, at an eternal twenty-nine degrees Fahrenheit, covers half the land. Twenty-thousand-year-old mastodons are mined from this earth and have been served as pièces de résistance at an Explorers Club banquet in New York. Hot springs puff vapor into chill air. Winter days are five hours long, in the north even shorter as the sun rises only a few degrees above the southern horizon or does not rise at all. Human hibernation is forced on all but a few, because unprotected flesh freezes instantly at sixty below. Winter gloom brings cabin fever, and even the placid Eskimo is sometimes pushed into a brief eerie madness. Engines are seldom turned off at forty below and colder, because they will not start again. Tires on sitting automobiles freeze with one flat side, so that klumpety-klump is the winter song of Fairbanks.

Summer days are twenty hours long, in the north even longer, as the sun sinks but does not really set, leaving its light behind. With summer lightness comes a giddiness in man and beast. Birds fly all night, man dances and makes love all night, as if to disprove the belief that energy cannot be stored up and spent another time. Alarm clocks are set not to rouse people from sleep but to remind them that despite the light it is time for bed. Sundogs arc the sky when the real star is invisible below the horizon. Twilit high noon; bright midnight.

Wild creatures are beyond counting. Seals, otters, whales, walrus; fish in solid schools; mountain sheep, lynx, wolverines, foxes, wolves as big as bears, bears bigger than oxen, moose as tall as Percherons; communities of nomad caribou, as many as twenty thousand in a herd, wandering across the tundra and south through mountain passes as the tundra unfreezes; ptarmigan, hawks, eagles, ravens, terns that fly eleven thousand miles in migration; mosquitoes so big and in such large numbers that they smother caribou by congregating in their nostrils and men swear they can see their wings flapping. Everything bigger than anywhere else.

Baranof, Valdez, Cook, La Pérouse are names on a coast explored in the 1700s by Russians, Spaniards, Englishmen and Frenchmen.

But other peoples were here first. Eskimos, people unique in all the world, physiologically adapted like the polar bear and Arctic fox to withstand cold, and intelligent enough to survive for twelve thousand years in a deadly land. Meek Aleuts, cousins of the Eskimo, reduced to handfuls by Russian gunpowder and by American whiskey wages. Interior Indians, handsome, straight, slim, speaking tongues related to that of the faraway Navajo.

Greed. A colony always, its abounding wealth skimmed by generations of exploiters who extracted timber, furs, fish, sea mammals, gold, and oil, and left the land and its aboriginal peoples flayed, the livelihood of the humans gone, hope of merging into the conqueror's culture nil. Outsiders who struck it rich left. Those who remained to grow old in Alaska have a gentleness in their manner and an innocence in their eyes that make one wonder if in Alaska the good die old.

Roads? What roads? In 1924 there were none. Trails are usable by dog teams only in winter, streams usable only in the short summer. Alaska's wealth and remoteness brought men by the thousands: adventurers and romantics on the last frontier; solitary, gold-seeking sourdoughs, some as gentle as the Aleuts; prostitutes and barkeeps and outlaws; bankers and engineers, merchants and entrepreneurs, scoundrels and saints, liars and philosophers, poets and scientists, teachers; men seeking something, men fleeing something. The Wild West lives.

From Canada's Arctic border on the northeast, to Attu at the western tip of the Aleutians, the Great Land sprawls for 2,500 miles, covering 586,400 square miles—as much as the twenty-three smallest of the United States combined—spanning four time zones and encompassing the nation's northernmost, westernmost, and easternmost points, as it reaches beyond the 180th meridian, eight degrees into tomorrow. Because Alaska is so far away from the equator, the distortion of a Mercator map makes it impossible to comprehend its spread west and north. It is so empty that in areas larger than some states there are no humans, and there are regions that as late as 1940 had not been explored. The Fairbanks school district is larger than the four smallest states combined.

Nothing said about Alaska can apply to all of it. Anything said about any of Alaska is inadequate. Alaska is a bewilderment of geographical, climatic, geological, historical, mythological, and human ingredients. Alaska cannot be described, much less explained. Yet almost everyone who has lived there, especially half-baked poets, must make a try.

12. ANCHORAGE

Noel Wien arrived in Alaska, in Seward, early in June 1924, a veteran aviator twenty-five years old, with 538:50 hours of flying time to his credit. By contrast, Ben Eielson had only twenty-four hours of solo time when he bounced from the .ground in the Fairbanks Jenny in 1923, hardly more than four hundred hours when he died in Siberia. Bill Yunker, thirty-five, slim as any model aviating man of the day, met Wien at the dock in Seward. Together they supervised transfer of the precious crates from the ship to a flatcar of the rail train that met each ship. The Alaska Railroad was one of the wonders of the engineering world. A trip over its 470 miles from seacoast Seward to permafrosted Fairbanks required two full days, with a lunch stop at Anchorage, an overnight pause at Curry on the Susitna, and lunch the next day at Healy in the Alaska Range. The 114-mile stretch up the Kenai Peninsula to Anchorage from Seward wound through mountains like the Alps and alongside waterways resembling Norwegian fjords.

Anchorage had been established on the northeast end of Cook Inlet in 1914 as the construction headquarters for the Alaska Railroad line from Seward to Fairbanks.

With completion of the railroad in 1923, Anchorage shrank from its peak population of six thousand to about two thousand. It retained that number because it had become the outfitting and jumping off place for mines in the Kuskokwim. Businessmen had begun to speculate about attracting sports fishermen and hunters, now that the railroad had opened some of the Interior.

As in other white Alaskan communities until after World War II, there were no "natives"—no Indians or Eskimos—on the streets. They still lived in their ancestral lands. For a few more years their hunting culture would be undisturbed and life-supporting, and they would not be forced to scavenge the edges of the white man's settlements. Substituting for aborigines in the role of second-class citizens in 1924 Anchorage were foreign laborers of the "bohunk class," as a Seattle newspaper noted,° who had been paid thirty-seven cents an hour when work started on the railroad and were housed in a "reserve district" outside of town.

Yunker told Wien that Rodebaugh, their employer, had instructed him to unload the Standard at Anchorage, assemble it, and have Wien joyhop for a while to make expense money. So sensational was the arrival of an airplane in Anchorage that Wien was to do much better than "make expense money." In expectation of the arrival of the airplane, gangs of Anchorage residents had worked free of charge to prepare a landing field, filling and leveling a three-hundred- by two-thousand-foot strip (which now is a park running east and west along Ninth Street) some distance south of town. The crates were put aboard a chain-drive, solid-tired truck and moved to the "airport." Yunker turned his tweed cap around on his head so that the visor was in back, signifying resumption of his function as aircraft mechanic, rolled up his sleeves,* and went to work.

Anchorage was a real nice town, laid out square up on the bluff above Ship Creek and the inlet. The railroad depot was down in the draw, about one hundred feet below the town, just where it is now. They told me Anchorage was much newer than Fairbanks. There weren't any buildings out at the airport, no hangars. It was next to the Gill home, and Gill had a big family of children and a machine shop in town. While Yunker and I were putting the ship together— it never was much of a job in those days—Gill was making a spare gas tank from drawings Yunker made for him. The Standard only carried thirty-five gallons of gas, in a tank ahead of the front seat in the fuselage. That wasn't near enough to set out over that wild country to Fairbanks. The thirty-gallon tank Gill made was

° Merle Colby, *A Guide to Alaska, Last American Frontier*, Federal Writers' Project (New York: Macmillan, 1943).

streamlined to fit under the center section of the upper wing. Yunker put in a line from the new tank down to the main tank. When I figured the main tank was nearly empty, I would turn a valve and the thirty gallons would come down with gravity.

One thing I remember so well. The field was covered with about three inches of the finest dust I ever saw. When I took off with the wind from the south, the cloud of dust the Hisso kicked up was big enough to just about cover the entire city of Anchorage. They all were pleased to have an airplane there, and nobody complained. This was the first airplane to carry passengers in Anchorage. I was in the air two days after we arrived, taking up two passengers at a time in the front cockpit, ten dollars each for a fifteen-minute ride. My first hop was a test hop on June 4, and in the next month I joyhopped more than 170 people, making seventeen hundred dollars for the Rodebaugh company. I spent my twenty-fifth birthday on June 8, 1924, flying around Anchorage.

Some city people came and asked me if I'd do some stunts for the city on the Fourth of July celebration, and I said sure. A good crowd gathered that afternoon. The day was overcast, with the base of the overcast at about four thousand feet above ground level, hiding the tips of the Chugach Mountains. I went up to three thousand feet and did some loops and wingovers and tailspins and then tried something I'd always wanted to but never had a chance to. I went up into the overcast, flying pretty steep for two or three minutes, then stalled and shut the motor, kicked the rudder over, and began a spin. The crowd didn't know where I was until I suddenly came spinning out of the clouds. I was told it was a very exciting thing to see and it was just as exciting for me. I finished with some low loops and wingovers and landed. It was the first stunting at Anchorage. The old Standard performed well, and the Hisso ticked over in great shape. Yunker was an expert mechanic.

Beginning about the first of July that first summer in Anchorage, Wien received daily weather reports from three stations along the Alaska Railroad. Telegraphed by station agents, these came from Curry, 110 miles north; from Cantwell, at the entrance to Nenana Canyon which cleaves the Alaska Range; and from Nenana, where the muskeg over which he would fly after transiting the range meets the Tanana-Yukon Highlands. From Nenana the rails wind north-eastward through these hills to Fairbanks.

A report from the west would have been useful in predicting weather along his route for a day following, but he was not aware then that he probably could have received such from the Army Signal Corps at McGrath and Ruby. The Army had taken no official notice of and volunteered no assistance to Wien's impending grand voyage northward to begin work at Fairbanks. Yet the few people in the untracked wilderness of Alaska owed their continuing existence to willing cooperation. Even the military, on the Outside often immobilized in mummy wrappings of red tape, participated in this family enterprise. As it turned out, a report also from his destination would have saved him an agonizing hour of blind flight. He was later to believe that a warning should have been sent to him from Fairbanks by Rodebaugh.

From his hotel window each morning, Wien could assess the current weather conditions by looking toward Mount McKinley. If its eminence was visible, he could conclude that he would have clear weather for at least the eighty miles to Talkeetna, and perhaps all the way to Cantwell, where Yunker reported a landing field was being scratched in riverside gravel. Yunker also reported that sand bars suitable for emergency landing lay on almost every bend of the Susitna, Chulitna, Nenana, and Tanana, the major rivers along which or near which their route would take them. Wien's chief worry was the possibility of low clouds over the Alaska Range, making Nenana Canyon impassable. Despite word of the sand bars and the possible Cantwell strip, he knew that a landing short of Fairbanks could be a disaster.

July 4, the day of his stunting exhibition, had been overcast. The mountains to the north were obscured, leaving a horizontal, slotlike opening over the marshes between them. Such inviting openings in mountain-country sky elsewhere had swallowed many an unwary pilot by closing in behind them. The following day, however, Anchorage sparkled and McKinley rose so clear that Noel thought he could make out the folds in its flanks. Reports from the stations were favorable. This was the day.

Noel told Yunker that if all continued well, they would take off around midnight on their great adventure. "Be sure, won't you, that the ship's in good shape and we've got a full sixty-five gallons of gas in the tanks?" he asked the mechanic. A night flight, during the coolest part of the twenty-four-hour day, would likely be smooth, as there would be less chance for thermal updrafts to develop. Darkness would be no hazard. The Alaska summer night is bright, even so far south as Anchorage.

13. PLUCKY AIRMEN

Word spread around Anchorage that "our airplane" was going to leave that night for Fairbanks. Even the least worldly of citizens understood something of the significance of the attempt. The train trip took two days. This Wien fellow had told somebody that he would be there in four hours. Excitement spread. A crowd gathered at Gill's field early in the evening to wait and see. Yunker poked and pried at the Standard. Wien waited in his imperturbable way, briefly answering the excited questions of the crowd. History was going to be made this night—maybe.

Takeoff was at 2:30 A.M., July 6. There was no wind. Noel, remembering downdrafts in other mountain country, was grateful for this. The laden Standard bounced and bobbed across the dusty field, raised its tail, bounced some more. It rose into the air, settled back down, rose again. Noel kept the nose level for a few seconds, allowing the Hisso to thrust the craft to top speed, then tugged gently on the stick to begin his climbout. He banked and turned left, straightened out on a climbing course approximately north, and headed for the water where Cook Inlet narrows into Knik Arm. He waggled the Standard's wings, the aviator's hail and farewell.

Noel removed from his jacket pocket the Alaska Railroad map that he had studied already a hundred times. The scale was not accurate, but the major loops and curves were shown and the stations were dotted in. The tracks went about thirty miles northeast from Anchorage to the end of Knik Arm, where they bridged the Knik and Matanuska rivers. Then they swung back westward for some thirty miles. At Willow they turned north. From there it was roughly north by east 285 miles to Fairbanks, through country that even fifty years later was some of the wildest and remotest on earth.

Because the night's visibility was almost perfect, Wien decided to save twenty-three miles by flying north over Knik Arm and the marshes and picking up the railroad where it turned northward at Willow. He estimated his total flight distance to Fairbanks to be just over three hundred miles, fifty-six miles shorter than the rail course, for he would straighten out the bends. Without a wind, his cruising ground speed of sixty-five to seventy miles an hour would complete the flight in about four and a half hours. With five hours of fuel in the two tanks, it was a tight fit.

After crossing Knik Arm, Wien leveled off at two thousand feet, throttled back two hundred revolutions, and looked around and below him. The Susitna River, dotted with sand bars and joined by hundreds of veinlike creeks, flowed north-south through a flat area about forty miles wide that was pocked with thousands of lakes. It was not unlike the desolate lake area back home between Cook and Bemidji in northern Minnesota. During the Ice Age, this country, for some three hundred and fifty miles between the Alaska Range and Kodiak Island, was covered by a four-thousand-foot-thick glacier. To Noel's right were the Talkeetna Mountains, 8,800 feet at their highest. To the left was Mount Susitna, a Tanaina name meaning "Sleeping Lady." In winter its 4,400-foot crest is covered with snow in the form of a supine woman—head and face, neck, breast, clasped hands—reposed as if on a catafalque.

On the Standard's nose, magnificent Mount McKinley rose from ground mists that were beginning to form. It seemed close ahead. From the valley at about two thousand feet above sea level, this incredible massif soars to a pinnacle 20,320 feet above sea level, a continuous thrust upward of 18,000 feet that is unmatched even by Everest. Noel saw four major glaciers and several lesser ones that grasped the range like fingers. In every direction isolated men slept in log cabins or worked at lode or placer mining for gold. They could not be seen from above. Pack trails and winter sled routes

Noel Wien, left, and Bill Yunker, right, stand with passenger beside the Standard J-1 shortly after Noel's arrival in Anchorage, June 1924. In this Hisso-driven, 150-horsepower airplane about 170 Anchorage residents went for their first joyhops, and on July 4 Noel put on the first stunt exhibition to be performed in the area. Courtesy of Noel Wien

Jimmy Rodebaugh, Eddie Hudson, and Noel at Weeks Field, Fairbanks, in July 1924, with the Alaska Aerial Transportation Company's two Standards. In the background is the hangar built for Ben Eielson's mail plane. Courtesy of Noel Wien

Noel and his passengers, Mr. Ingraham, a mining engineer, and his secretary, Billie Saunders, on a flight from Fairbanks to Kantishna in 1924. Fog forced Noel to make his shortest landing ever in Alaska, on 300 feet of rocky sandbar in Bearpaw Creek. Courtesy of Noel Wien

Noel starting up the Standard at Wiseman, May 1925, on the first flight to land beyond the Arctic Circle. Courtesy of Noel Wien

were invisible in the timbered greenness of the lower rises and across the lowlands beneath the airplane. It was a fine start for a fine flight. Yunker twisted around in the front cockpit and gave Wien a hand salute of exhilaration and confidence.

Eighty miles from Anchorage the Chulitna River comes down from the left to meet the Susitna in a juncture that looks from the air like a tuning fork. Here was Talkeetna, a metropolis of seventy persons and a depot. Although he had been flying toward it for more than an hour, Noel thought McKinley still seemed to be the same distance away. It had appeared to fill half the sky almost from the flight's beginning. Captain George Vancouver of the British Royal Navy had seen this "stupendous snow mountain" in 1794 from his ship far south in Cook Inlet. The Russians called it Bolshaia Gora, "big mountain"; the Tanaina Indians called it Traleika, "the big one"; and the Tanana Indians called it Denali, also "the big one." ° Denali it was called by early explorers and exploiters until an unimaginative prospector changed it in 1896 from this beautiful word to the surname of a forgettable politician. Similar has been the fate of many Alaskan features. Only the year before Wien's momentous flight, President Warren Harding had visited the Great Land to drive a spike on the Alaska Railroad at Nenana. In honor of this occasion, Salchaket Lake near Fairbanks suffered a change to "Harding Lake."

From Talkeetna, the railroad continues to follow the east bank of the Susitna. Twenty miles farther, it turns about twenty degrees east and enters a narrow canyon bordered by hills that reach 2,500 feet above the now racing river. The canyon sides are covered with birch. Curry, a station and a roadhouse for railroad overnight stops, came and went under the biplane. Twenty miles beyond Curry the railroad makes a ninety-degree left turn into Chulitna Pass, bends back ninety degrees to the right, and climbs up a rapidly rising slope toward a unique geographical site. This is the lowest pass through the Rocky Mountain cordillera. When Noel had flown the continental divide in Montana he had been forced to push his airplane to 12,000 feet. Here the divide is only 2,400 feet above sea level. Mount McKinley was now over his left shoulder. Behind and ahead were dozens of peaks from 10,000 to 14,000 feet, yet Noel was

° Colby, *Guide to Alaska*, p. 281.

flying the divide at only 4,000 feet. He began a climb to 8,000 for the leg through the Alaska Range. The Standard was performing beautifully, gauges at safe readings, motor roaring in key.

About twenty miles beyond the divide was Cantwell. Even Wien's practiced eye could not locate the landing field that Yunker told him was in preparation there. Unlike localities shown on Outside road maps, most of the "towns" here were only lone buildings that served as station and station agent's home. Some of these Noel had not been able to find in the wilderness below. Just ahead, the railroad dived into Nenana Canyon for its transit of the Alaska Range. The canyon walls rose steeply to more than six thousand feet along both sides. Far below, the river twisted and turned and bent back upon itself and the rails followed. The Nenana River ran north. The ones he had followed up to the divide flowed southward.

I hadn't been worried at all, although this was the first flight from Anchorage across this unsettled country. If we weren't following the railroad, I might have worried. But following a railroad was the best possible way to navigate, and I had been doing that since I started flying. There were no airports anywhere below. I had checked the elevations of the stations on the railroad map and at first could hardly believe that we would fly through these big mountains at so low a level.

We turned into the canyon at Windy, and it was smooth even there, although the name does describe that place. McKinley was off to my left as we turned in. The canyon was narrow and the river below was too fast for sand bars. There didn't seem to be any places where I could have landed. There were creeks running in from left and right, but they were in pretty steep sides too. The railroad went through three tunnels. It was real rough country.

About halfway through the canyon, I could see a cloud front far ahead of us that was solid from the ground up to about ten thousand feet and as far west and east as I could see. This was the first sign of trouble we'd had on the whole trip so far. I thought after a while that maybe it wasn't a cloud but was a dust storm. It seemed to have such a squared-off top. When we got a bit farther I could see a bluish tint in it and I decided that it must be smoke.

We came to the end of the range and flew out over the muskeg that stretches thirty to fifty miles between the range and the Tanana River. I was glad to be out of the mountains and over flat, green country—I didn't know then that you couldn't land on muskeg in the summer—but I was plenty worried now because I could see the railroad lines disappearing into the smoke. And I saw the faint outline of some more hills. I started looking around for a landing place.

A big river came down from the east and from my map I figured that was the Tanana and that Fairbanks was about fifty miles straight up that river, about ten miles longer by railroad. Nenana, the little village where the Tanana and Nenana join, was in the clear, and I felt a little better. There was a little bit of hayfield there, about seven hundred feet long, that I figured I could land in—I did use it later—but decided to give it a try through the smoke.

Across the place where the rivers meet, the hills run off to the right and go up about thirteen hundred feet above the railroad. The railroad skirts around them and goes northeast up Goldstream Creek to Fairbanks. I nosed the Standard down to about two hundred feet over the railroad and we crossed the river bridge and swung around the hills. Then we entered the smoke.

My visibility forward was nothing. Soon I found I was down to one hundred feet over the railroad. This was real bad. I could see straight down by cross-controlling and twisting the ship to one side to look straight down.

Bill Yunker didn't seem concerned—at least, he didn't try to give me any advice. I couldn't ask him for any, because he was in the front and I couldn't holler against the wind. I wanted to ask him about tunnels, if there were any more along here.

I tried to look up every now and then to see ahead but was afraid to look forward too long. I was afraid the railroad would turn under us and I would lose it. If I did, that was it, because I didn't think I could ever have found it again in this visibility. And I couldn't count on being able to get back to Nenana and the clear air because the railroad twisted so much and I wasn't exactly sure which way Nenana was.

I made up my mind that if I lost the railroad, I would just climb and turn south and try to get back over that smooth green country this side of the range.

Then the visibility got too bad and I thought I'd have to land on the railroad. It would have been a bad landing, but that could be our only hope.

We had just gotten into the smoke when it was three hours since we'd left Anchorage. Now we were in this smoke with two hours of gas at the most. Here we were, trying to bring the first airplane up from Anchorage. Rodebaugh and his friends had been wired that we'd left and they were waiting to welcome us. The whole thing might end up in a wreck on the ties or, worse, by smacking into a mountain above a tunnel.

Then it was 3:30 since leaving Anchorage. We barged ahead, flying twisted over to the right so I could see down, following the rails back and forth. I didn't see any of the stations that the map showed were along this stretch. Pretty soon I was too busy to even worry. I kept my eyes down on those rails and my hand and feet loose but ready on the controls, making every turn. My eyes began to sting a little from smoke getting into my goggles. I could see nothing but the airplane itself and the rails. I kept my head down.

The stories that appeared about this flight in years afterward had people asking me about the big bridge at Hurricane Gulch and me asking what bridge, giving the impression that we had flown under the bridge. This couldn't have happened, of course. I was following the rails, above them, and I never could have flown *under* them. Besides, that three-hundred-foot-high bridge at Hurricane is way back near Chulitna Pass, a long time before we got to this smoke. Bridges weren't any problem at all. Tunnels were a problem. Fortunately, there weren't any more of them.

At 3:40 from Anchorage, Yunker suddenly waved his arms and pointed down. It was a cleared space left of the rails, the experimental farm run by the new college. Then I saw the college building up on a hill nearly as high as we were. About three miles more and I saw the railroad depot and a little river or creek. This must be Fairbanks, but it was in solid smoke also.

Bill Yunker waved his arm and pointed to the right and I turned that way and got a scare when I saw a high smoke stack. I banked away. This was part of the Northern Commercial Company power plant on Second Avenue, about two hundred feet tall. In a few seconds I saw the race track and knew this was Weeks Field. I was going to land there even if it wasn't, because a race track was home for an old barnstormer.°

Yunker had told me to avoid the middle of the field, as it was soft. Ben Eielson had busted up his De Havilland mail ship there a few weeks before and that was when the post office canceled his contract. I landed—in a three-point landing—along the north side, just inside the track, and taxied on up toward a frame of a hangar. Eielson had built it. It was just a frame, with no sides, and only part of a roof. There wasn't any fence around the track. There was a wooden grandstand on the northwest side. It stayed there into the 1930s, even after the Road Commission had graveled the infield and the track had been turned into the airport.

Four or five men were at the hangar, Jimmy Rodebaugh and some of his friends. They had been up all night waiting for us. They came running to the plane and before I could stop the motor Bill Yunker jumped down and ran up to one of the men and waved his arms.

"Why the devil didn't you let us know about the smoke around here?" he yelled. "We've been in this stuff for eighty miles. You want to lose your plane and pilot without ever laying eyes on them? Not to mention me?"

He was yelling at Rodebaugh, who was a short man, about five feet five and forty years old. He was stout, wearing bib overalls and a white shirt, with a black mackinaw and a black derby. It was a momentous occasion for him and he was laughing in a giddy way. He didn't answer Yunker, just shook his hand and slapped him on the back. The smoke had been covering the Tanana valley for about two weeks. I don't know why they didn't tell us about it, except that smoke never looks as bad on the ground as it does in the air and these people weren't flyers. Yunker was really peeved, but I figured we'd made it, so no use yelling about it.

Rodebaugh came and shook hands and said, "Welcome to Fairbanks, Wien! I didn't know if you'd be able to make it in all this smoke, but I sure am glad to see you. Congratulations!"

He had been in Alaska for years. He was first with the private narrow-gauge railroad from Fairbanks to Chatanika, then went with the Alaska Railroad when the government got that built. He had a wife but no children and had saved his money, I guess. He'd made

---

° The baseball field/race track was named for John W. Weeks of Massachusetts, who was appointed secretary of war by President Harding in 1921.

some money trading furs along the railroad. He had enough to start the Alaska Aerial Transportation Company, buy the two Standards, and hire Yunker and Sampson and me. He was the sole owner of the company. He had taken flying lessons somewhere Outside and had soloed; but he didn't care much for it, and didn't like to fly cross-country at all. Rodebaugh was intelligent and quite a salesman and a hard bargainer. I liked him. He paid me once a month, like he agreed, and didn't miss a date during the two seasons I worked for him.

Art Sampson took me over to the house he'd rented on Lacey Street. Sampson was a big, tall fellow, six foot three, with wavy black hair, and real nice. He was from Ben Eielson's home town in North Dakota. During the month or so he'd been at Fairbanks he'd flown very little. He took up joyhoppers, he liked that, but he didn't want to fly cross-country and that's where the money was, carrying passengers, freight, and gold.

"This is bad country, boy," he warned me. "Those old Hissos in Rodebaugh's planes have never been overhauled. You're going to go down one of these days, if you fly cross-country, sooner than you think. And when you do, how're you going to walk out? This is just not walking country. Wait until you see it. I've been over it, and I know. It's just not aviation country." Sampson talked slow and serious.

"I learned to fly in Dakota where there's fields everywhere. Here there's nothing but swamp, brush, spruce timber, and mountains. Rodebaugh's got a flight all set for you to Brooks, a mining place north about sixty miles. Wait until you see what's between here and there. You couldn't make a good landing anywhere, so maybe there's no use to worry about how you could walk out. You just won't be walking."

He wasn't a coward by any means. He was intelligent and was just being honest. Warning me was a friendly thing to do, because he knew that if I decided to leave too, he might have to stay. Sampson liked Fairbanks and the people, who he said were friendly and had the pioneer spirit. Nobody locks their doors, he said, and everybody knows everybody else and trusts them. "You'll like this town," he told me. He said that Ben Eielson was a real nice fellow and that he might be coming back.

"But I just can't feel that it's worth it to me, to fly up here,"

Sampson said. "I can live without flying in this kind of country and in old airplanes with old motors."

He flew joyhoppers and some students for a few more days, and then he left Alaska.

Wien did not see the newspaper story about his arrival that appeared that evening in the Fairbanks *News-Miner.* "Plucky Airmen Bring 'Anchorage' to Interior; Fast Time Made over Unknown Course" was the headline. The lead paragraph of the story reported: "Arriving over Fairbanks at 6:16 A.M. this morning, the airplane Anchorage, ship No. 2 of the Alaska Aerial Transportation Company, successfully completed the first flight between Anchorage and Fairbanks. The flight was made in the fast time of 3 hours and 45 minutes, and was accomplished without incident. Pilot Noel Wien was at the stick, with Mechanician William B. Yunker as passenger."

Without incident? True to character, Wien had not volunteered to the *News-Miner* reporter the harrowing facts. The story was five paragraphs long, hardly enough to memorialize a flight that linked the Golden Heart of Alaska to the coast. Men who had been in Anchorage that morning had arrived in Fairbanks less than four hours later. By rail, the trip would have taken them two days. By any other method then possible, all of which required some foot work, the trip would have taken weeks.

14. FAIRBANKS

The smoke cover lay over Fairbanks for nearly two weeks after Wien arrived at the outpost, preventing his flying the charters already accepted by the eager Rodebaugh. One day, when visibility

widened enough so that hills to the north could be faintly seen, Noel
took off for Brooks, a mining location ninety miles north by trail,
fifty miles on a direct line.° Paying passenger was Luther C. Hess,
wealthy Fairbanks banker who owned property over much of the
Territory and was recognized as the Interior's economic arbiter.
Hess was flying off to inspect his holdings at Brooks, hoping to make
in an hour a trip that had taken him four days of fighting hills and
mosquitoes on the ground.

Deadheading in the front cockpit with Hess was Rodebaugh, who
went along both to share the excitement of the inauguration of bush
flying as well as to direct his pilot in following the dog trail. This
latter was more easily proposed than done, for even the most
familiar landmarks when seen from the air for the first time are
often unrecognizable. There was no compass in the Standard, Noel
had only a general idea of where Brooks was, and his map was not
detailed enough to be of much help. Rodebaugh's ability as aerial
guide was not to be tested that day, however, for just over the first
ridge the three adventurers met a solid curtain of smoke. "The hills
ran left and right across our course," Wien said, "and I wasn't going
to go down low in that like I did to follow the railroad from Nenana.
Railroads run in valleys and cuts, and you can follow them low."
Wien turned the Standard's nose around and deposited his disappointed passengers back at the Fairbanks race track.

Rodebaugh later was sometimes irritated by Wien's caution, but
this time he had seen for himself what his pilot faced. "I wouldn't
have known where to tell you to go," he admitted to Wien.
Impressed with the pilot's decision, and happy about it, was Mrs.
Hess. "I was worried," she told a friend, "when I got to the field and
saw this young boy who was going to fly Luther to Brooks. I didn't
expect Luther to get back. I couldn't believe that this boy knew
how to fly that big airplane." †

He did not fly it again for a week. He became so absorbed in
discovering the uniqueness of Fairbanks that some mornings he did
not even go out to the field to pat the springy fabric of the old
Standard, a failure for him as shocking as Cactus Jack's neglecting

---

° Gold was discovered here in 1914 by N. R. Hudson and Jay Livengood, along a creek
later named for Livengood. Stampeders founded a village nearby, first calling it Brooks. It is
now called Livengood. Once housing several hundred persons, the village lost its post office in
1957, and by 1969 was home to only one man living among its abandoned buildings.

† Related to author by Mrs. Barney Hanson in 1969 during interview in Fairbanks.

to curry Ole Paint. Fairbanks, almost in the center of Alaska, about one hundred miles south of the Arctic Circle, came into being because a boat ran aground on a mud bar there.

Capt. E. T. Barnette's supply boat had steamed up the Tanana in 1901 and turned into the narrow Chena in an attempt to push as far as possible. Eight miles up the Chena was the mud lump. The boat stopped, the captain said, "This is as far as we go," the goods were unloaded, and a town was founded. True to Alaska tradition, at a town meeting two years later the place was not named Barnette, which would have been appropriate, but was named in honor of another political immortal, an Indiana senator who was later Teddy Roosevelt's vice-president.

Gold was discovered in 1902 about ten miles northeast of the mud bar. Word spread and stampeders raced in, two thousand miles up the Yukon and Tanana from the Seward Peninsula, down the Yukon and up the Tanana from Dawson, and by land from every direction. They found a trading post already established nearby and a wise man taking the mercantile road to sure wealth—supplying the gold seekers, few of whom ever hit it so well.

Though gold worth millions was to be stripped from the area, few sourdoughs of the individual and partnership variety were to realize wealth. Most of the gold here was too hard to get. It was deep placer gold, the precious metal lying on bedrock at the bottom of eighty to one hundred feet of frozen gravel. Sourdoughs worked over the surface with their pans, making a stake but working their lives away. They were followed by men with sluice boxes, then others with flumes, then derricks and steam shovels. Finally, great dredges moved in for the final assault, ingesting and excreting acre after acre as they worked through the deep gravel of ancient stream beds.

Noel and the dredges arrived about the same time. Only completion of the railroad made dredging possible. The huge, boatlike dredges were shipped in pieces over the railroad, dragged to the sites, and erected. The major operator was the Fairbanks Exploration Company, a subsidiary of United States Smelting, Refining and Mining Company, which bought up old claims in all directions within the thirty- by fifty-mile Golden Heart.

Fairbanks in 1910 had been a genuine metropolis of the far north, with 3,541 residents. By 1920 there were only 1,155. There were

fewer than that, and jobs for newcomers were nonexistent, when
Noel arrived in 1924. The dredges brought revival. By 1930 the city
had grown to 2,101 living on the payrolls and purchases of the
dredges. More than one hundred million dollars in gold—this was
the "real" money of the young 1900s—was taken from the
Fairbanks gravel. When the dredges finished their work, Fairbanks
again shriveled. The dredges remain in the spots where they
chewed their last bites, perfectly preserved in the dry arctic air, the
woolly mammoths for later ages. Fairbanks was resurrected by
arrival of the military in World War II, and its economy has been
based on its presence ever since. Full realization of its potential as a
supply base for Arctic Plain oil development would bring another
boom.

Noel felt at home. He was surprised to find afternoon temperatures going to 90 degrees. He had already been regaled with stories
of 60 below in wintertime Fairbanks, 82 below at Snag nearby in
the Yukon. This meant that men in the north endured temperature
ranges of 150 to 170 degrees. Both heat and cold in the Interior,
however, were tempered by dryness and the rarity of strong winds.

Fairbanks, with its dirt streets, board sidewalks, log cabin homes,
false-front buildings, roughly dressed men, and few women, was like
a relic of the Wild West of the 1880s. Prices were marked to the
nearest quarter. Pennies were not in use, for who had space and
strength to carry around a load of chicken feed? Paper dollars were
rare, and men strode down the dusty streets in step to the clank of
silver dollars in their pockets. That was real money. Out in the bush
pennies, dimes, and nickels were useless. The smallest coin in
circulation at the roadhouses along the trails was the quarter. On
the Yukon and beyond, everything was priced in multiples of one
dollar, and cartwheels were the smallest coins.

When Sampson left Fairbanks, Noel moved into the hotel on
Second Avenue.° Because of the local depression, he got a single
room. When times boomed, hotels sometimes had to ask strangers to
share a room. But there were few tourists in Fairbanks in those
days. Lone sourdoughs and those working in pairs were out on the
creeks shoveling for glory. Some of those who had no stakes and

° Sampson became head of the aviation department at the State School of Science at
Wahpeton, Minn. In 1940 he organized the Minnesota Civil Air Patrol. Retiring in 1953, he
operated a repair shop at Battle Lake, Minn., until his death in 1961 at age sixty-one.

those who had been laid off by the big works sat around the small hotel lobby talking incessantly about the "next hole," the one at the end of the rainbow that would bring them fortune.

Besides *cheechako*, Noel heard a few more words—*skookum* (physically strong) and *siwash* (to sleep in the open)—of the old Chinook trading jargon that had come up from the coast and was dying out. What little construction work there was in Fairbanks had to be done in the summer when a few inches of the permafrost could be melted, and such work went on around the clock in the perpetual daylight. Industrious men lifted corners of their cabins that had sagged into the gravel and stuffed in sand to level their walls. Around the few cabins ruled over by women, gigantic pansies, marigolds, and other flowers bloomed so brilliantly that they seemed to be fake.

Fairbanks, Noel discovered, sat where the Tanana-Yukon Highlands came down from the north to end at the valley of the Tanana River. The old rolling hills covered with spruce and birch reached 100 miles northward to the Yukon Flats, attaining heights of 5,400 feet. South of Fairbanks, and for 150 miles east and west, was the muskeg of the valley. Fifty miles south the muskeg ended at the Alaska Range, one of the most magnificent upthrusts on earth, arcing 275 miles east and west just below the Territory's waist. Often visible from Fairbanks were the crags of Mount Moffit at 13,000 feet; Mount Shand, at 12,700; Mount Hayes, 13,800; Mount Hess, 12,000; and Mount Deborah, 12,300. On winter days the fleeting sun set behind Mount McKinley, 165 miles away. Fairbanks is at 147°43′15″ west longitude, as far west as Tahiti; 64°50′43″ north latitude, farther north than Reykjavik. It is the only "city" within an area of 227,000 square miles.

I liked Fairbanks right away, the people and the town. The long daylight was so interesting. In Anchorage it got a little dark around midnight, but up here it was light all night in July. The baseball team played on weekends, and on June 21 and July 4 they always started a game at midnight sharp, just to indicate that this was the farthest north city in the country.

There was a complete change in my living. I couldn't get to bed. I wanted to stay up all night. I walked the quiet streets and looked at the sky, went to the movies, stayed up to chat with the young fellows and old sourdoughs in the hotel lobby. They all sat there and chatted with anybody who came in, leaned over the counter and talked with the clerk. They wanted to know all about me and about flying and the circus days and every hour I had in the air. And they told me about Alaska, about the north and the cold and gold. It seemed nobody slept, just stayed up. You really had to discipline yourself to get to bed. I was a regular chatterbox and I found talking with any of these fellows as easy as chatting with my brothers and sister or with George Babcock. I never did get homesick in Fairbanks, because I was home.

I'd look into the stores at night. Lavery's grocery was on the corner and the prices weren't bad, because Fairbanks was in a depression. Fifty cents a pound for butter, and a honeycomb was fifty cents. That was high for Seattle, but not for Fairbanks. My room cost me thirty dollars a month, and I made out all right and ate well. I didn't have to buy any clothes, just odds and ends. Bloom's was the hardware store. They had outfits for prospectors, guns, traps, big eighty-by-eighty-inch sleeping bags, all kinds of boots, and drill parkies that you wore over your fur parky° to protect the fur from wearing. The movies were at the Empress, and they still had silent pictures in the thirties, years after talkies came in. They changed pictures three times a week, so I went three times a week. I saw everything, but I liked westerns best.

They had dances, which I went to. I also went to the ball games and began running. I did a little curling, too, and fished for grayling.

Sampson told me about the rough country, and I knew he was right, that sooner or later I would go down. So I wanted to get in the best shape possible to walk out, even though he said I'd never be able to walk out. So every night I began going out to the race track, Weeks Field, to run at a good trot three or four times around the half-mile track. I ate carefully, skipping breakfast. If I had a job the next day, I'd go to bed around eleven; but if I didn't, I'd stay up until two o'clock or so and make myself go to bed then. Rodebaugh didn't say anything about being at the airport every morning. I kept up my running for nearly thirty years.

There was a young fellow, Eddie Hudson, who wanted to learn to fly. The smoke was still too bad to see far, but it was good enough

---

° Spelled parka, but always pronounced "parky" by sourdoughs.

for local flying. We went up on a joyhop, and Eddie wanted me to stunt him. I made seventeen loops in succession without losing any altitude, and then spun down to land. After this, I heard that my reputation was getting a little bad. Some older folks were worried about flying with me, so I quit stunting. I told it all around town that I never stunted with anyone who didn't want to, and even then not with everybody who wanted to. When I would take a joyhopper up and they leaned outside on the first bank I made, I knew they were scared, so I wouldn't stunt them even if they asked me to. I wouldn't even do a steep bank with them.

Finally, on August 19, 1924, Wien made the long-awaited flight to Brooks (Livengood), opening wide the gates for the age of Alaska bush flying in which a thousand fine pilots won their wings. With Rodebaugh and Hess in the front cockpit, Noel put the old Standard into the air from Weeks Field. He had noted during his two weeks at Fairbanks that there was little wind on the surface, learning from old-timers that this was a constant condition. Taking off and landing at Fairbanks, where he had a good twelve hundred feet in the track infield and about two hundred feet of cleared overrun, would be no problem. He wondered, however, about the short strips he would find in the hills and how difficult it would be to land with no slowing help from winds.

Once again he topped the first ridge, sailed out over Goldstream Creek, along which the railroad ran, and this time ridge after ridge of timbered hills were visible. Following Rodebaugh's pointing finger, he climbed out to about five thousand feet, enough altitude, he estimated, to clear anything he could see ahead.

At the end of Goldstream, Rodebaugh signaled a slight left turn and then pointed straight on a course that was 300 degrees magnetic; but with no compass in the plane, Wien could not be entirely sure of his course.

Ridge after ridge fell behind the Standard. They were heavily timbered, with only occasionally a rounded, smooth dome poking up from the expanse of trees. Along the occasional clear spots, Noel was able to see a stringlike line. This was the dog trail. Rodebaugh had told him there were nine cabins along the trail—home for prospectors and trappers—but Noel could not spot any. Rodebaugh had told him also that there were plenty of farmers' fields around

Fairbanks that would be good emergency landing places, but he could find few of these either. The only possibility for putting down that Wien saw on this first flight to Livengood (Brooks) was a mountain dome, the highest on the route, that reached about thirty-two hundred feet above sea level. It had only a few hundred feet of rounded space on it, but it was clear of timber.

Fifty minutes after takeoff, Rodebaugh turned and yelled back to his pilot and gestured downward. This must be Livengood. Noel banked and looked down. He saw a cluster of cabins on a hillside, a stream below. There did not appear to be an airport, a strip, even a field. He circled. He circled again, over timbered hillsides and a rocky, narrow stream with no sand bars. Rodebaugh yelled back and pointed north across the stream. Noel saw a clearing about six hundred feet square on a hillside.

He set up an approach, heading southwest. The Standard was old and wrinkled, but her controls were solid. Noel stuck her in exactly the attitude he wanted, settled down over the creek, the trees, sensed that his ground speed was low enough to let him land safely, pulled off power, and put the plane on the ground at thirty-five miles an hour. It stopped with room to spare.

Rodebaugh tumbled out of the craft, bubbling with happiness at the success of his first venture, clapping his grinning pilot on the back. The grin was Wien's wildest show of emotion in months. Even the dignified Hess felt something of the zest of the moment. The Livengood "airport" was less than a mile across the draw from the village, but the walk down and then up was about three. Noel and Rodebaugh went with Hess. While the banker visited his gold properties, no doubt startling a few unprepared managers, Rodebaugh bounced about the streets and dumps and promoted his miracle transportation company. "Miracle" was hardly exaggeration. They had brought Fairbanks to within an hour's travel of Livengood. It was a trip of several days during the winter on the frozen dog trail. In the summer, the trail was impassable; the journey via the Livengood River took two weeks. Miners went to Livengood in the winter, and the soonest they could get out was after the next freeze-up. Now men in airplanes could go to Livengood and back in a morning, maybe any morning in the year.

Even the least imaginative panners and muckers in Livengood could understand what it meant to them also, in obtaining supplies, preventing starvation, repairing equipment, replacing equipment, sending out gold for safekeeping in Fairbanks, obtaining medical help, and summoning the law. No doubt the thought of an occasional whoopee in the "big city" crossed a mind or two.

Advantages that bush flying brought to the large-scale mining and pelt operators are fairly obvious. But aviation meant even more to the single prospector and trapper, for it opened up areas that were impossible to reach in any other way. For example, a loner trying to reach an isolated location in winter—which he could not reach at all in summer—would have to feed half the total load he could carry to his dog team, the "fish burners." He could not haul enough supplies to last a winter, much less through the following summer, the only season during which he could wash down his dump. An airplane could take such a man, and a partner too, five hundred miles into the bush, deposit them, and then make regular runs to resupply and to bring them out. The old sourdoughs were not to make use of the airplane that first summer of bush flying, but from 1925 on they were a major source of revenue for Rodebaugh and the other bush operators who followed in 1926.

15. BUSH

When Hess had finished inspecting his property at Livengood, the trio returned to Fairbanks, a flight of 1:15, making 2:15 for the round trip. Wien was to fly thirty hauls into Livengood that summer. About two hundred fifty men worked there at small gold operations, all needing goods and services; it was close to Fairbanks, making several round trips a day feasible during the twenty-four hours of daylight.

But Rodebaugh sent his pilot in every direction. Noel flew to

Circle Hot Springs, 90 miles northeast over the Tanana-Yukon Highlands, 140 miles by trail, where natural hot water heated the roadhouse to seventy degrees above even when it was sixty below outside. Circle Hot Springs was a resort at the center of a mining district. Many miners came in from the wilds to spend the winter there in comfort. Before descending to land, Noel could see the Yukon Flats beyond the highlands, the mighty Yukon itself distinguished by its size and muddy color among the thousands of lakes and tributary streams. This was a promotional flight of a sort. The Springs' owner, Frank Leach, had scraped off a sixteen-hundred-foot landing strip below his resort—population seventeen—and wanted to let Fairbanks people know how easily it could now be reached.

A few days later, Wien set out with Charley Peterson, a mechanic summoned to repair machinery at the Salchaket Mining Company works on Caribou Creek, sixty-five miles east of Fairbanks. Noel was told that Caribou was at the headwaters of the Salcha River that flowed southwest into the Tanana.

"I'll show you where it is," said Charley, who had never been near an airplane. They found the Salcha without difficulty, then flew up it, circling from time to time while Charley scratched his helmet and whistled into the windstream, confused at the sameness of the landscape below.

Noel flew farther up the Salcha, or at least what he thought was the Salcha, keeping the largest stream he could see under him. At the point where he was deciding to turn around and return to Fairbanks he saw a column of smoke rising ahead. He headed for it. It was his destination. Anticipating a problem because the plane was overdue, men at the mine had lighted a brush fire. Noel put the Standard down on a small, bumpy field that had been cleared somewhat, hit a rough spot and slowly began nosing over. He cut the motor and luckily the propeller stopped exactly straight across, saving a cracked prop. The flight back to Fairbanks was cold—the Interior's two-week autumn was nearing—and thereafter Noel wore a wool-lined flight suit and warned his passengers to bundle up Alaska-style.

Two days later, he flew Norman Wimpler of the U.S. Bureau of Mines to Eagle on his annual inspection of placer operations. Eagle, on the Yukon River six miles west of the Alaska-Canada border, had once been a city of eight hundred residents; in 1924 it had fewer than one hundred. To it in the dead of winter in 1905 a solitary foreigner came by dog sled in order to send a message from the U.S. Army's Fort Egbert. The message was to Fridtjof Nansen in Norway, and it said something about the sender having reached King Point in the Canada Arctic and being iced in for the winter. He then turned around and mushed back the 350 frigid miles through the Brooks Range and down the slope to the Arctic Ocean and his ship, the *Gjoa*. He was Roald Amundsen, and in just this way did he announce to the world-famed Nansen that he had sailed the Northwest Passage, the first captain in history to do so.

Alaska's first bush pilot, on his trip to Eagle, headed north from Fairbanks. He wanted to pick up the Yukon River first and follow it, thinking that flying direct would get him lost. The Yukon was well mapped; at least, its bends and turns were well located, although some of the villages were misplaced as much as fifteen miles. After 3:45 in the air, Noel found Eagle and discovered that abandoned machinery and boilers (the metal junk that is ubiquitous in the northland) would prevent his landing on the deserted fort's parade grounds.

He put the Standard down on a sand island, guiding it among willows on the approach. In the past, Wimpler's inspection trip had taken him three weeks, steaming down the Tanana River and up the Yukon to Eagle. Today he had made it in less than four hours.

Clouds were building and snow seemed in the offing, so Noel decided to return to Fairbanks direct, over the highlands, rather than take the 220-mile river route. By heading southwest, he thought, he would meet the Tanana where it turns north toward Fairbanks, and could follow it home. That is, if he didn't meet some other rivers in between and mistake them for the Tanana. Fortunately he did not, arriving at Fairbanks in 3:15.

"Yesterday's flight was the longest attempted by Pilot Wien in his Alaska work," reported the *News-Miner*. "He appeared not to have been fatigued when he landed last night, altho the cold, constant hum of the motor and nervous tension caused him to seek rest shortly after the plane was put away."

Following a trip to Chena Hot Springs, fifty miles northeast, with two passengers, one a child, Wien made the first flight into the Kantishna country. Rich mines of copper, gold, zinc, lead, and silver were being worked here, in the lowlands due north of McKinley. A mining engineer and his secretary, a frequent passenger mix, were Noel's charter. These two were to have quite an adventure, for, after two days of trying to get through poor weather, Noel was to land them among solid mosquitoes on a sand bar twenty impossible miles from their destination.

The Alaska Range was not visible when the three took off from Fairbanks, but the horizon to the east was clear. Kantishna was 140 miles southwest. Wien planned to fly down the Tanana River to Nenana, then over the muskeg, crossing the Nenana, Teklanika, and Toklat rivers, to the Kantishna River, remaining north of the hills and the range. He thought he could remain low enough to get through, but when he made the turn around Chitsia Mountain, he found the overcast down to the ground ahead of him. Nevertheless, he continued on and tried to fly up Bearpaw Creek and then Caribou Creek (a different one) toward the mines. No use.

I turned back northward, and it was still clear in every direction but south, the way I needed to go. I flew around the rim of the foothills again and headed back to Fairbanks. Over the Toklat I saw a fine sand bar and decided to land to see if we could wait out the weather. The engineer was very anxious to get to his work. There wasn't any wind and the approaches to the bar were clear and the bar was a real long one, so I set up and put her down.

The rocks were bigger than I thought they'd be, but we didn't bust anything. But I never landed again on a sand bar without dragging it at least once, no matter how good it looked from above. That night, when it started to get dark, I told the engineer we'd have to go back to Fairbanks or else spend the night on the bar. He said, "Let's go to Nenana and stay in the hotel and then try again tomorrow." That's what we did.

The next morning I couldn't see the range, but we took off again. He was very anxious to get to work and kept pushing me, but the weather was just like it was the day before. We couldn't get through to Kantishna, even flying just a few feet above Bearpaw Creek. He told me to land them somewhere as close as I could if we couldn't get through.

I found a cabin near a little bar on Bearpaw Creek. The bar was only about three hundred feet long and we were very heavy, what with the two of them and their camping and business gear. I knew it would have to be a perfect landing. There was a little wind (I could see smoke coming from the cabin), and I had to come over some spruce to land into the wind. The trees were about fifty feet high and they were about one hundred feet from the beginning of the sand bar. I knew I had to put the wheels down right on the edge. I came over the trees at the edge of the river, chopped power right over them, flared out over the river, and made a three-pointer. The bar was hard-packed gravel and we stopped right quick. I was pretty proud of that landing.

I didn't slip the ship to get it in. I never did that. Straight in was always best control for me, the most accurate way to put down on the first ten feet of landing space. I'd get the sing of the wires proper for my lowest airspeed, come in with power, chop it off, and plunk her on. If I was slipping, it would be too easy to come in at a slight angle and wipe off the gear. That would have been the end in Alaska in those days. The pilots who sideslipped were just afraid to get down to their lowest speed on approach, then the only way they could lose altitude at the last minute was to sideslip. Lots of them lost their wheels. A lot of pilots sideslipped every time as a way of showing off, because they'd do it even on long fields.

We couldn't have taken off from that bar nohow, with three people in the Standard. It was the shortest place I ever put the old Hisso into, three hundred feet. The fellow in the cabin near where we landed put the engineer and his secretary up for the night, and then they walked on to the Kantishna. I heard they had quite a walk through the mosquitoes and the soft trail.

That summer I also made my first flight to the Kuskokwim, taking Tom McKinnon in to look over his property at McGrath. McGrath was a good-sized place about 280 miles southwest of Fairbanks, right down a sort of trench in the Kuskokwim Mountains where the Kuskokwim and Takotna rivers meet.° Bill Yunker had replaced the auxiliary gas tank with a bigger one, giving the Standard seventy-seven gallons, and I used up all but twelve gallons on this trip.

° It was good-sized in Alaskan terms. McGrath had about one hundred persons, was a supply point for inland mines, with much of the goods reaching it up the Kuskokwim River. Dog trails crossed here.

Population figures throughout are taken from Colby, *Guide to Alaska*, or Donald J. Orth, *Dictionary of Alaska Place Names*, Geological Survey Professional Paper 567 (Washington, D.C.: U.S. Government Printing Office, 1967).

I had a Road Commission map with me, but it showed nothing but the sled dog trails and the features you saw when on the ground. Most of these didn't show from the air in the same way. The rivers were more accurately drawn, but there were so many of them and they all looked so much alike that it was easy to get lost. You could find almost the same exact features in a half a dozen places on a dozen rivers. Later, when I got to memorize the Alaska Range, I could use my angle to it to tell about where I was or where I had to go.

There were some cabins marked on the map, but nothing was marked accurately enough to give me mileage checkpoints so I could figure my ground speed. I picked up the Kuskokwim and started down and came to the Takotna. We'd been flying 4:45. I circled a slough on the river that looked exactly like the spot that showed McGrath on the map. McGrath should be right here, I thought.

Well, I couldn't see McGrath anywhere, or any cabins. It's got to be further along, I figured. I must be going slower than I thought. So I started back down the river thinking I'd go that way just a few minutes. We were just about out of gas.

Suddenly I saw it, the cabins at McGrath. What I thought was the Takotna wasn't it at all. I'd been still following the Kuskokwim and hadn't reached the Takotna yet.

There wasn't any time to pick out a landing spot, so I just headed for the first sand bar I saw, a smooth one with black sand and no rocks, just around a bend in the river from the old town. My narrow, three-inch tires cut into the sand four or five inches and we stopped quick. We'd been in the air five hours and twenty minutes. I never knew the old Hisso would fly so long. It was a three-week trip by dog.

I stayed overnight at McGrath, filled the gas tanks, and flew back to Fairbanks. It took a mighty long run to get off that soft sand bar. I stopped at Nenana on the way back and gassed up. You always had a wind up that trench, I learned, blowing right in your face from McGrath to Fairbanks, and it didn't take much to cut your ground speed to forty. That made every hop back from McGrath a sort of serious one. They had this gas at Nenana and McGrath because the gas boats were replacing the steamboats on the river. In later years we built caches of gas at places all over our territory.

My biggest thrill that first year wasn't these first flights, or the first one over the Arctic Circle, my last flight of the summer, but a short hop back from Livengood. A miner gave me his poke of gold dust to put in the Fairbanks bank for him. This was done all the time: the miners never asked for a receipt, just handed over their gold. The poke was about eight inches long and three inches thick and made of caribou hide. It weighed more than nine pounds, because in it there were about 150 ounces of dust, worth about three thousand dollars, or twenty dollars an ounce.

I put the poke under my seat on one of the floor boards. There wasn't any cupboard or container to use. The safest place was on the board by my feet. These boards were used to slide your feet on in using the rudder. Under the boards was just the old fabric covering.

Well, after flying awhile I felt down to check on this poke, and it wasn't there. I felt around as best I could in all directions in the cockpit and it was just gone. It must have slipped off the board onto the fabric.

That was the wrong kind of thrill to have, and I was real worried. Five years is just about the life of fabric before it gets brittle and rips and tears. This old Standard was about eight years old, and the fabric had holes in it and was pretty loose. A nine-pound poke could easily rip a hole in it and drop from the plane. That was a terrific worry. You could put a rip in the old fabric just stunting.

Back at Fairbanks, I landed as easy as I could and didn't even taxi, just stopped out on the field. I dived headfirst down in the cockpit and started looking. The poke was there. It had slid off the floor board and vibrated back, but it hadn't bumped a hole in the fabric.

I still don't know if I would have been legally responsible for replacing that gold, but I know I would have had to do it somehow. I had been able to save only four hundred fifty dollars during the summer, so I would have had a long siege of hard work to pay that man back. Flying was coming to an end because of weather, and there weren't any jobs in Fairbanks. I don't know how I could have made it good. I was more scared over that poke than over anything in all my flying. Those sourdoughs trusted you, so you just couldn't let them down.

Wien's final flight that summer was one the entire Interior had been awaiting, the first beyond the Arctic Circle. A miner and his son wanted to fly from Fairbanks to Wiseman, a gold-mining outpost 80 miles north of the circle, 185 miles northwest of Fairbanks. The community of several hundred hardy folk had been established in 1911 on the middle fork of the Koyukuk River in the Brooks Range. By water it was 1,300 miles from Fairbanks. In winter a dog team trip required two weeks.

By now the Standard, despite Yunker's wizardry, was showing signs of weariness. Her radiator was clogged with minerals from Fairbanks water, and it had been pinched in uncounted places to nip leaks. Wien, his two passengers, and a full load of fuel took off into the blue sky and headed for the Yukon. They crossed the mighty river at Stevens Village, a place Noel recognized, and flew toward the Brooks foothills.

A few miles beyond the Yukon they passed the Arctic Circle, but the momentous fact that they were the first people to cross it in flight did not register on the pilot's mind. The terrain remained the same, but ahead he could see virga from low clouds over the rising hills. In a few more minutes the Standard entered light snow as it climbed to top the hills now rising toward five thousand feet.

Noel found that with his load he could not reach higher than four thousand. He banked left to skirt the first shoulder of hills and flew out over the Kanuti Flats in an attempt to pick up the Koyukuk. Before he reached even the south fork, however, the snow became too heavy for safety. He could not see ahead.

He turned southeast and made several probes into canyons in the range, to no avail. The snow was too thick, the canyons too narrow and too deep, the ship too heavy to climb above the storm. To his passengers' great disappointment, their pilot again turned southeast and returned to Livengood. There were three inches of snow on the ground. They had been in the air 5:15, the Standard had only minutes of fuel left. The three were so stiff with cold that they had to be helped down from the cockpits.

After gassing, they took off for Fairbanks, arriving there with the Hisso thrashing like a harpooned beluga. One magneto was out, one plug was missing on the good one, and the vibration was frightening. It was October 8. Interior temperatures were going toward the bottom of the thermometer and the snows had begun. The temperature would not climb back to zero for nearly eight months, not a flake of snow that fell would melt until May. Liquid-cooled motors would no longer run. People could not fly in open cockpits. It was time to shut down Alaska's first bush flying operation for the long winter.

Wien had flown 139:05 hours in Alaska. His success converted many doubters, and Fairbanks businessmen enviously eyed Rodebaugh's operation. Having demonstrated through Wien that aviation not only was possible in Alaska but was uniquely suited to coping with its empty spaces, Rodebaugh now thought about all-year flying. What equipment would he need in order to fly in the Interior winter, he wondered. Noel told him that at a minimum he must have an airplane with an air-cooled motor and an enclosed cabin.

In the States, despite the efforts of pioneer commercial organizers, most of the flying being done was still regarded by much of the public as a dangerous stunt. Transport was adequately provided by water, rail, and the growing highway webs for automobiles and trucks. Who needed to risk his goods or his neck in a flimsy man-carrying kite? Alaskans of all strata, however, instantly saw the value of air travel. It was in the figures: sixty miles an hour to anywhere, as against fifteen miles a day to the accessible places.

Alaskans took eagerly to the airplane, dragging with them every conceivable kind of household and personal item so that aircraft often looked like Mexican rural buses. Freight was stuck here and there around the passengers and in their laps. Groceries, canned goods, dry goods, odds and ends stuffed under the seat, on the sides, on the floor boards. Sleeping bags sat on laps, suitcases and bedrolls protruded from the cockpit, spades and picks were tied on outside.

Almost everybody in Alaska took at least one moose and one caribou every year, but there were no beef cows in Alaska, making beef a dreamed-of delicacy. Iced beef was boated from Seattle to Seward and sent from there to Fairbanks by rail. Almost every flight Wien made carried an order of beef for some village store, wrapped in layers of burlap. Often this was not sufficient; sometimes it thawed and dripped through.

A spare wooden propeller was carried strapped to the fuselage at the lower wing, for noseovers were common. The Standard's instruments were an inaccurate altimeter, an oil-pressure gauge, and a water temperature needle. Noel carried a small compass, a mosquito net, and a Luger pistol. He had no other survival gear, for he had not learned the necessity for such foresight. Secured between fabric and wires in his cockpit were pliers, monkey wrench, screw driver, and a Boy Scout knife. Thus equipped, he started out on flights to places he had never heard of over terrain no airman had dreamed of in nightmares.

He thoroughly preflighted the Standard, a practice not yet general throughout aviation. He measured with a stick the fuel in each tank; checked bolts in the flipper, aileron, and rudder controls; drained the sediment bulb in the fuel pump; checked the oil; tested the wires; looked at the turnbuckles.

He developed a fits-and-starts technique for takeoff from the tight Alaska landing places. The Standard took off in a nose-level attitude, then needed to be held down to allow speed to build. But hills and spruces ringing the landing spots prevented a continued nose-down flight. Noel's "feel" led him to a sawing takeoff in which he alternated back pressure, release, back pressure, release on short takeoffs to get the ultimate quick climb from his craft.

Landing techniques also needed to be adapted to Alaska conditions. Power should not be pulled abruptly or completely on a Hisso, because a sudden cooling of the heated motor would warp the valves. Yet those hills and trees around sand bars and short fields made power landings impossible. Noel learned to cut power only at the absolutely necessary moment and for only the absolutely necessary duration, and he observed the limits so expertly that hundreds of landings caused no damage to the Hisso.

He carried also the Road Commission maps that showed dog trails, even after he found them of little use. He soon learned to distrust the directions given by his passengers. He absorbed the elements of topography, memorized the rivers, lakes, mountains, flats, and their relation to each other. His inborn sense of north-south never failed him; usually, when lost, he was able to find a feature that he knew from which he could trace his way to safety. If all else failed, he learned to fly downriver: little rivers lead to big rivers; big rivers have cabins on them.

He looked as he flew. He remembered Sampson's words, "Wait'll you see that country. You couldn't make a good landing anywhere." Noel was to prove Sampson wrong, many times over, but it was not through luck. He studied the land constantly, and he saw places where he thought he might be able to put the Standard. "This kept me so busy," he said, "I didn't have time to think about the danger of flying there."

Some men would have felt the weight of the vast loneliness of this land, in which a man had a hundred thousand square miles under his view during a two-hundred-mile flight, with perhaps no other humans in all that expanse. Even in the 1970s the vastness of Alaskan space and the insignificance of a lone man's relation to it sometimes produced a sense of unreality, of awe, of ineffable unease, of something like fear.

"I was too busy to be lonely," Noel said.

16. OUTSIDE

Wien rode the train south to Seward, took the S.S. *Alaska* to Seattle. Rodebaugh told him before he left that Eielson's old lean-to hangar would be roofed and sides would be nailed to it. One of the Standards would be sheltered there, but the other would have to remain outside through the winter. Noel warned his employer that snow must regularly be swept from the wings or the wings would scrape the ground when the ship emerged from its mound of ice in the spring. Rodebaugh made certain that Wien understood he was expected to return to Alaska in the spring and resume his job.

The post office inspector for Alaska gave Noel a letter of introduction to whomever it may concern in the department's air mail service in the States. Although he did not say so then, this prescient man was concerned about airplanes taking over Alaskan mail routes from the dog mushers and was recommending Wien for a flying postman's job Outside. Noel took the day coach from

Seattle to Omaha, traveling the "cheapest way," as he always did. Omaha was a stop on the transcontinental air mail route between New York and San Francisco.

At Omaha he looked up Slim Lewis, one of the more famous of the mail flyers, who was not only dashing and glamorous in Noel's eyes but kind as well. He took Wien out to the line, where the Alaskan thrilled at the sight, feel, and sound of the great De Havilland D.H. 4s that the air service used. These big airplanes had served as bombers for British and American forces in the World War. The American version was powered by a twelve-cylinder, 400-horsepower Liberty that pulled it to a high speed of more than 120. Noel longed to fly one of the husky craft, but, assuming there were regulations against outsiders joyhopping, did not ask permission.

Neither did he ask for the job the Alaska dog mail advocate hoped he would find. He intended to return to Alaska; he had given Rodebaugh his word. Besides, he said, "they wouldn't have taken me on. I didn't look like an air mail pilot. They were all older, taller, more sophisticated, more rugged looking." He had nearly seven hundred hours command time, a fifth of it over the wilderness of Alaska, and had begun to perfect techniques that would allow flying man to conquer Alaska; yet his attitude toward the mail flyers was like that of a hero-worshiping kid.

"I had so much to learn," he said, "and these were like flying knights. Those big airplanes, with that great motor . . . it was more than I'd ever handled."

He watched Lewis make a night takeoff, the first one he had seen, for the next mail leg west to North Platte, with burning flares marking the runway edges. "It was amazing," he said. "Hair-raising!"

Noel continued on to the home farm in northern Minnesota. Big brother Ralph, now married and still struggling with his auto repair business, pumped Noel for information about Fairbanks. Noel told him of the depression there and said he could not recommend Alaska as a place to find steady work. Sister Enid had married and was living in town. Fritz, two years younger than Noel, was working in an auto body shop in Grand Rapids, Michigan. Sigurd, twenty-one, and Harold, fourteen, remained at the farm.

Although Noel could not identify it, there was a new quality in his father's manner that was very pleasing to the young man. It was respect. Although he did not put it into words, Papa Wien for the first time looked on his second son as a man, a working man, now that he had left the unproductive foolishness of barnstorming, playing games in the sky, and was actually working, hauling freight and passengers every day. Perhaps the airplane could be more than a toy after all. The family spent a cozy Christmas together, swapping small necessities as gifts, quiet, contented.

A few days later, Noel received a message (wireless to Seattle, by wire from there) from Rodebaugh asking if he would look around the States to try to find an airplane with an air-cooled motor and an enclosed cabin. Noel replied in the affirmative, Rodebaugh wired two hundred dollars for expenses, and Noel took a train to Minneapolis and then headed east. He soon found that there was no such craft to be had in the country, although there were rumors of such to be tracked down, and word of "almost as good" craft to be checked out.

He went to Dayton, Ohio, birthplace of the airplane. No such ship here, he was told, but the Waco people at Troy, just twenty miles north, might have one—there had been some talk. . . . Noel had not heard of Waco, and evidently neither had the people of Troy. Although it was a tiny town, Noel had to find the factory for himself. When he found it, he saw four men working on what may have been the first Waco 9, a trim, three-place biplane powered with an OX-5 that was in production from 1925 to 1927.

The craft Noel had heard about was there. It was a four- or five-place cabin biplane of most peculiar aspect, with a 250-horsepower BMW motor. The pilot's cockpit was open, behind the cabin. Noel regrets he did not take a photograph of this machine. "It was a funny-looking ship," he said. "I tried to find out what the stress analyses showed, but they didn't have any paper on stress. They'd just started building a plane according to their ideas, without testing them. All I could find out about specifications was that the motor weighed 700 pounds. They hadn't been able to sell this ship, and I decided it wasn't what Rodebaugh wanted. I went to New York, to companies I'd heard of, the old-timers in the business."

Wien rode the interurban to Mineola, took a room near the airport, and called on the Curtiss people at their airport across a ravine from the Army's field. George S. Ireland, who later designed the Ireland Neptune amphibian, was kind to the young flyer, although Noel was anything but impressive with his humble manner. Curtiss could not meet the Rodebaugh specifications, but Ireland telegraphed Douglas and Wright.

Wright had available a Huff Daland Petrel equipped with the new Whirlwind, a nine-cylinder, 220-horsepower, air-cooled radial. But the Petrel was open cockpit, and Noel thought Rodebaugh would want passenger comfort more than air-cooled power. He saw plans for a beautiful Bellanca-designed monoplane with a six-place cabin, also with a Whirlwind.

"They wanted badly to sell me one," Noel said, "but it couldn't be ready for a year. Spring was coming and we had only a four-month season and couldn't waste a day waiting." In that plane Clarence Chamberlin flew the flamboyant Charles Levine thirty-nine hundred miles from New York to Berlin in 1927, a few weeks after Lindbergh's classic flight.

"This was a beauty, just perfect for us," Noel said. "For $12,500. But we couldn't wait." He dealt personally with Charles L. Lawrence of Wright Aeronautical Corporation, a designer of the great air-cooled engine series.

As a final suggestion, Ireland sent Wien across the Hudson to Hasbrouck Heights, New Jersey, to find the American company recently started by Anthony Fokker, the Dutch designer who had gained world fame by building fighting planes for Germany during the war. Wien met the great man himself. Fokker and his sales manager, R. B. C. Noordyn, took the prospect back to Mineola and at Curtiss Field showed him the curious aircraft Wien was to buy.

This was a Fokker F. III, a giant, single-motored craft, a monoplane that stood about twelve feet tall at the center of its massive cantilevered wing. Fokker pioneered this type of wing, which was structurally self-sufficient, requiring no external bracing. Behind the plane's huge, flat nose, set to the left side and forward of the wing, was the pilot's open cockpit. The aviator rode there like an aerial stagecoach driver, wind-whipped and isolated from his passengers.

The five passengers traveled in baronial splendor in a compartment enclosed in the fuselage and set with three large, oval windows on each side. Two sat on upholstered chairs, three on a sofalike bench, their feet on carpeted floor, soothed by shiny plush walls fitted with glass flower holders. It was as ornate as an 1890 Pullman car.

From the side, the craft was so unexpectedly long that, standing on its stubby landing gear, it resembled a winged dachshund. The ailerons were similar in appearance to those of the dreaded German Fokkers of World War I. They protruded behind and wrapped around a bit forward of the huge wing's trailing edge like swellings. Span was fifty-two feet six inches.

At the right side of the pilot, but partitioned off by bulkhead and cowling, was a 240-horsepower BMW motor powerful enough to haul the massive machine and its twelve-hundred-pound payload through the sky at ninety miles an hour. But the motor was liquid-cooled. Noel paused. Furthermore, from the looks of it Wien estimated that it would take at least one thousand feet to stop after it touched ground. There were not many one-thousand-foot smooth spaces in Alaska. The Fokker had no brakes, but Noel knew of no plane with brakes.

The airplane had been built in Holland in 1921, before Anthony Fokker had left his Dutch plant to come to America. It had been flown by KLM on European passenger routes. It looked much like the Fokker T.-11 that in 1923 had been the first craft to fly nonstop across the United States. Army Lieutenants J. A. Macready and Oakley G. Kelly had covered the 2,520 miles from New York to California in twenty-six hours and fifty-six minutes. The series had stamina, and Alaska demanded that.

Noel came to love the Fokker F. III, but he was not stricken at first sight. He pondered and poked and finally asked for a test hop, a demonstration ride.

"Oh, no," came the reply, "we cannot let you fly it. You are not covered by insurance. You know that."

They were right, of course. But then, how could he go about discovering if he should recommend purchase of the ship? If he went for a ride with the Fokker's pilot, he would have to do so as a passenger back in the club compartment. He couldn't sit outside in the pilot's lap. There was a peephole in the forward bulkhead through which a passenger could watch the back of the pilot's head, but that would not tell him anything about the craft's performance and handling characteristics.

He sent a message to Rodebaugh describing the aircraft. Its price was $9,500. In order to buy a third airplane, Rodebaugh had organized a firm, the Fairbanks Airplane Company, with several local businessmen. The others had invested cash and the old OX-5 Jenny that Ben Eielson had flown in 1923; Rodebaugh had invested his two Standards and a going business. Rodebaugh would be company manager. He and his new associates evidently were impressed with the Fokker name, for, liquid-cooled motor notwithstanding, they messaged back for Wien to buy. They wired $9,500. Then, and only then, was Wien able to find out what kind of a flying pig was in the poke that he had bought.

Boy, oh boy! What am I going to do with this thing? That's what I thought when I tried to fly the Fokker. The rudder pedals had hinges at their base and they started fluttering like a butterfly as soon as I gave it some throttle. It was a strange feeling, being so high up and out front on the nose of the plane. That big motor roared and cooked up a lot of heat right there by my side.

I taxied awhile, trying to get the feel of the ship, and could feel that rudder flutter as soon as it started rolling. The airplane had a balanced rudder, with no vertical stabilizer. I don't think there was any aerodynamic reason for this kind of control surface, except it was easier to move. But once it started to move, it wanted to get out of control, flipping from side to side. When you'd open the throttle, the ship would start off like a snipe, swaying from side to side.

After a while I began to get the feel of it. I decided to give it a try and gave full power, then slowed up my feet so I met the controls. There was never another rudder like that. The tail came up and I let it run and then gave a little pressure and the ship took off.

I didn't want to try anything yet, just to see if it would fly and if I could fly it. I went up a few hundred feet and made a shallow circle around and came into the wind. A monoplane sailed long, I had heard, and this was the first monoplane I'd flown. That first day I just did some takeoffs and landings and steep turns. Once I knew how to handle the rudder pedals, I got to like the way it flew.

This was early in February 1925. Over the next fourteen days I flew the Fokker on twelve hops, and by that time I had mastered the rudder. I knew I had to work on that ship to be able to fly it onto the twelve-hundred-foot field in Fairbanks.

I had passengers on just about every hop. The Fokker mechanics and helpers wanted to ride, and I took some of the stockholders in Atlantic Aircraft. That was Fokker's American company. Only three people paid for their hop. The Fokker people arranged to crate the ship and send it by boat around through the Panama Canal. That was the cheapest way to send it.

I went back to the farm at Cook and there was another telegram from Rodebaugh. He said that Bill Yunker had gone Outside and wasn't coming back and would I try to hire a mechanic for two hundred dollars a month.

Well, when Ralph heard about that, he let out a whoop you could hear on the Mesabi Range. He was always a little more lively than the rest of us. "That's for me!" he said. "Let me try to sell the garage and I'll take the job." He was real excited about getting out of a little town and seeing the world. There was some Viking in him, too. His wife would come up after we had gotten settled in Fairbanks, and she seemed all for it. Ralph had studied at the Sweeney Auto School in Kansas City and was a fine mechanic.

I don't know why Bill Yunker wasn't going back. He liked it so much and was so happy there and always told me of the great future we all had there. Maybe his wife needed him at home in Minnesota. I never did see him again. He was an awfully nice fellow.°

Ralph and I took the steamship *Alaska* from Seattle and bunked in a little two-bunk room. We went to all the entertainments, including the dances. Ralph liked everything he saw and everybody liked him. He was big and friendly and more outgoing than I was. He never regretted his decision for a second. He never did go Outside before he was killed.

Everybody asked me about flying, and prospectors and old-timers wanted to know whether I might fly them to their diggings in the bush. I said I'd have to see where it was first, that I couldn't promise.

Ralph really had a good time. He got a kick out of everybody calling everybody by their first names, and the nicknames he heard, like Two-Step Louie, One-Minute Tom, Pretty Pete, and Highpockets John. All the way up it was so warm and Ralph said he didn't believe me about Alaska being cold. But he wasn't in the Interior

° Yunker became maintenance superintendent for Northwest Orient Airlines at the Twin Cities. He died in the 1960s.

yet. When we got to Fairbanks it was about March 20 and it was thirty below zero.

We stayed one night at the hotel and then moved into a cabin I had started buying, and lighted fires in the wood cook stove and the wood heating stove in the middle of the room. This cabin was on what is now First Avenue. It was called the old Hamilton home, and had been Bob Crawford's home. Bob was born in Dawson but was raised in Fairbanks. He became a composer and teacher and Army flyer, wrote the official Army Air Corps song, and became famous.

The cabin cost eleven hundred dollars. I made a down payment before I left in the fall of 1924 and began making monthly payments when I got back with Ralph. When Julia, Ralph's wife, came up, I was going to sleep in a bunk fitted into a little shed that stuck out from the back of the cabin, sort of like a wanigan. Ralph and I had had to get up to Fairbanks and get the old Hisso Standards in shape, but Julia wasn't coming until June. They were going to live in the main cabin.

Snow was still on the ground, the breakup hadn't come yet, so we couldn't do any flying. The Hisso Standards were in surprising shape, even though one had been outside all winter. It was so dry, there wasn't any rust, and Rodebaugh had kept the snow off the wings.

We tested the radiators by running water mixed with alcohol through them, and were pleased to find that they wouldn't need any soldering. No problem with the steel wires, they just needed tightening. We put new spark plugs in and the motors were ready to go without overhaul. The fabric was more brittle than ever, but that couldn't be helped. Grade-A linen gets brittle sooner than the Grade-A cotton that was used later for covering.

Wien met the bosses of the new Fairbanks Airplane Company. All the officers and most of the stockholders thought they had executive prerogatives. Richard Wood, president of Fairbanks National Bank, was president of the company. Other officers and investors were Rodebaugh; Fred Struthers, manager of Waechter Brothers Meat Market; Robert Bloom, proprietor of a general store; Robert Lavery and Hal Bailey, partners in the grocery store; and Ed Stroecker, cashier at the bank.

Wood, Lavery, and Stroecker spent much time asking about the

Noel's second landing, in May 1925, at Frank Leach's Circle Hot Springs resort, on the first field in Alaska to be cleared specifically as a landing strip. Frank Leach (left) and Joe Mehern (right) are clearing and dragging the plane, with cracked but still usable propeller, from the spring-thaw mud. Courtesy of Noel Wien

The Fokker F. III before takeoff on June 5, 1925, on the first commercial flight between Fairbanks and Nome, with four passengers and 500 pounds of baggage. Ralph, in cap and coveralls, and Noel, in leather jacket, stand just to the left of the Pullman conductor. Passengers are on the right, local dignitaries on the left. Courtesy of Noel Wien

Noel, Capt. George H. (later Sir Hubert) Wilkins, and Ben Eielson in Fairbanks, March 1927, beside one of the long-range Stinson biplanes Wilkins was to use in his Detroit *News* expedition. Courtesy of Noel Wien

Noel and the Fokker, which he flew occasionally for the Fairbanks Airplane Company in 1927, after his own company, Wien Alaska Airways, had been formed. Courtesy of Noel Wien

operation, giving little pep talks to Rodebaugh, Ralph, and Noel. And nagging.

"How come you're not flying today?" Lavery would ask Noel, after the season had begun.

"Well, just look at the weather," Noel would reply.

"It looks good to me."

"This wind means there's bad weather coming," Noel would say.

Noel was to find that the new men thought airplanes and pilots were like wagons, mules, and teamsters and should be hauling on an eight-to-six schedule seven days a week.

17. ARCTIC

There is more than one Alaska. The terrain and topography that the aviator so painfully learns to read during the summer disappear with the fall and do not return until after breakup. When Wien took one of the Standards up to begin the 1925 flying season, it was as if he had been snatched to another world. The land below was white, solid white.

There was no flowing Chena River, no broad Tanana. There was no green muskeg dotted with lakes. There were no dark spruce, bright birch and aspen and alder covering the rises. There were no cabins and dusty streets and trails stringing out of town. Everything was flat white, with only occasional relief provided by a spruce showing part of its green through the white mantle. Only the Mainelike hills, visible to the north after he had gained one thousand feet or so, seemed familiar.

In the almost windless Tanana Lowlands, snow falls and stays; it does not drift to bare one expanse and pile high on another. All

heat- and vapor-producing mechanisms, including human and
animal lungs, send frost into the air to cling to all it touches. Ralph
and Noel had tramped down a bit of a runway so that the Standard
would be able to take off, but even Weeks Field was momentarily
gone.

A flush of concern at the sudden disappearance of the familiar
passed through Noel. Then gradually his sharp eyes began to pick
out detail in the white. Thin, stumpy willows edged what must be a
stretch of the Chena. A different light reflection indicated a road on
which snow had been packed into ice by wagon and auto wheels.

He banked and saw below a moving dot amid whiteness. It must
be Ralph walking across the field. Noel realized that the smaller
landmarks along the routes he had flown the summer before would
be of little use for eight months of the year. Even finding familiar
destinations would require the discovery of new landmarks for
determining the route. He had worried about the sameness of the
terrain in the summer. It was far worse now in this dazzling,
pervading white.

In May and June the frozen land unclenches and allows its
burden of ice and snow to melt and flow seaward. Another Alaska
emerges. The rivers become torrents in the mountains and spread
out across the muskeg and tundra like lakes. Gushes of water race
down every slope. The top two or three inches of the earth begin to
melt and join with water to become mud with a nearly chemical
affinity for feet and wheels.

As the snow gradually melted from Weeks Field, Noel found that
the ground was so well drained that only the soggy spot in the
middle turned to quagmire. As the days grew longer in dramatic
leaps of five and six minutes daily, morning low temperatures rose
beyond zero and then beyond freezing. The 1925 ice breakup in the
river at Nenana occurred at 6:32 P.M. on May 7, and a stunned
sourdough finally hit it rich, winning nearly fifty thousand dollars in
the annual sweepstakes. It was an early breakup.

Before the ice cracked and began moving downstream, however,
Noel had made fourteen flights, achieved his history-making landing
beyond the Arctic Circle, and become the first bush pilot to be
downed in the Alaskan wilderness. Among his late April flights was
his first to Tanana, near the ancient Indian village 150 miles west

down the Tanana River, where that stream joins the Yukon. Since the coming of the white man, there had been several trading posts there, and in 1925 it was a sizable city of three hundred persons. The Standards had not been fitted with skis (that idea had not yet come to the pioneer aerial transporters), so Noel made a wheel landing on the frozen Yukon, whizzing down the ice and achieving a personal record for length of landing roll.

He made several hops to Nenana, one to Beaver on the Yukon, then a well-ballyhooed flight to Circle Hot Springs, taking one Joe Meherin, salesman for Smith and Wesson. Meherin took "S&W" signs to the airfield, stood them up against the Standard, and invited city dignitaries and airplane company officials out to be photographed beside the plane. Meherin had chartered the plane to take him also to Fort Yukon, which would have been the first flight to land beyond the Arctic Circle.

But Wien learned his first lesson about the breakup when he landed at Circle on the field that had been so friendly the previous summer. The Standard rolled out and hit a thawed spot. The wheels sank to the axle, and one blade of the propeller twanged into the mud. The tail went up, then flipped back down as the propeller acted like a spring.

Noel made a careful inspection of the prop—a dark, well-polished wooden Hamilton—and found a slight crack. He told Meherin the trip to Fort Yukon was canceled; in fact, they might not even get back to Fairbanks safely. Because of the heavy load of samples Meherin had insisted on carrying, the spare propeller had been removed from the Standard's side. While the disappointed promoter stamped off to attend to his business, Frank Leach, the resort owner, hooked up his team of horses and hauled the Standard from the mud.

When the pair landed at Fairbanks, they received a message that had arrived in Circle after their takeoff. It was from Fort Yukon, saying that the river had broken up there, the bars were under water, and there was no place to land. Later that summer Wien flew several times into the city of three hundred persons that had been founded in 1847 as a Hudson's Bay Company trading post at the Yukon's farthest north reach. In all, he made twelve flights that summer beyond the Arctic Circle to inaugurate the era of Arctic aviation. Amundsen was then at Spitsbergen, where his aircraft had been shipped, and would make his first Arctic flight two weeks after Noel first landed beyond the Arctic Circle.

On that day, May 5, 1925, Noel's career was nearly terminated. The flight was to Wiseman, the camp in a Koyukuk canyon that a snowstorm had kept Noel from reaching the year before. His passengers this time were Harper Workman, returning to his mines from Outside, and a Mrs. Wheeler. Robert Marshall, in his book *Arctic Village*, calls the flight "one of the great events in Koyukuk history." [*] The Army had established a wireless station at Wiseman two weeks before the flight, and local residents of the mountain village knew a plane was coming. In Marshall's book, an Eskimo girl named Dishoo tells the story of the airplane's arrival:

> It flew over the town and up toward the roadhouse, and we all ran up toward the roadhouse. Then it started to circle around, and we all ran around back of the roadhouse. Then it came back again in front, and then it flew back, and then it flew front, and then it flew back again, and we all followed it. . . . We ran around and around in the snow. Everybody was running, old men, old women, little children. Seemed like they were all crazy. . . . It circled around and came lower and lower, and all of a sudden it landed out there in the bar in the river.
>
> There was about two feet of water in the slough between the roadhouse and the bar. I ran into the slough and the water came up to the top of my boots. Then I looked around to see if any one was coming, and they was all coming after me. So I ran as hard as I could, and behind me I heard everyone in camp splashing in the water.
>
> Jimmy Tobuk and I were the first to reach the plane.[†]

What Dishoo called flying to the front and to the back was Noel's careful examination of the bar on which he was to land. He found that the snow had melted from about four hundred feet of it, giving him a fair strip. He noted "people running in all directions and right through the water over to the bar when we landed."

In hailing the flight, Marshall wrote that "civilization was no longer three weeks to three months away, but only a matter of two or three hours. . . . Small wonder that [Alaskans] should regard Noel Wien, the first aviator to land in the Arctic, as one of the greatest heroes in the world, and that the adulation which they conspicuously withheld from the more advertised explorers should

[*] *Arctic Village* (New York: Smith & Haas, 1933), p. 134.
[†] Ibid., pp. 132, 133. Dishoo became Mrs. Joe Ulen, and her son, Benny Ulen, became a pilot for Wien Air Alaska, lineal descendant of the airline Noel founded in 1927.

be given to this modest pilot and his colleagues. . . ." Not until six
years later did the first automobile come to Wiseman.

The elated Wiseman residents could not let Noel return to
Fairbanks without a ceremony to stamp the day as special. The
whites haled him to Martin Slisco's roadhouse, where he was guest
of honor at a banquet. Then they convened a special meeting of
Igloo No. 8 Pioneers of Alaska and made the pilot an honorary
member of the northernmost chapter. This was the most solemn
honor the people could confer on anyone, but Wien did not fully
appreciate the importance until later, as he began to learn how
proud the old-timers were of their chronological primacy.

Worried about the weather, Wien finally managed to escape the
hospitality. He bought twenty gallons of fuel for the Standard, at
$1.60 a gallon. This gasoline, packed ten gallons to the wooden case,
had been sent in by dog sled. The only other transport to Wiseman
before the airplane was by boat from Bettles, laboriously poled the
last fifty miles up the Koyukuk. After straining the gasoline through
a chamois—an improvement over felt hats—Wien took off alone on
a flight that nearly became his last.

I started out on a direct line for Livengood, instead of following
the rivers in zigzag fashion, because I thought the landmarks were
good enough so I wouldn't be confused. On my southeast course
there was first the mountain range, then the fairly wide valley of the
Koyukuk south fork, then another range, then the Yukon Flats,
thirty miles wide in that part. From the Yukon near Stevens Village
I thought I could pick up Livengood Dome, if I was high enough,
and home on that.

The first sign of trouble was when I got up to about six thousand
feet and hit a lot of turbulence. Those big Standard wings took the
wind and, the plane being slow on the controls anyway, we did a lot
of jumping around. On my first ground check, the south fork, I
figured my ground speed was only about thirty miles per hour. But
that couldn't be, I thought, until three hours passed and I wasn't
even at the Yukon yet.

When I could see the Yukon, it was going south in big loops and I
figured from my map that I'd been blown west. About a mile down
from the Rampart roadhouse was a long streak of blue on the river
which was clear ice with no snow on it. I landed and when I got

down I was real glad to find that the wind had died. I'd been 3:20 from Wiseman, the same as it took me from Fairbanks to Wiseman, and I figured later that my speed had been thirty-nine miles per hour. I had almost no gas left.

I started walking back to the roadhouse and met the owner about halfway. He went on back and brought me twenty gallons of gas on his dog sled. I felt that was plenty, it was very expensive, and with the wind calmed I was only an hour and a half from Fairbanks. I needed only eighteen gallons for that. My oil was low, but I didn't take any on, thinking I had plenty.

The whole population of Rampart, about forty people, came down to watch. This was the first ship to land there and not even some of the whites had ever seen one. My worst mistake was in not asking the old-timers if there were some cabins or villages or trails in the area.

I took off and circled back to get up over the mountains. When I got over them at about six thousand feet and turned toward Livengood, I was standing still. The nose was pointed to Livengood, but the mountains stayed right below me and didn't move. I just sat there hovering.

Then I thought, I'll never get to Fairbanks this way. Airplanes can't fly into sixty-mile-an-hour winds. They can fly, but they can't get anywhere. So I turned right and thought I'd make Nenana and get down on the Tanana there. I got to Manley Hot Springs flats in no time and went down low, but the wind was just as strong. I was about thirty-five miles from Nenana now, trying to fly to it but was being carried sideways to the south.

That wind was something! Pulling at my face and really screaming in the wires. I'll bet the old Standard had never been in anything like that before.

My gas was getting low now and, even more serious, the oil pressure was dropping. I kept looking for places to land but didn't see any. I found out later I was within fifteen miles of Manley Hot Springs and there were two little fields there I could have landed on. I could have turned and that wind would've had me there in five minutes. But I didn't know about it, so I just kept trying to get to Nenana, holding the nose left and being blown to the right, to the south.

I drifted over the Tanana and sideways up the Kantishna, about one hundred feet above the ground, toward the Alaska Range. Under me was flat muskeg with some clumps of trees, snow was covering the ground everywhere. I never heard anything like that shrieking wind before or since. I recognized where the Toklat comes into the Kantishna; I kept in full left rudder, but floated on to the right up the Toklat, getting farther and farther from Nenana and Fairbanks.

I'd been watching the oil pressure gauge get lower, and all of a sudden it hit bottom. I pulled up the nose a bit to bring oil to the pump, and the gauge went back up. Then it went to zero again and I pulled the nose up and got a little reading. I had to keep putting the nose back down because if I flew nose high, that wind would flip the Standard over on the back.

There were some lakes I might've landed on, but they were breaking up and I would've lost the airplane. I was thinking the whole while that I had to save the airplane, no matter what.

The oil pressure was gone again and pulling up the nose didn't do any good, so I knew I had to go down or the engine would be ruined in seconds. I picked out a bar on the Toklat and nosed down toward it. When I got down to about ten feet, the wind was weaker there, but I still landed at only about fifteen miles per hour.

I landed on a foot of snow that was melting fast. Just as I touched down, the right wheel caught on something and that wing went down into the snow and we stopped right there. There was a piece of driftwood under the snow. It spread the gear and broke the cross cable between the wheels. The oil pressure was zero and the gas was zero. I turned the motor off.

18. DOWN ALONE

He was alone, more absolutely alone than even this private man had ever been before. Attempting to hold a southeast course from Rampart, Wien had been blown eighty-five miles due south and away from the Tanana flats. He was as far from Fairbanks as he had been at Rampart. The plane was sitting at the southwest edge of the Tanana Lowlands, forty miles southwest of Nenana, but Noel might as well have been on top of Denali. No one knew he was there. No one would come searching.

Between him and Nenana were a dozen streams of varying sizes, of varying depths, and in varying stages of breakup, the temperature of their water about freezing. In the gravel along the streams were stumpy birch, alder, and willows. In between the streams was tundra, marshy, boggy, undrainable ice-earth, now in its intermediate stage between winter concrete and summer muck.*

There were patches of stunted spruce. The elevation was five hundred feet above sea level. Frost heaves called pingos stuck up here and there like bumps on the arctic prairie. Toward the east a prominence, like a rounded butte, reached several hundred feet above the surrounding bog. Its sides were mostly bare except for lichens and other ground-hugging flora that grew also on the level tundra. On top were spruce, birch, poplar, and aspen.

It was 10:45 at night. The twilight was deepening. Stationary lenticular clouds, evidence of the vicious wind aloft, streaked the sky above. The temperature was thirty-five, and Wien was not warm in his cotton flight suit.

---

* There are two differing definitions of tundra. According to one version, it is flat land with permafrost underneath. The other says tundra is treeless, flat land. The terrain that stood between Wien and life was treeless in parts, forested in others; but it was all permafrost.

He sat in the cockpit. There was no sound in the world except the hum of the wind in the Standard's wires. He was hungry; the Wiseman feast, nine hours before, seemed like days ago. He was tired, having flown for ten hours that day, half of it under intense strain.

Well, first he could eat. He still had two of the three whole-wheat rolls he had bought that morning at the Fairbanks bakery. He ate one. He could doze, and he did, sitting upright in a fuselage cradle that rocked gently in the wind.

He awakened about 2:30 A.M., at full light, and climbed from the cockpit onto the lower wing. Time to start walking. He had no pack, no food. He ate the last roll. From the cockpit he took pocket knife and Boy Scout ax, razor sharp, put the knife in his pocket, hung the ax from his belt. He had a metal match can. His Luger was in a holster on the belt of his thick twill breeches. His shirt was a thick-layered blue wool. Gray woolen socks folded down over the tops of knee-length leather boots. Long johns were underneath all.

He climbed atop the upper wing and looked around. There was the Alaska Range with Mount Deborah and Mount Hess to the left, Mount McKinley on the right. He turned around and saw the Tanana-Yukon Highlands, hazy where they end in the thirteen-hundred-foot shoulder at the junction of the Tanana and Nenana rivers. It looked to be quite close, but he knew it was at least forty miles away. He was lucky, he thought, to have gone down within sight of his two most easily recognized landmarks.

He stepped into the front cockpit, then onto the lower wing, looked again into his rear cockpit, picked up the Road Commission map and put it in a pocket. Jumping to the snow, he started walking northeast.

On the bar the going was easy. The foot-deep snow was slushy and his feet moved easily. The Toklat was running a bit, but had not broken up. There was some snow on its ice surface, some jagged ice sticking up. Rivulets of water coursed in streaks along the surface of the ice. He picked a spot not too deep and waded across. So far so good, although he recalled that his boots were not waterproof and would get soggy.

Then he reached the tundra.

Before I'd gone an hour, I wasn't sure I could make it, although

I'd been running every day to get in shape for something like this, and a doctor in Duluth told me once he'd never seen a stronger body than mine.

There seemed to be a trail of some sort, a moose or caribou trail, but there was no footing on it at all. I'd take two or three steps through the soggy snow and mud, and one leg would go down to the hip. I'd pull it out and take a few more steps and, again, down to the hip. It became harder and harder to pull my legs out of the slush. Even when I'd reach a little grove of spruce, where you'd think the ground would be hard, it was almost as bad.

I thought I was in top shape—no carousing, I didn't smoke, I didn't even drink tea or coffee. I felt I could take anything. But after about an hour of this I just fell forward and couldn't move.˙

I laid there and used all my strength just to move my hand up under my cheek to keep it out of the snow. I couldn't have wiggled a toe even if a grizzly was heading for me. I rested for a half hour, laying in the snow, and got a little strength back. I was able to get up and plow along for a half hour, then I fell again and couldn't get up or move another foot. A few mosquitoes buzzed around and I just let them.°

My boots were soppy wet now, no better than cloth, and my feet were getting numb with cold. If I'm out here overnight, when the sun goes behind the hills, I wonder how it'll be. I pulled myself up again and started dragging on.

Strangely, I seemed to be gaining strength, or maybe it just seemed like that because I wanted it to, but I could go a little longer now and laid there a little shorter time when I fell. But it took me eighteen hours to make the first ten miles.

I went on for two more hours, falling and resting, and then about eleven at night stayed down for about five hours on the edge of a slow-running stream that followed down the Toklat. I chopped off some branches from the short spruce there, piled them up against the butt of a bigger tree, and fell down on it, covering myself as well as I could with spruce boughs. It sure was cold and I would doze off and then come awake and doze off again. I couldn't stop shivering. I put my face in my arms to keep the mosquitoes off.

° Vilhjalmur Stefansson in *The Friendly Arctic* (New York: Macmillan, 1932) calls mosquitoes "the one serious drawback to the North." A University of Alaska biologist has said that at some times of the year, in certain parts of Alaska, the mosquito swarm weighs more than all other "animal" life combined. And this is a land of big animals in big herds.

About three in the morning I got up and looked at the stream. It was deep and the ice had broken up, so there was nowhere I could walk across. The banks on both sides were about four feet high, straight down to the water. On the edge of the stream I picked a spruce with a butt about ten inches across and started chopping.

It was slow work, even with my sharp ax, because I guess I was pretty weak. It took about two hours. I chopped so it would fall across the stream—about twenty feet—and I hoped the spruce would reach. When it fell, it went into the water and bounced, so the butt end was about three feet out into the water, and the top missed the other side by about the same distance.

The middle of the tree bowed down about a foot under the water, with skimpy branches sticking up. I started across this tree, wobbling and bouncing and trying to keep my feet on the skinny trunk, which was getting thinner, and holding onto the branches.

I knew that if I fell, it would be the end, because I'd freeze. There wasn't enough dry grass, brush, or wood to make a fire; at least, I hadn't seen any.

When I got across, I had to climb the four-foot bank and that was as hard as cutting the tree. It took me a half hour to make it, because I kept sliding back down and there wasn't anything close to the top that I could grab.

For this second day I wanted to make the butte or dome that rose a few hundred feet, and I wanted to get on that and look for Nenana again. The going was just as bad as the day before, and I kept going up to my seat in the muck, pulling out, falling down, resting, and then pushing on once again.

I got to the dome and started up. There were many deep gullies in it, although it looked smooth from a distance, and there were bear tracks all around, quite large, a grizzly without a doubt. I had a half-dozen cartridges, but that little Luger wouldn't even sting a bear.

I was so tired and the going was so hard and I was so hungry that thoughts of running into a bear didn't bother me much. The immediate problems were all I could cope with without borrowing some possibilities. The bear took bigger steps than I did, but I tried to walk in them through the snow.

A big plate of ham and eggs kept coming to my mind. I sure was hungry. I ate snow for thirst, but my mouth seemed to stay dry anyhow. Every now and then there'd be a cranberry bush that would have dried berries from the season before. They puckered my mouth but they seemed to be good for me.

The snow was deep on the dome and the gullies were trouble, going up and down in them and walking extra trying to go around them. I walked and crawled. There were thick bushes in the gullies, willows and high-bush cranberries I guess. I couldn't make the top and had to stop and go to sleep. It was miserably wet, laying out on the slope. I was soaked through now and remember wondering if I'd wake up.

But I woke up around 3:00 A.M., right on schedule, and crawled up to the top of the dome.° Nenana hill was in the right direction, but it didn't seem much closer than it had from the wing of the Standard. I couldn't make out any cabins, and couldn't even make out the high railroad bridge over the Tanana River there. It was sort of disappointing, but I couldn't do anything about it, so started down the other side of the dome and across the tundra again.

I was real hungry now and kept thinking about ham and eggs. Ice was still on four or five streams and I could walk across them through a few inches of water. I couldn't feel my feet anymore. I kept thinking, I've got to get to Fairbanks, the Fokker's coming and there's nobody else to fly it. I have to get to Fairbanks and fly the Fokker.

This was my second full day on the tundra. There was a bad stretch of burned-over spruce trees about four feet high and very close together. They were bowed over across the way I wanted to go. This was tough walking, forcing my legs between them and through them and pushing them aside. And sinking into the muck also.

About the middle of the third day I hit a trail, not a moose trail, and this was like a boulevard compared to what I'd been on, even though it was not easy walking over the bumps and niggerheads.† Nobody ever found out how to walk on niggerheads. The breakup was making the trail unusable. I found out later this was the sled

---

° Detailed charts now show this as Wien's Lookout.

† Niggerheads remain unabashedly and innocently in the Alaska vocabulary despite expunging efforts of antidefamationists. They are tussocks of tough grass set in ball-like clumps of earth. It is thought the name came from their resemblance to the coiffure of the Sudanese tribe called "fuzzy wuzzy" by the British, and was applied by British stampeders. The tussocks vary in size, says Stefansson, "from grapefruit to pumpkin."

trail from Nenana to McGrath and the Iditarod, and I'd been only ten miles north of it where I went down. That was only about twelve miles from Knight's roadhouse on the trail. I didn't know it was there.

I came to another deep-running stream, the Teklanika River I guess, and it was too deep to wade. Alongside the trail I found two old wooden gas cases, used for carrying two five-gallon cans of gasoline. Somebody had used them for a boat in the summer. There were also some sawed-off logs about four to six feet long—probably stove wood.

I pulled the nails out of the cases with my ax and nailed the three longest logs together with the wood from the cases to make a raft. I gave a big shove, jumped on, and sailed almost across before the nails pulled out of the rotten logs and I went in to my knees. But I got my hands on the other bank and pulled myself out.

The next stream was not broken up and I crossed on the ice. I knew I was getting near Nenana and I kept going. It was so much easier on the dog trail, but I still stumbled and fell and lay down awhile, I was so tired.

I got to the Nenana River about a mile below the village. It was wide and running fast with ice cakes. I heard barking and snarling and saw a man across the river feeding his dogs. I whistled and hollered and after a while he rowed over in a big skiff. He lived on the side I was on and took me to his cabin and cooked up a little clam chowder. Boy, did that taste good! I hadn't eaten in three days. Then he rowed me across the river to the Nenana side and I gave him five dollars and walked the mile into the village.

Nobody asked him a question. Four days' whiskers prickled a face blackened by mud and exposure. His flying suit was frayed and skinned from the burned spruce and uncountable falls. He was caked with mire, staggering from exhaustion, gasping with a deep chest cold. Haggard, he had lost twenty of his 165 pounds.

The first Alaska bush pilot had walked in from the first bush downing, a feat he had been warned could not be done. He had been lost for four days, had walked and crawled for sixty hours across eighty miles of tundra. But when he turned up at Nenana, nobody asked him a question. Other men, celebrants of the river breakup the day before, were still staggering about town. They had whiskers, they looked like coal miners, none dressed like dudes. So, Wien was just one more sourdough, his looks and behavior nobody's business but his own.

It did not occur to Wien that at Fairbanks there might be men concerned over his plight. Groggily he walked to the village hotel, went to the restaurant, and ate the plate of ham and eggs that had been on his mind for days. He went out to the hotel desk and asked for a room.

When the clerk saw his name on the register, he exclaimed: "Noel Wien! Why, ain't you the aviator they been looking for?"

Noel said he was an aviator, yes, and he had just walked in from the Kantishna. "Look, fellows," the clerk called to the lobby sitters, "this here's the aviator they been looking for out of Rampart."

He turned back to Wien. "You have to call Fairbanks right away," he said earnestly. "They've been calling up everywhere and telling people to have you call if you showed up."

Fred Struthers answered Wien's call to the airplane company. In answer to Struthers' excited questioning, Wien reported that the Standard was all right, that he needed sleep and would call again after he had rested. He went to his room, but slept poorly despite the ordeal he had been through.

Next day he was a celebrity, the *cheechako* who had walked from the Toklat to Nenana during breakup. "Only a *cheechako* wouldn't know you can't do that," sourdoughs said, shaking their heads.

Wien phoned Fairbanks. Dick Wood, company president, said he had arranged for Noel to get to Fairbanks aboard a railroad gas speeder that was leaving Nenana that day, so he would not have to wait for the triweekly train. The gas speeder was an open vehicle like a handcar, but powered by gasoline motor. "That was about the worst part of the whole experience," Wien said, "sitting in the open wind on that thing, flying along the eighty or so miles to Fairbanks. I nearly froze."

A hero's welcome was waiting at Fairbanks. Several dozen residents were at the station to see him return from the dead. Ralph grabbed him in a bear hug and half pulled him through the mob of people who clamored to hear about his miracle. "Old timers in this country," said a *News-Miner* story, "do not need to be told what his experience must have been, wading continuously through snow, slush, streams and swamps, plowing through underbrush, shivering with cold and wet clothes at night and fighting off hordes of Alaskan bat-sized mosquitoes which he mildly termed 'uncomfortable'!"

For the next few days Wien rested and treated his cold. He learned that an attempt had been made to begin a search. A prospector named Ed Young had gone to Rodebaugh and told him he was a former Army aviator and offered his services. Young, who had not flown for years, made a test hop in the second Standard, but the motor overheated and ran rough. Rodebaugh, prompted by the worried Ralph Wien, then had Eielson's old Jenny hauled out. Ralph worked at it and Young made a hop. But on landing he hit Eielson's soft spot, nosed over, and cracked the propeller. Young would have searched between Fairbanks and Rampart and Rampart and Livengood, however, and it is doubtful that he would have come within forty miles of the Kantishna. His offer was a courageous one.

A few days after his return Noel and Young flew the Jenny with a replacement propeller to the Toklat in an attempt to retrieve the Standard. The river had broken up and was flowing over the bar where the Standard sat. There was no place for the Jenny to land; the Standard could not have been taken off. En route back to Fairbanks Wien landed the Jenny at Nenana to refuel, although Fairbanks was only forty miles farther. Once bitten in this country, Wien was not going to pass up a fueling stop.

Unable to shake his cold, Noel was put to bed by Ralph and his wife. He was down for several days. Meanwhile, Rodebaugh and Ed Young took the train to Nenana, hired an Indian and his boat, and went down the Tanana to the Kantishna and up that river to the Toklat. The Toklat, a glacier stream, had receded from its flood, and the trio had to walk up it, carrying gear, grub, tools, gasoline, and oil. It took them two days of walking to reach the Standard. It was over its axle in sand, the lower right wing covered with silt. They dug it out, patched the wing, replaced the broken landing gear wire, fed it oil and gasoline, and Young flew it back to Fairbanks alone. Young later became a bush pilot and was killed in a crash at Livengood.

As newspapers from the States arrived in Fairbanks, friends brought them to Noel. His story had received wide coverage. One newspaper headlined in red ink: "Lost Alaskan Pilot Alive." Persons who know the taciturn Wien will sympathize, even over a half-century gap, with the Fairbanks reporter who wrote: "To get a complete story from Noel of the three days and nights overland would be almost impossible. For while he seems not to be shy, he doesn't understand that the trip was not just all in a day's work. When told that his trip was a story of world interest and that the New York Times had wirelessed asking for details, he merely remarked, 'Is that so?' and laughed the short quick laugh that is so characteristic."

19. LOOKING

Wien's view of his Toklat feat as just a routine performance may have toned down his description of the ordeal to reporters, but it did not prevent his realizing how ill-prepared he had been. For one thing, he had been foolish not to carry some kind of food. Having the two buns with him was unpremeditated good luck; but two buns would not have been enough to sustain his strength had he been another day on the tundra.

When he returned to flying the Hisso Standards after mid-May, he took with him a canvas bag filled with emergency items. These included enough concentrated and lightweight foods such as raisins and dried apples and apricots to allow him to live several weeks; a cup and a small kettle; and his waterproof case of matches—more important than food, miners and trappers told him, except in the three summer months. As ritualistically as he checked his airplane before each flight, Wien thereafter checked to see that the emergency poke was in its place on his seat.

Secured between a longeron and the fabric in his cockpit was an ax with a thirty-inch handle, longer than his original one. He discarded the Luger in favor of a long-barreled .30-caliber Mauser pistol with a stock that could be attached to convert it to a rifle. "That was a very fine gun," he said. "It could even get you a caribou. You could blow up a ptarmigan with it, and shoot squirrels and rabbits, which I did."

When there was room, he took also a pair of trail snowshoes for walking on semihard snow. He tried always to find space inside for these items rather than tying them outside and losing speed on the already slow craft. His few tools were in the small opening in the turtleback behind the pilot's cockpit.

There was no danger of loading a Standard out of balance, even with passengers and encumbrances sticking out so that it looked like a flying porcupine. There were no compartments abaft the pilot's cockpit; everything was carried in the wing area. He could load it over gross, but he could not load it outside the balance envelope.

"We didn't worry about balance," he said, "until we got the cabin airplanes that had the cabins and baggage compartments in back of the wing area. The Fairchild 71 was very critical. It had a narrow chord wing, the cabin extended back of the trailing edge, and baggage was back of that. You had to watch it close."

As the planes grew, so did Wien's emergency gear. By 1929, when he began flying the beautiful Hamilton Metalplane that made history's first flight across the Bering Strait to Siberia, he carried enough to keep a squad of people alive for some time. There were drill parkas and mukluks because, he said, "some people were determined to fly into the bush with oxfords on. I had a lot of trouble getting people from Outside to dress proper."

Food rations, packed in a five-gallon gasoline can, included luxuries in Wien's later airplanes: salt, sugar, jam, cornmeal, oatmeal, bread, canned butter, coffee. There were kettles and pans for cooking over a two burner Coleman. In winter he carried another gasoline can into which a door and a round hole had been cut. A pipe could be fitted to the hole and run outside and a fire built in the can-stove to keep downed people warm in a small tent that was also part of the package. Snowshoes were standard. In addition to a small rifle Wien sometimes had a Savage over-and-under with a .22 barrel on top and a 410-gauge shotgun barrel below.

During the first month of his first season in Alaska, brother Ralph Wien formed the habits of painstaking care that were to make him one of the finest aviation mechanics in northern flying. He had never seen before any of the engines that were entrusted to him. There were no handbooks, no manuals to direct his work. To succeed, he needed to be a man of intelligence, resourcefulness, and inventiveness. He had all these qualities, and something more—a protective regard for his younger brother, Noel.

"Ralph was very fond of Noel," said Sam White, the Maine-born dog musher, Arctic surveyer, and bush pilot. "He stopped some people from putting things over on Noel before it got started. He looked out for Noel. Noel was the leader, but I think Ralph would have assumed the leadership if he hadn't cracked up at Kotzebue. He was gone so soon. He was the leader when they were boys, because he was older. He was more aggressive, in a very nice way. He was no toughie or anything like that, but he was so big that people just didn't want to find out how tough he was."

The big mechanic was more open, more communicative than any of his younger brothers, the only one who showed his emotions. Of the five brothers, only he used more than "gosh" and "gee whiz" as expletives. Under severe provocation, such as hammering a thumb, Ralph would wring his hand and say, "Damn, oh damn."

Ralph rented a cabin on Front Street, rigging it with auto repair and overhaul equipment and the very expensive tool set he brought from Minnesota. He soon had a substantial auto, truck, and machinery business to augment his work for Fairbanks Airplane and built not only on his knowledge and skill with engines but on his ability to adapt, devise, and invent. Nothing came before his responsibility to the airplane company's machines. Noel was his chief concern, and he pampered the Hissos and Standards.

Noel was flying every good day. Early each morning Ralph went to Weeks Field. He looked at the points, cleaned the strainers. If Noel had noticed a magneto hesitation or drop in revolutions, Ralph cleaned the plugs. He kept the oil at the proper level, changing it as often as his money-conscious employers would allow. Gasoline came in fifty-gallon drums, to which Ralph fitted a hosed pump. He and Noel would fill the Standards' tanks, straining the gasoline through a chamois. "Fuel was contaminated so often," Noel said, "that the only rule to go by was that all fuel was dirty. If you treated it like that, you'd get by. I always expected to go down for some reason or other, and this was one problem we could do something about ahead of time."

The Hissos were old. They consumed twelve gallons an hour, with little difference between climb and cruise consumption. There was no mixture control, no flow gauge. If a flight was to be conducted at unusual altitudes, Ralph would make a mixture adjustment in the carburetor; but almost all flying was done between 400 and 8,000 feet. Although the image of Alaska to Outsiders is that of a mountainous state, the elevation of Fairbanks at Weeks Field was only 400 feet. The highest Noel reached during his first two years in Alaska was 11,500, in order to top fog over Nenana Canyon in the range.

In 1925 there were no required overhauls or inspections, not even federal inspection, of aircraft. The first Department of Commerce laws regulating aviation went into effect in 1926, but not until 1928 did inspection reach Alaska. The inspector was Ben Eielson, having returned to work for Captain George Wilkins, and he issued motor mechanics licenses to everyone who had worked on airplane engines. Noel also received one. Any pilot, especially any pilot in Alaska, was at least a fair, if not better, mechanic, school-trained or not.

Ralph took the Hissos to his downtown shop when they needed major work. He built a tripod derrick of poles, block, and lines, and he and Noel removed the motors and eased them onto the bed of a secondhand truck Ralph had bought. "It wasn't long before Ralph knew everything about those Hissos," Noel said, "all the tolerances and clearances and how every part fitted."

Ralph's wife arrived in June and moved into the Front Street cabin. Noel bunked in the lean-to addition to the cabin along with the wood supply. Instead of rent from his brother, he received housekeeping services. Ralph was a homebody. Occasionally the three adults went to a movie. Because of his size, Ralph was soon tapped by a baseball team and became its star pitcher. "I hated to catch him," Noel said; "he was so fast I didn't even like to play pitch and catch with him in the yard."

Before the Fokker arrived, Noel flew sixty-six hours, including the first aerial timber cruise and the first "mercy flights," as they were later christened by Outside newspapers. The cruise was 175 miles along the Tanana and Yukon rivers to the village of Tanana, and allowed Wien's passenger to estimate the cover on more than five thousand square miles. Such a tour could have been made on the surface only after freeze-up and would have taken months. By air it took 4:30.

One day a miner came walking and running in from Nome Creek, more than fifty miles during the breakup. He said his partner in a little gold dredge was up there dying and I had to go get him and bring him to Fairbanks.

How this fellow'd made the trip, I don't know. Most of the way he came down the cat trail [Caterpillar trails were forged where possible along dog trails for use in winter hauls], but it must have been as bad a trip as mine from the Toklat. Nome Creek is about forty-five miles northeast of Fairbanks, in the upper Chatanika country.

This fellow said he thought his partner, Charley Updyke, had pneumonia and was surely dying. I asked him where he thought I could land an airplane up there and he said he'd picked out a smooth dome that would do fine. Rodebaugh and the company officers said for me to go, so I got the sourdough in the front cockpit and we started off. He was going to guide me and I told him when we got there to yell back to me and point to the landing place.

Well, he found the dredge right off, but the dome he pointed to, about two thousand feet above the creek, I didn't like at all. There were only about two hundred feet of level on top, and it was all covered with moss with no smooth places where I could see any shale. If there was shale underneath the moss, I could count on a pretty good landing. Also, there were many big, dark spots in the moss, and that meant wet, soft spots. I figured I was sure to bust the airplane if I landed there.

I picked out a spot on the north side that seemed to me to be a little harder looking, after I flew over it three or four times. I found the wind, came into it, and aimed the Standard to stall going uphill, on a stretch about two hundred feet below the top. All the way in, it didn't look like any place to be landing an airplane, but they'd told me to go in, so I was going.

Now the Standard was a good ship for three-point landings. The shock cords were good, and it would stick if you pulled the tail down and stalled about six inches or a foot over the ground. It didn't glide level, so the nose was down and you had a good view for a safe landing.

But this time I was coming down on a field that was going uphill away from me steep. To keep from sticking that long nose into the moss, I had to pull back and put the tail down higher up than a foot off the ground.

We hit at about thirty miles per hour and took a couple of bounces that could have flown us right over the top of the dome, but we stopped just about at the highest point and I was greatly relieved.

We heard a man hollering and saw him coming up the slope from the dredge below. It took him a half hour to get to us, climbing about two thousand feet at a forty-five-degree angle. He said the sick man was better, or said he was, and he was not going to be carried up to the dome but would walk.

"Well," my passenger said, "we'll see about that," and started down the dome with the other fellow. After a while I saw three fellows way down below start climbing back up. The one in the middle, the sick fellow, was walking, but the other two had a piece of conveyor belt around his seat and each one had an end of it and were hauling the sick man along. After about an hour they got to the top.

While they'd been gone, I checked the ship and found about four inches of one tip of the propeller gone! That was the beautiful dark Hamilton wood propeller that I'd cracked at Circle Hot Springs. Lucky it busted off on the ground, because it could have caused trouble with vibration if we'd been in the air. It must've hit the moss when we bounced.

I had a spare propeller tied to the fuselage, a skinny wood one we called a toothpick propeller, but I found out I didn't have a Stilson wrench with me. The fellow who'd walked in to Fairbanks went back down the slope and came back in about forty minutes with a pipe wrench and we changed propellers.

Charley Updyke was in the front cockpit most of this time, and after I'd been there about two hours and a half I was ready to try a takeoff. Like landing, I wasn't any too sure I could do it.

With one of the fellows on each wing to steer, I taxied up to the top of the dome. The way was soft and there were bumps and holes.

I had to take off down the other side of the dome, because I needed the wind to help me.

When I got to the top, I saw the dredge and the creek about two thousand feet below, and saw the slope ahead was much steeper than on the side I'd landed on. There was about two hundred feet of fairly level run on top, then a sharp drop-off at more than fifty degrees. The tops of the spruce trees were just below the drop-off, and then there was another lower dome beyond.

There was no sense waiting and looking, because I had to make a try. I got the motor up to full revolutions and then signaled the two fellows to let the wings go and we shot off across the top of the dome.

It couldn't have been better. Just at the drop-off the nose went down and we were flying. I kept the nose down a few seconds and then pulled back a little and we flew out over the trees with a little to spare.

I got Charley Updyke to the Saint Joseph's Hospital in Fairbanks and they found one of his lungs still worked and they pulled him through. I didn't like landing on a dome and figured the ones I'd already picked out as good emergency spots weren't so hot.

Certainly Noel Wien was a hero in this first mercy mission in Alaska aviation. But there was another hero—the unnamed sourdough whose devotion and stamina compelled him to walk fifty miles to Fairbanks through the breakup, make a flight to Nome Creek, help haul his ill partner up the two-thousand-foot slope, and then go back down the mountain to return again with a wrench.

In late September a *News-Miner* story reported: "Once again the call for help came from the wilderness and was answered yesterday when word came from Brooks that Jack Irvine had been hurt on the tram-way and needed immediate medical attention. The aeroplane at once responded to the call and the injured man brought to Fairbanks. The trip was made more hazardous due to darkness falling before the plane returned here, making the landing a ticklish proposition."

On these and other flights Noel added to the store of original knowledge that was to determine the techniques used by all wise bush pilots. "I was often tired from flying that summer," he said. "There was a stress and strain because I worried about the old ships and the old motors. Their slow speed was a bother. I never flew relaxed or daydreamed, but was continually looking for possible landing spots. Where would I land now? Could I fly to that bench over there if the motor conked out? I was looking, looking, looking."

The Standard's glide ratio was poor, acting like a built-in headwind against a volplaning craft. With the nose down at about forty-five degrees, the Standard would glide at perhaps four to one, hardly better than a brass bedstead would. Wien said he never heard of the deliberate stalling of a powerless airplane—where there was altitude enough—so as to stop the propeller and gain a little more glide range. Perhaps with all those struts, wires, blunt surfaces, and the proportionately heavy engine, a stall would cost more than a stilled prop would add.

"You had to learn to drag a possible landing spot at the lowest possible altitude," Noel said about bush airfields. "A spot could look much different from five feet up than from twenty-five. The throttle was on the right, so I'd look out the left while making an approach, but on strange bars I'd twist from side to side to watch for gullies, driftwood, holes, and rocks. The Standard was so narrow that this was easy."

Pilotage—contact navigation by which an aviator gets from here to there by looking at the ground and picking up anticipated checkpoints—had developed a helpful if unofficial literature in the States by the mid-1920s. Pilots leaving on a first hop between two points often could find in writing a list of checkpoints to watch for: railroads, rivers, lakes, roads, cities, parks, stockyards, polo fields, golf courses, canals, aerodromes, power plants, high church steeples.

There were no such guidebooks, of course, for Alaska when Wien arrived, and there were no parks, canals, golf courses, church steeples, few villages, and no cities. Of lakes, ponds, rivers, and mountains, there were thousands, hundreds of which looked identical. Worse, clusters of features such as a lake, a river, a dog trail, and a roadhouse looked so like other clusters that a pilot could be thrown off by many miles. Worse still, new identical features appeared and old ones disappeared.

Sam White said he used two small, side-by-side lakes as one checkpoint in flying from Fairbanks to Beaver. "One time," White recalled, "I got to where the lakes were supposed to be and there were three lakes there. I thought I'd made a bad mistake and was off course. I circled around and checked and looked off in the distance for other checkpoints and did some calculating. Everything else seemed just right, except the three lakes down there instead of two.

"I finally decided I was on the route, and went on north and picked up my next checkpoint. I found out later that a fire some years before had burned off some of the vegetation around the two lakes, and there was a big ice crystal underneath the ground. Without the vegetation the sun got to it and finally melted it, and the ground on top caved in and there was a third lake.

"Those ice crystals were a lot of trouble. They were left over from the glaciers, and were solid pieces of ice and not ice mixed with dirt like the permafrost."

Wien's "looking, looking, looking" paid off that summer, and so perhaps did his experience at Nome Creek. On flights to Livengood he had studied the highest hills along the route. These made up a ridge about thirteen miles long, halfway between the villages, that rose to more than three thousand feet, dramatically higher than the surrounding prominences. At the south end of the ridge, around which the dog trail skirted, was Wickersham Dome, 3,207 feet, named for James Wickersham, early Alaska federal judge and long-time territorial delegate to Congress.

We had just put a new Hisso in the Standard, that is, it was a used Hisso that was given a major overhaul in the States and Rodebaugh had bought it to replace one of our old ones. I was flying from Livengood with two passengers. One of them was an insurance man who went to Livengood to adjust a fire they'd had at a sawmill, and the other was a tough old miner.

There were some low, scattered clouds, and I was flying at about twenty-five hundred and approaching Wickersham Dome. I was looking at a ledge at about three thousand feet, fairly smooth, six hundred feet long, that I'd look at every time I passed as the only place between Fairbanks and Livengood I might make a landing on.

Suddenly water spurted out of the radiator all over the three of us. The water pump had busted. I didn't know that yet, but I knew we couldn't fly without water to cool the motor.

That water was getting on the plugs also and they spit and sputtered. I had to get up to that ledge and I had to climb about five hundred feet to do it with no water.

I jammed the throttle forward and the motor spit a bit and caught and I went wide open up for that ledge, hoping to make it before the motor froze up with the heat. We made it, in a cloud of steam, and it was a right good landing. Even without brakes, the six hundred feet was enough to stop on.

We were about twenty-two miles from the nearest roadhouse, the one down at Olnes just south of the Chatanika. There was a telephone there and we could get help from Fairbanks, if we could get to Olnes in the first place. That wasn't a sure thing, because the insurance man was one of those Outside people who went into the bush wearing Oxford shoes.

It was not bad at first, getting down from the smooth dome, but then we hit the dog trail. It was after breakup and there wasn't any snow and not much mud, but there were those bunches of grass they called niggerheads.

They grow up about a foot out of the ground and the grass leans out of the tops to all sides. They're so close together that you can't walk between them, and if you step on them hard they turn your ankle no matter where you step.

Nobody ever figured out how to walk on these things but the best way was to try to jump on top of them, stepping very quick and light, and this gives a tundra walker a very funny gait, like a kangaroo.

The insurance fellow gave out in the first mile. He kept saying, "I can't make it, I can't make it," and the old-timer and I didn't think he would either. His ankles and tendons were giving way. We helped him, one on each side of him, and he put one foot in front of the other slow and painful; we had to stop about every five hundred feet and let him rest and rub his ankles.

After about twenty hours we got to Olnes and we phoned and a car picked us up from Fairbanks. The next day I flew back to the dome in a Jenny with a mechanic-pilot who had just arrived. We busted a tire on landing, but I took a spare because I had seen plenty of holes on the dome. We fixed the Hisso and flew the planes off the dome.

20. NOME

"The mosquitos at the ball park seem in no way to affect the many people who have visited the plane," a *News-Miner* story reported on June 4, 1925. "At least, they have failed to keep the crowds away."

The compelling object that was drawing crowds to Weeks Field was the giant Fokker F. III that had arrived in Fairbanks by rail and was being assembled by Ralph and Noel. Crowds attended every step, gathering at the station to watch the arrival of the train with two flat cars carrying the aircraft, at the depot the following morning to witness unloading of the parts, and at the flying field to see wing joined to body. Many were confused to note only one wing and doubted that one would be sufficient.

Presiding over each performance was Jimmy Rodebaugh, at his jolly best upon finally seeing his monster purchase arrive in Alaska. Among the crowds were the other officers of the airplane company. They, like Rodebaugh, were anxious to get the Fokker into the air where it would more than double the revenue realized from any of the three company biplanes: five passengers instead of two at an average of $1.00 a mile; 500 pounds of freight averaging $.40 a pound on short flights, $.75 on flights longer than 60 miles; and there would be room also for mail if any could be wangled from the post office in the future.

Assembly of the Fokker was uncomplicated. The plane fitted together like a model airplane. The empennage bolted to the aft end of the fuselage, the two-foot-thick wing joined the top of the fuselage with four bolts. Control wires were easily strung. But assembly took time, because of the size of the parts and the customary Wien deliberateness.

The *News-Miner* was enthusiastic. "Pullman equipment has nothing on the interior of this airship," read one story. "Red upholstered chairs and settee, easily opened windows, vases for flowers and drapes and leather fittings—all tend to make the ship not only exceedingly comfortable looking but exceedingly beautiful looking. Even the exterior has an aristocratic look. A dull green finish, anything but gaudy, gives one the feeling that all the equipment is safe and substantial. A trip to Nome is to be made in a few days, taking one day to go over and another for the return trip." In view of the wonders Wien had already wrought in air travel, the reporter can be pardoned his almost parenthetic mention of the most ambitious plan of the summer, a round trip to Nome on the Bering Sea, 570 miles from Fairbanks.

With the last bolt in place, the Fokker fueled and oiled and watered, Noel ran up the motor and then took off for a forty-five-minute test hop. The racket of the 240-horsepower engine and its long scimitar propeller thrilled the spectators. Noel met the rudder flutter perfectly and the great bird flew beautifully, but Noel decided after the first landing that the ball park was not big enough. At its longest dimension, Weeks Field was twelve hundred feet. The Fokker needed a nine-hundred-foot run after touchdown. It had no brakes and its skid was a shovel type, three inches wide and six inches long. A sharp skid would not have dug in deep enough, for the craft was so light on the empennage that Noel could pick it up and walk the tail around without help.

It would be too risky to try to bring in the Fokker when fully loaded over the Northern Commercial Company woodpile at one end of Weeks, or the thirty-foot spruce at the other, hoping to get down in time to have nine hundred feet of landing space left. Operations with the Fokker were moved east to a field owned by Paul Rickert. Here there was a north-south length of fifteen hundred feet, not roomy for the Fokker but more comfortable than Weeks. It was from Rickert's field ° that Captain Wilkins mounted his unsuccessful Polar expeditions of 1926 and 1927, with Noel as one of his pilots for a time during the latter year.

° This field was in what later became the vee formed by the road into Fort Wainwright and Cushman Street, where the Alaska Highway enters Fairbanks.

The day after his test flights, Noel made four joyhops, taking five riders each time, then in the afternoon made his first cross-country in the new machine, hauling two passengers to Livengood. The following day he took in three others.

During his approaches to the uphill mountainside field there, the seat of his pants tingled as it had not done in some time. "I had to stall it all the way in," he said, "about five miles over stall and hold it just exactly there."

The Fokker proved itself a bush craft, but it took a Noel Wien to fly it. The second pilot hired by Fairbanks Airplane that fall refused to fly the plane. On an indoctrination hop with Ralph back in the cabin to keep him company, this man began yelling, "He's gonna stall! He's gonna stall!" as Noel dragged the long, thick-winged craft in on her prop.

As hundreds of Fairbanks residents watched, thirteen people lined up at 10:00 P.M., June 7, to have their photograph taken standing in front of the Fokker. Little Jimmy Rodebaugh, casual as ever in coveralls, was at the left. On the right were Bostonian Norman C. Stines, a mining engineer, proper in breeches and matching jacket, boots, white shirt, and sober tie; and two women. The intrepid Stines, engineer for Fairbanks Exploration, had chartered the Fokker for fifteen hundred dollars to fly him and the two women members of his party, Midge Downer and Mrs. Dayo, to Nome.

Others posing, all in their Sunday best, were Mayor Frank de la Vergne of Fairbanks; airplane company stockholders Mr. and Mrs. Wood, and a Mr. and Mrs. Frank Gordon, store owners, and Fred Struthers. Ralph Wien in coveralls stood beside his pilot brother in boots, breeches, leather jacket, and cloth cap. A curiosity was a uniformed conductor of the Alaska Railroad, who would pretend to dispatch the historic flight.

After the passengers and Ralph climbed through the tall door into the cabin and settled themselves in the upholstered seats, Noel secured the door and swung up to his postillion mount beside the motor and under the leading edge of the thick wing. One more photograph was made, of Mayor de la Vergne handing Noel a letter addressed to the mayor of Nome. Good-byes were exchanged, and Noel engaged the booster magneto to begin starting procedure for the six-cylinder BMW. It never failed.

After a long takeoff run between lines of autos and trucks, the Fokker was airborne at 10:45, carrying 1,350 pounds, placing it over the Fokker's posted gross of 4,800 pounds. Alaskan pilots flew with overloads well into the 1940s. Even Noel Wien, the most conservative of all, did not hesitate to do so when he knew it was safe, until CAA inspectors convinced the bush flyers that their rules were going to be enforced.

Climbing at three hundred feet a minute, the Fokker banked left in a climb as Noel felt for a wind to raise it over the ridge so he could fly westward down Goldstream. There was no sense of elation or of expectancy, just an attention to the business of flying, although this flight and the return to Fairbanks, being the first long-distance hops accomplished in Alaska, gave Alaska communications and commerce a quantum shove from stone age to air age. By boat in the summer down the Tanana and Yukon and across Norton Sound, Nome was about 1,100 miles and three weeks—fifteen days at the very speediest—from Fairbanks. By winter dog team it was 735 miles and four weeks. By air it was to be 570 miles, which in the Fokker would take less than seven hours.

Noel set the big, slow prop at 1,200 revolutions after reaching four thousand feet, and the Fokker cruised west at ninety miles an hour, passing Nenana on the left, Manley on the right, and picking up the Yukon at Tanana village. From here on the country below was new to Noel. His plan was to follow the wide Yukon to where it turned sharply south after receiving the Koyukuk River, 300 miles west of Fairbanks. He would leave the Yukon there, continuing westward over the mountains between Nulato and Norton Bay and along the coast to Nome.

Noel carried Coast and Geodetic Survey charts of the Yukon and Bering coast, and faith in the accuracy of old-timers who told him that the Yukon was studded with sand bars that would give him emergency landings along its entire length. The faith proved to have been misplaced.

We were supposed to land on a sand bar at Ruby and gas up. That was the little mining village where the Black Wolf Squadron landed.° Not having been down that way, I trusted that the

° Brigadier General Billy Mitchell considered Alaska a key to air defense of the United States and to world transport. In 1920 he persuaded his superiors to let him send a flight of

company people and old-timers knew what they were talking about. But the Black Wolf Squadron flew the Yukon in August when the river was low. We were making the trip right after breakup and the water was flowing heavy and every bar in the Yukon was covered.

I should have used my head when I got to Tanana and saw no bars in the river and turned back while I still had gas to get to Fairbanks. But I thought maybe the bar at Ruby was a special high one. When I got there at 12:45 in the morning, there was no bar

We continued on, hoping to get over the range from Nulato to Norton Bay and along the beach somewhere to land where they might have gas, or to get on to Nome if I still had enough gas left.

The Fokker was performing well, so at least that was a plus. About forty miles on from Ruby, though, we ran into stormy weather. Heavy, black clouds covered the whole Nulato range from north to south and we hit heavy rain.

I didn't know how much rain the motor would take, not having been in rain with the Fokker before, but I remembered the OX-5 and wondered. I didn't know what the country was in any direction except back the way we had come, and I didn't have enough gas to scout around for a way through the storm. The only thing to do was to turn back.

By now we couldn't get all the way to Fairbanks, and there wasn't any place to land at Tanana. The bars were under water there, and the parade ground at Fort Gibbon that was closed down in 1923 was less than six hundred feet long.

I had been watching the ground all along, as usual, and had seen a skinned-off place on top of a hill above Ruby. When I saw it I remember thinking, I hope I don't have to try to put the Fokker down there. Now I was heading back to try to do just that. At least we'd be near a town where people could come and pick up the pieces.

When I got back near Ruby it seemed we had a little wind from the south, so I came across the Yukon heading for that skinned place, a little round hill. The Fokker would stall at about fifty, so I came in just barely over that, crossed the Yukon, and flew over the

airplanes to Nome from New York. Four Liberty-powered D.H. 4s, led by Captain (later General) St. Clair Streett, made the epic trip. Mitchell waved good-bye to the squadron at New York, but so sensational was its success that the greeter on its return was General of the Armies John J. Pershing, giving the operation a three-star escalation in importance.

village and toward that cleared spot about three hundred feet over the town. I aimed for the edge of the cliff.

We nicked some brush at the edge of the cliff and I plunked the ship down with the skid about ten feet inside the cleared space. We set down solid without bouncing, and ran uphill a couple of hundred feet and got to the top. It was a baseball field, I could see that now, and just over the highest point we rolled down and toward some spruce. Then we hit a soft spot and started a noseover.

Wien hung on helplessly as the Fokker's tail rose up, the nose went down, and the entire plane slowly somersaulted onto its back. The pilot unstrapped himself carefully so as not to fall out of the cockpit. He walked down the underside of the wing and opened the cabin door. Chairs, baggage, freight, books, and all four people were in a jumble, but no one was hurt. Stines was verging on huffiness, but the calm way Noel said, "I'm glad you're not hurt," seemed to choke off the threatened complaint. The two Wiens set the cabin right and helped the passengers from the plane. Then they assessed the damage to the Fokker.

The propeller was shattered, and about a foot of the balanced rudder was crushed down. That was all. It was something of a miracle. Noel had set down in four hundred feet a plane that needed a nine-hundred-foot landing run and, instead of smashing it and five people, had left it needing only a new prop, some tube straightening, and a piece of petticoat to become flyable again. Had Noel touched down a few miles faster, the plane would have done a fast flip when it reached the soft spot, and more than a few inches of rudder would have been crushed.

A crowd gathered, as one will even at Ruby, Alaska—population 125 in 1925—at two in the morning. The unexpected visitors from aloft were taken down the bluff to the roadhouse, where they slept a few hours. On arising, Stines decided that he had done his flying for the meantime, and hired a small boat to try to catch up with the regular Yukon steamer. He intended to ride the steamer to Saint Michael on Norton Sound, and from there take another scheduled boat along Norton Sound to Nome.

There was no question what Noel would do. He was not going to leave the Fokker and he was not going to abandon the Nome flight if he had a choice. As soon as the Army Signal Corps radio station opened later in the morning, he messaged Fairbanks Airplane, reporting the crack-up and describing the damage.

In reply Dick Wood said he would grab a spare propeller, hop on a boat, and try to make the 220 river miles to Ruby in two days. With the river high and flowing rapidly, this was possible in one of the gasoline launches that were appearing on the rivers and beginning to compete with the wood-burning steamers.

Stines and entourage set out downriver while Noel and Ralph set to work on the Fokker. They had volunteer help in abundance, for the entire village turned out. They removed the four bolts that secured the wing and, while one gang lifted the nose of the upside-down fuselage, another slid the wing out from under it. With the aid of a tripod derrick, the fuselage was set on its wheels. The thick, cantilevered wing weighed nine hundred pounds. The tallest men of the village heaved it to the top of their reach and placed one end of it in its slot. Carefully they walked the wing up and across the fuselage until it slipped into place; Ralph bolted it down.

Now the rudder. Ralph skillfully reshaped the mashed tubing, and village women produced cloth for patching the fabric. The community effort reminded Noel of how farmers in Minnesota during his boyhood had pooled their labor for threshing and harvesting.

The Fokker was ready to receive the new propeller when Wood puttered up in the gas boat on the second day after the plane had left Fairbanks, having covered the distance to Ruby in a record thirty hours. Noel took on about fifteen gallons of fuel, making a load of only fifty-five gallons. He faced a short takeoff, and even without Stines, his women, and baggage, it would not be easy.

"It was kind of tricky," Wien said. "I had to take off the same way I'd landed, because of the wind. We taxied back to the edge of the field and turned around. The run was uphill, then flat for about one hundred feet, and then a bit downhill for about two hundred feet. With Ralph and Dick Wood in the cabin, we bumped along and made the curve on top and turned downhill and scraped through the brush at the end with our wheels and were off okay. I don't think anybody ever landed there again, even in an emergency."

Back toward Nulato they went, keeping course with the Yukon,

Noel and the Stinson biplane, in September 1927, just after he had inaugurated the first scheduled air service in Alaska—one round trip per week between Fairbanks and Nome. Courtesy of Noel Wien

The Stinson biplane, first plane with air-cooled engine and enclosed cabin in Alaska, landing in 1927 at village of Kobuk, north of the Arctic Circle. Courtesy of Noel Wien

Calvin "Doc" Cripe (top) and Ralph Wien (bottom center) giving the Stinson's Wright Whirlwind, 220-horsepower engine a top overhaul after a year of successful flying in 1929. Courtesy of Noel Wien

Noel and the Stinson at Candle in March 1928 after six-day blizzard with temperatures down to five below zero. Thirty-five-mile-per-hour winds blew snow under and through motor cover and packed it hard on the outer surface of the engine. Courtesy of Noel Wien

in flood more than a mile wide in places. A new vibration shook the Fokker. It was very slight but noticeable to Wien, alert for changes in sound and feel.

North of the river there were hills up to five thousand feet above sea level; for thirty-five miles south of the river were flats dotted with almost uncountable lakes and ponds. The mountains on the north made the sharp southward bend with the river beyond Koyukuk and followed along the right descending bank almost to the Bering Sea.

Just south of Koyukuk was Nulato, the site of a Russian trading post established in 1838. A fog often hung over the eighty miles of mountains from there to Norton Sound. On more than one later flight Noel was forced to feel his way down the Yukon and to try to creep under fog along the coast to Nome. On others he was able to follow the dog trail downriver to Kaltag and then go under the fog through a canyon past Twentytwo Mile Cabin and Old Woman Shelter to Unalakleet on the coast, and then northward and westward around the edge of Norton Bay.

On Noel's first flight, however, the sky was spotless and Noel flew the Fokker due west across the mountains from Nulato. Despite its new and worrisome vibration, the Fokker maintained ninety miles an hour in cruise, and the longitude lines on Noel's chart came and went rapidly. (At 64°30′ north latitude, the globe is pinched to less than half its equatorial diameter, so converging longitude lines are less than thirty miles apart.)

There, coming up out of the distant haze, was water—Norton Bay, and beyond it to the left, Norton Sound. It was just a matter now of following the coast to Nome. The blue-gray water was covered with whitecaps. The land was dun-colored and curiously desertlike.

Three hours and forty minutes from Ruby the Fokker swooped down over Nome and along the beach whose black sands had once been so permeated with gold that wildly rich claims were measured by the inch and tens of thousands of expectant stampeders worked their long toms side by side for more than twenty miles.

The Fokker circled the village—home of about one thousand whites and Eskimos—and dipped for a landing on the parade ground of abandoned Fort Davis, four miles east on a spit formed by the Nome River and the sea. The Black Wolf Squadron had landed here five years before, and the six-hundred-by-fifty-foot strip had again been cleared of driftwood so Wien could land.

The Fokker had left Ruby during the night and completed its flight before the Army radio station at Ruby had opened. No message was sent to Nome, and there was no crowd at Fort Davis. Three days before, however, the entire Nome population had waited on the spit all night, picnicking, singing to the Nome Brass Band, celebrating the great event to come.

Almost before the Fokker had been unloaded and secured, however, a welcoming crowd began to arrive. About fifty men, women, and children descended upon the spit. The excitement was understandable, for Nome residents were among the most isolated of Americans. Each year a final ship made it to Nome in October, and from then until late June the frozen seas prevented passage. During that time, the only goods that reached the village came once a week by dog sled from Nenana, 674 miles away on the Alaska Railroad. Only five hundred pounds of mail and freight could be brought at a time. If all connections were precisely made, a letter or package dispatched from Seattle would be delivered in Nome six weeks later. Often the gap was ten or eleven weeks.

"After the last ship each fall," a Nome resident said, "we had no more new eggs until the next summer. The ones we had on hand had to last all winter. The whites got greener and the yellows got redder as time passed. How did they taste? Why, divine! When the first ship from Seattle came through the ice the next June, folks rushed down to the stores to buy the first eggs off the first lighters. And they were always disappointed. 'They don't have any taste at all!' was the cry."

The fastest trip from Fairbanks to Nome in the summertime was fifteen days, and all connections had to be made. "No section of Alaska has more cause to bless the coming of our airplanes," Mary Lee Davis wrote in her book *Uncle Sam's Attic*, "than has far-lying winter-frozen Seward Peninsula. What used to mean a dreaded, entire summer's delay-ful inspection trip for mining engineers, road commission men, geologists, bishops, school superintendents, governors, politicians, and all the scores of commercial people who had to make the Nome trip regularly each season, can now be accomplished in comfort and ease, over the week-end." °

Therefore, arrival of the Fokker in 1925 was an even more notable event in Nome history than arrival of the annual new eggs. Unfavorable takeoff winds kept Wien in Nome for fourteen days before he could make a triumphant nonstop flight back to Fairbanks. But while he was still in Nome the community's leaders already were organizing pressure on behalf of building a landing field and obtaining air service. In September the Nome *Nugget* reported that approval had been given by the Road Commission for an airport up Bessie Creek, a mile and a half from the beach. Although Bessie Creek (or Gold Hill) field was built in 1926, it was not until a year later that Nome got its regular service from Fairbanks, when Noel, Ralph, and a Fairbanks photographer named Gene Miller joined to buy a Hisso Standard and opened for business at the new Nome airfield.

Engineer Stines, who started it all (but didn't finish), arrived in Nome one day after the Fokker. At that, he beat the straight river–Bering Sea time by more than a week. While waiting for a west wind so they could take off from the short sandspit with full tanks, Noel and Ralph made two joyhops, taking up four passengers at a time and charging ten dollars each.

"We couldn't do many hops," Noel said, "because there wasn't much gas in Nome. Some had been left for the Army flyers of 1920. I used up just about what we had left in the tanks, and then stopped flying. I filled up a full ninety gallons for the flight back to Fairbanks. There was not much wind, so I was able to get all the way back nonstop. When I checked the gas with a dipstick, I found we had two gallons left. The flight back took 6:55."

These milestone flights failed to gain the notice they might have if they had been conducted closer to population centers or undertaken by a well-promoted explorer who needed publicity in order to raise funds. Noel's walk in from the Toklat was widely written up. It was sensational. Perhaps there is something unsensational about a commercial flight. Compared with some European countries, the United States seemed to be surprisingly backward in developing

° Mary Lee Davis, *Uncle Sam's Attic: The Intimate Story of Alaska* (Boston, Mass.: W. A. Wilde Co., 1930), pp. 147, 148.

commercial aviation. Wien's Fokker was the only large cabin aircraft he could find in the entire country in 1925, and it had been built in Holland. The United States was to work itself into a frenzy over aerial stunts and over the exploratory flights of Wilkins and Byrd and the dramatic trail-blazing of Lindbergh and Chamberlin, but relatively little public interest was directed to the infant organizations struggling to make flying a business. Commercial airlines were firmly established in Europe a half-dozen years before the first United States transcontinental mail route was granted in 1927. Planes were being built in Europe for passenger comfort and long-distance load carrying for a decade before appearance of the Ford Tri-Motor in the United States.

In Nome, one of Noel's passengers on a joyhop was Ada Bering Arthurs, the stunning seventeen-year-old daughter of a genial descendant of Ulstermen and a Minnesota-born mother. Tall, dark-haired, alternately sparkling and solemn, Ada had a way of looking disconcertingly at a man from challenging dark eyes beneath wide, level eyebrows. She had known Amundsen, and later met Lincoln Ellsworth and Umberto Nobile at Nome. While out for a stroll when she was thirteen, she and a Nome matron had been the first to greet the Black Wolf Squadron when the De Havillands dropped suddenly from the sky and landed at Fort Davis.

Early in June 1925 Ada had just graduated from high school. She had hung out a window in the Arthurs home watching for the airplane from Fairbanks. Noel Wien did not notice the intense young woman among his passengers, but during her short flight Ada went to the peephole in the cabin's bulkhead and looked at the back of the helmeted head of the man she would marry.

PART III

21. HIATUS 1926

Wien continued flying past freeze-up in 1925, until it got too cold. It was the first such flying ever attempted in Alaska. Ralph diagnosed the Fokker's vibration as a bent shaft, racked up in the noseover at Ruby. In the first major test of his ability as an airplane mechanic, Ralph built an engine from parts of the damaged one and parts from a spare that had been bought with the plane.

As Noel became more expert in handling the giant plane, he became devoted to it. Although exposed to the elements in the open cockpit, he remained cozy with his feet almost touching the radiator forward and the big BMW in-line heating the cowling beside him.

He flew the big ship past McGrath to Takotna, a river landing at which the Road Commission had built an "airport" and in its pride couldn't wait to have it tried out. It was to serve the McGrath-Takotna-Ophir mining district. Noel had several passengers and some freight going in. His return load was to be the body of a former Fairbanks postmaster who had died in McGrath. The body was being poled up the shallow river eighteen miles from McGrath to Takotna.

When Noel arrived at the landing, he saw that the "airport" was a skinned place on a shelf about five hundred feet up the side of the hills. It was not more than one thousand feet long, with a decided hump midway, and spruce and aspen grew right to the edges, dictating a high approach.

I tried to get in there, though I felt it was no use. I came in one way, just skimming in at about fifty, and touched down, but I was already four hundred feet down the field and the spruce were

149

coming up fast. I had to give it the gun. I felt so sorry for the corpse's friends who had been poling all night and half the day to get it to Takotna.

I tried to land the other way, but again, because of the high approach, couldn't get down in time. I had to go back to McGrath and land on that black sand bar that I was familiar with. It was pretty soft and we had to get help to drag us to a harder place before we could take off.

I phoned Takotna over the eighteen-mile phone line and told the people there what had happened and why I couldn't land. The road commissioner there, the one who had built the airport, said that the field was very ample and that under the circumstances I should try landing just this one time.

Well, I replied that I knew I couldn't get in there safely and that even if I did, by some miracle, we would never get out again. There wasn't enough run to get the Fokker off and over those spruce. But I couldn't have gotten in there any kind of way.

They had to pole the body back to McGrath in the big scow, and I sure felt sorry for those fellows. But there wasn't anything else we could do. They just didn't understand about the plane being limited. I had to carry full tanks, a full ninety gallons of gas, because we had to get nonstop back to Fairbanks. The Fokker couldn't land in the seven-hundred-foot field at Nenana, and there was nowhere else to get fuel.

The road commissioner was mad because he thought he knew how an airport should be laid out. That field was never any good, even after they cut the trees down at the ends, but later we could get in with slow airplanes like the Standards and after ships came in with brakes. They got the body back to McGrath in only eight hours, because they were going downstream that way. I waited for the body there and then flew it to Fairbanks.

I went to McGrath again that summer in the Fokker. My passenger back to Fairbanks was H. Y. Groshong, who had been in the Takotna country since 1905. We got to Fairbanks in two hours and a half, and Mr. Groshong said when he went in twenty years before, it had taken him twenty days from Nenana to the McGrath area. He sure was excited about the progress. The newspaper wrote up the story about him, like it wrote up just about every flight we made the first five years. There was always a crowd of sightseers at

The storm-damaged Stinson on Lake Minchumina on December 26, 1927, after having been blown two miles across the lake during a gale the night before. Courtesy of Noel Wien

The fur ship *Elisif*, when found by Noel, ice-bound three miles off North Cape, Siberia, in 1929. Courtesy of Noel Wien

Chukchis and *Elisif* crew members loading the Hamilton with 1100 pounds of bailed white fox fur pelts after Wien's flight from Nome to the ice-bound ship in March 1929. This was the first flight from the United States to Soviet Russia. Courtesy of Noel Wien

Noel, wearing jacket of Australian wombat with wolf-skin collar, beside the Hamilton Metalplane in March 1929. Courtesy of Noel Wien

the Fairbanks field to see the airplane come back: the wireless station would tell everybody that the ship was on its way in and a crowd would gather.

On one flight I brought in 240 pounds of gold in bars. That was worth over $75,000. I flew the Standards 98:30 that season, flying them when there wasn't much load or when the destination was a place where the Fokker couldn't land. I flew the Fokker 157:15.

A new man was hired by the company at the end of September. He said he was a pilot and a mechanic and he gradually began undercutting Ralph and me with the owners, saying Ralph was no good and I didn't fly enough. I had to turn back from one trip in the Standard when I saw the oil pressure was twenty instead of forty-five. It turned out that this fellow had set the pressure to read only twenty, saying that's what it should read. That was very dangerous on the Hisso. Another time I had to turn back with the Fokker when it started throwing oil. It was escaping from a poor fitting this fellow had made between cylinders. These things were worries, and when Ralph was no longer in full charge of keeping the ships in shape, I didn't see how I could keep on flying them.

My last hop was to Eagle and back on November 14. By this time the weather was getting cold, down to forty below, so we couldn't fly the Standards because of the open cockpits. But the Fokker had the cabin for passengers and I was warm beside the engine, although exposed. This new fellow took charge of fitting skis to the Fokker. He had them made at the hardware store in town without asking Ralph and me for any advice. They were short and stubby, with a sharp turn-up at both ends, and they were attached on a weak-looking stand. I didn't like their looks but agreed to try them out. They folded over sideways at a slow taxi, and that was the end of the Fokker on skis.

Ralph and I resigned from the company and he spent his time at his garage and got a job shoveling coal at the N.C. powerhouse. I went Outside, because a Harvard man named Robert Alexander Pope wanted me to fly to the North Pole. The new fellow at Fairbanks Airplane wouldn't fly the Fokker, and neither would most other pilots who came after. It was just left to rot and be torn apart. It got a bad name it didn't deserve. On normal-sized fields I liked it better than any other ship available at that time. During the 157:15 hours of flying in 1925, it grossed more than $15,000. All together, the company made a profit on it and that includes the initial purchase price of $9,500, or $10,000 by the time they got it to Fairbanks.

The "new fellow" referred to by Wien became widely hailed as one of the two worst scoundrels in Alaska aviation. It was not Wien's way to point out to Fairbanks Airplane Company owners the defects in this man, even to protect himself, and it is not Wien's way to "say bad things" about him even after nearly a half century.

Rodebaugh tried to talk Noel out of quitting. He told the pilot, "You'll be back when the new season starts next spring." Noel did not return. Rodebaugh went into business with the "new fellow," buying an OX-5 Waco, and the Fairbanks Airplane Company hired twenty-three-year-old Joe Crosson from San Diego as its pilot. Crosson flew in the Antarctic with Wilkins in 1928, and became one of Alaska's most distinguished bush pilots and a friend of Noel Wien. In the 1940s he and Noel were partners for a while in an aviation maintenance and supply business.

These were sad days for Ralph and me. We'd had jobs with a great future and now because of one man the opportunity blew up in our faces. The company investors thought this new fellow was just great and I was no good. I had gotten hard-skinned after a while, and didn't take orders from them that could get me in trouble.

I wasn't going to bull into things, get lost, be forced down, run out of gas. There were so many dangers in this big country in those slow ships. You could get lost suddenly and not be able to find things to recognize.

Every minute I was in the air I had to know exactly where I was, how far to a village, to a reference like the Yukon, to spots where I could put down in an emergency, how many minutes I had left in the tanks.

I had to depend on myself for all this, to get back. None of these people could do anything to help me once I got into the air, so I wasn't going to accept their statements and estimates of the weather or anything else that had to do with the flying. I relied completely on myself for this and on Ralph for the repair and keeping up the ships, and naturally this made some of them mad. But I went my way and did what I had to do.

I learned a lot about flying in Alaska. Between Fairbanks and Livengood and Wiseman there were just a few places to put down. Wickersham Dome was one, if you were in a Standard with wheels, but it wasn't really good. In the summer the Yukon at Stevens Village was passable, landing on a bar. I found it was better to pick a gravel bar than a sand bar. Gravel was rusty colored, sand was dirty gray and usually softer. After Stevens Village there wouldn't be another safe place until sand bars in the middle fork of the Koyukuk about fifteen miles below Wiseman.

In early spring there was just Wickersham Dome, because everything else was covered with water or soggy from the breakup. There were some domes north of Stevens Village that might have been all right, but I'm glad I never had to try them. They looked like that Nome Creek Dome.

In wintertime, on skis, there were more places to land, so many more than even on floats in summer. All the rivers, lakes, the tundra, muskeg, almost every place offered places to land. The domes weren't good in winter, though. There was wind up there and that meant the possibility of snowdrifts, and snowdrifts can bust an airplane as easy as rocks. And you couldn't judge the wind on a dome unless you had power to circle and find out, so you might go down on one with a tail wind and that would blow you right on over the top.

When I couldn't see any smoke, bending trees, or ripples on water to judge the wind, with power I could circle shallow, about ten degrees bank, and as low as possible to the ground, and find the wind by the drift of the airplane.

Noel took the S.S. *Yukon* south to Seattle in November 1925. Several letters bursting with optimism were waiting for him in Seattle from Robert Alexander Pope, of the motor car and motorcycle Popes. He wanted Wien to keep himself available for the polar expedition, but he sent no money to help with the keeping.

He did not fly an airplane until March 6. It was a Hisso Jenny owned by Delmar Snyder, the old barnstorming "friend" who had lived off Noel in New Orleans. Snyder was organizing a flying circus and wanted Noel as one of his pilots. Wien, unable to hold a grudge or even entertain one, accepted.

Snyder's circus began its tour on May 10. There were two airplanes, two pilots, and George Babcock, the great wingwalker. Noel flew a Canuck, the Canadian-built Jenny with ailerons on upper and lower wings, less wing stagger, and a level motor mount that caused the nose to point into the sky when the craft was on the ground. It had an OX-5. One spectator at Elyria, Ohio, was Paul Whiteman, "The King of Jazz," who was appearing with his orchestra at a local resort. Whiteman was one of the first show business people to own an airplane.

Noel logged his one-thousandth hour while throwing out hand-bills over Danville, Illinois. After four months of barnstorming the Midwest, he received word from Pope that all was ready for the North Pole push. He packed his cardboard suitcase and took a train from Columbus, Ohio, to New York. He had six hundred dollars in saved wages from the circus. Snyder owed him two hundred dollars more and said he would send it along at the end of the month. He did not.

Wien went directly from the Grand Central Station to 36 West Forty-fourth Street. On Pope's office door, as on his letterheads, were the words "Investigation," "Organization," and "Finance." Pope was tall, ample of girth, richly dressed, impressively elegant. He talked in sincere tones, and enthusiasm radiated from him with enough force to quicken the pulse of even the imperturbable Noel Wien.

"I am delighted to see you, my boy. I sent for you to come to New York because any day now, maybe even this afternoon, the final pledges will be in and we can start for the North. I do not want to waste even twenty-four hours, so that is why I want you to be on hand and ready in an instant."

Pope took the pilot to lunch at the Harvard Club, obtained a two-week guest card for him, and helped him move into a room there. No word was spoken about money for expenses. When his two weeks were up, Wien paid his bill at the club and moved out. His six hundred dollars had been greatly reduced. He took a fifth-floor attic room at the Grand Hotel on Thirty-third Street and Broadway, farther removed in style than in distance from the

Harvard Club. His ceiling slanted, his bath was on the floor below, there was no elevator. "I didn't know much about a thing like this," Noel said, "so I didn't think it strange that I had to pay my own expenses."

Pope kept close track of the doings of Captain Wilkins, who was at Fairbanks trying to organize a polar flight. The Australian explorer, after years of Arctic experience aboard ships and afoot alongside dog sleds, proposed to use the airplane to investigate a theory that there was a land mass in the Arctic Ocean. He had a Fokker, powered with a single Liberty motor, for use as a supply plane, and a trimotored Fokker that he proposed to fly toward the pole with Ben Eielson. Pope wanted his All-American Alumni Expedition to beat Wilkins to a landfall, and he was relieved when Wilkins failed. Eielson flew gasoline supplies north from Fairbanks to Barrow, but both aircraft were damaged, other delays set them back, and Wilkins called off his attempt until the following year.

Noel hocked his watch and gold chain that had hung so proudly on his vest when he had arrived in New York in August. He met another of Pope's pilots, Leigh Wade. Wade, about thirty, was also a famous aviator. He had been overseas in the war and, as Lieutenant Wade, had been a pilot member of the army's around-the-world flight team in 1924. He, Canadian Pat Reed, and the Alaska aviator Noel Wien had been chosen by Pope to pilot the expedition that would be financed by donations from alumni of Pope's school, Harvard College. Wade soon left New York, declaring that Pope was a phoney.°

° Wade later returned to the army and became a general.

22. NORTH AGAIN

It was beginning to seem to the patient Wien that it was El Paso and New Orleans all over again. Just a few months before, there had been such high hopes. Richard E. Byrd on May 9 had announced that he and his pilot, Floyd Bennett, had flown over the pole from Spitsbergen, but that did not deter other seekers after polar fame. Some aviators and foreign newspapermen did not believe that Byrd had flown to the pole; their arithmetic told them that Byrd's aircraft could not have made such a flight within the time he was absent from Spitsbergen. During his wait in New York, Noel had met Byrd and the Norwegian aviator, Bernt Balchen, who had been hired by Byrd for his planned Atlantic flight. While he still had money, Wien had visited airports and aircraft factories in the area, talking aviation and airplanes. Byrd was aloof. Balchen, when he learned who Wien was, showed him some airplane skis he had designed. The two men were to meet often over the decades.

On one of his trips to Mineola, Wien had been awed by the sight of René Fonck's huge trimotored Sikorsky biplane in which the glamorous French war hero would attempt an Atlantic crossing. Igor Sikorsky himself was putting finishing touches to the craft. With seventy-five confirmed kills to his credit, Fonck was France's leading aerial ace of the world war. He was not destined to fly the Atlantic. In late September 1926, his fatally overloaded Sikorsky wallowed down the runway on its takeoff roll for Paris. Unable to become airborne, it ended up in a ball of flame in the gully that separated Mineola from Curtiss Field. Fonck and his navigator survived, but his mechanic and his radio operator perished.

By November Noel was reduced to his New Orleans regimen of one slim meal a day and long walks to forget hunger. Pope told him that the money was coming in just fine, but that he was banking it in a special account and would not spend any of it until $250,000 had been raised. In his pocket Noel had six dollars, the totality of his resources.

After Christmas, I had no more money at all, and everything was sold or in hock. I'd been in New York for five months and had walked over every step of it and the smell of food was too much. I lost more weight than I had on the walk from the Toklat. When thirty-five dollars came in from Ralph, I knew I had to use it to get out of there. I went to tell Robert Alexander Pope good-bye and he still seemed cheerful and talkative as ever and said he wished I'd stay but he knew I longed to feel that joystick in my hand again and the scarf whipping out behind me.

There weren't any flying jobs that I knew of. A whole year, 1926, was gone, and in all that year I worked only a few months. I went back to Cook from New York. The family was in bad times as usual and were existing but not putting anything aside. There weren't any jobs in the winter, so I helped out around the family place.

I determined somehow to get back to Alaska and I knew I would. I wrote to Ben Fall, a miner at Livengood, and told him that if he would send me three thousand dollars I would buy a Hisso Standard and get it up to Fairbanks and he and I would go partners in the airplane business. He wired me back, "On account dry season, mining here uncertain. For that reason can't tell what I will do until fall. New aviation company in Fairbanks. Keep in touch with me as I might take up your proposition conditions turn out favorable."

Noel received help from an unlikely source, a bank. Upon his father's suggestion, for the first time in his life he walked into a financial institution. He walked out with two hundred dollars, enough to take him back to Fairbanks. The unassuming Wien, in his own eyes still a "farm boy," was a celebrity in Cook, a daredevil aviator who had gained world-wide notice for his exploits as Alaska's first bush pilot. The Farmers and Merchants Bank of Cook lent him the money on his reputation and that of the Wien family.

About March 1, 1927, Noel started back for Alaska, accompanied by brother Fritz, then twenty-five, who had made his own financial transaction to raise money for the trip.

Thirty-below temperatures and unmelted snows of March welcomed Noel and Fritz to Fairbanks. The lean-to addition to the cabin on Front Street was now a nursery for Ralph's and Julia's son, who had been born in Fairbanks in 1926. Noel and Fritz slept on the floor in sleeping bags. Ralph, his garage business at low ebb, looked gaunt, but he still loved Fairbanks. "This is the place, this is the life," he solemnly told his brothers. Julia did not indicate agreement.

Ralph said that Rodebaugh had left the Fairbanks Airplane Company and had gone into business with A. A. Bennett, the pilot hired in late 1925, even accepting second billing in the firm's name, Bennett-Rodebaugh. They set up at Weeks Field, flying two Waco 9s with OX-5s and a Hisso Standard whose front cockpit had been covered for passenger comfort. All were biplanes. Bennett flew them constantly, cornering almost all the salesman and fur-buyer traffic between Fairbanks northeast to Fort Yukon and southwest to McGrath. Flying allowed these men to do in one day what required twenty days on the surface.

The old Fairbanks Airplane Company still operated from Rickert's hayfield, and had built a hangar on the edge. Bob Lavery became manager when Rodebaugh left. Joe Crosson, the new pilot, flew a Hisso Swallow, open cockpit, and only occasionally took up Noel's old Fokker F. III. Like other pilots who followed Noel in Fairbanks, Crosson was not fond of the Fokker. It was too much plane for the bush fields.

On his first morning back in Fairbanks, Noel rose early and walked the two miles to Rickert's, trying to regain the ice legs that allow a Fairbanks man to remain upright. Ice ruts ran down each street, cut and tamped into the thick ice by wheels and feet during the eight months of snowy winter.

No one was flying at Rickert's; in fact, neither airplane company had tried to operate through the Interior winter of 1926. The Wacos were hangared. The Fokker and the Standard were in the open, off to the side as if discarded. Another Standard that Noel had flown for the company in 1925 had been downed and abandoned in the Kantishna. Noel looked at the airplanes and felt a thump in his chest and a catch in his throat. The urge to fly was almost overpowering. He counted back to July 26, 1926. In nine days it would be eight months since he had been aloft. Maybe there was a job for another pilot here. Although he had not spoken of it even to his brothers, he knew that he would not fly again unless all particulars were of his own choosing. That meant, probably, he would have to be his own boss. He did not go look at Weeks Field.

Noel went back to the cabin and there met Captain George H. Wilkins, who had come to offer Noel a flying job. Dignified and commanding, the Australian explorer was then in his second season of attempting to fly from Alaska to Europe via an Arctic route. He knew the Arctic as few men did, having spent most of his life since 1913 exploring the frigid regions by ship and dog sled. Photographer, geographer, meteorologist, and aviator, he was to gain renown as a great navigator the following year when he flew with Eielson from Barrow to Spitsbergen. He was knighted as Sir Hubert Wilkins. Stefansson, whom Wilkins accompanied on several expeditions, said he had never known a harder worker than Wilkins. "A half dozen such men," he wrote in *The Friendly Arctic*, "would make an invincible polar expedition" (p. 291).

Wilkins and his Detroit *News* expedition had three aircraft at Fairbanks that year. One was a high-winged Fokker monoplane, single engine, in which Wilkins planned to make his intercontinental flight. The others were four-place Stinson cabin biplanes to be used to supply the takeoff base at Barrow. Wilkins had brought two pilots from the States, Ben Eielson and Alger Graham. The year before, Eielson and U.S. Army Major Thomas Lanphier had wiped out two of the Australian's aircraft when each stalled before reaching Rickert's field on landing approaches. Wilkins had learned of Noel's skill, especially with the big Fokker, which he had operated from what Wilkins called "the wretched field at Fairbanks." What better pilot than Wien to test-hop the expedition's planes from that field?

So, on March 18, 1927, Noel returned to the sky, joyfully test-hopping Wilkins' airplanes and thinking in the back of his mind that Wilkins had three airplanes and only two pilots, and perhaps. . . .

But as Eielson was taxi-testing the Fokker on skis, one ski cut through the deep snow and stuck in a furrow. Wilkins decided that the Fokker was too heavy for ski work. He would use one of the Stinsons for the Europe flight, the other as supply ship. That left the expedition with two planes and no need for three pilots. Wien was paid off after two weeks. He had two hundred dollars in his pocket, but that wouldn't last long in Alaska. He got a job as grease monkey and truck driver at Fairbanks Exploration's Chatanika camp, where Fritz was working, twenty-seven miles northeast of Fairbanks. The bush pilot was back at the controls, but of the wrong kind of vehicle. When another hand was needed, he helped drive steam points, metal pipes that were forced vertically into the permafrost and through which steam was pumped to thaw the earth for mining.

This work required no skill, no attention even, and Noel's mind was twenty-seven miles away on the old Fokker and Standard sitting at Rickert's field. If he could raise some money, and if Fairbanks Airplane would sell, he could go into the airplane business for himself. But the company hardly would sell to a prospective competitor, especially with Bennett-Rodebaugh already supplying cutthroat competition.

Suppose, though, he promised to go somewhere else to start his airplane company? Suppose he went to Nome? The Bering Sea village was the supply center for the entire Seward Peninsula. With airplane service it could also supply the Arctic coast. Noel recalled the warm welcome given him by Nome businessmen on his pioneering flight there in 1925. A landing field had since been scraped out on the hill north of the town, but no planes had yet used it.

If he agreed with Fairbanks Airplane Company to operate out of Nome and not Fairbanks, maybe they would sell him one of the old craft. If he could find some money, that is.

The dream became too compelling, and Noel quit the F.E. before a month was out, hitched a ride down to Fairbanks, and called on Bob Lavery. Lavery didn't know; he'd have to call some of his partners. "I guess maybe it'd be all right," said Dick Wood, "as long as he does go to Nome. It wouldn't be right for him to have gotten all this experience on us and then go into competition with us in the Interior."

Hal Bailey also thought it would be a good deal to sell one of the old, unused airplanes to Wien. "He won't be any competition anyway," Bailey sneered. "Every time he sees a cloud in the sky he won't fly. He won't be reliable enough for these sourdoughs when he's on his own. Let him have a plane."

They asked five thousand dollars for the Fokker, Noel's love and first choice. That was out of the question. They asked seven hundred fifty dollars for the Standard. Noel walked out and went over the old J-1. The exterior was pathetic. The old crate's fabric was stained, ripped, stretched almost loose enough to flap in the faint Fairbanks breezes. The radiator looked like a sieve. Wire wheel spokes were loose or sprung. Splices knotted the flying wires, even the control wires; ribs and longerons had been wood-spliced with bolts. It was a discouraging mess. But Noel knew that nothing was rusted, because nothing could rust in the Interior dryness; and that the best mechanic in the Territory—Ralph—was shoveling coal at the powerhouse and waiting a chance to use his skills again.

"Well, I'll see," Noel told the airplane owners and went back to town to canvass Second Avenue and Cushman Street. He joined the boys at the hotel lobby, stopped in at Harry Phillips' tobacco shop, looked in at all the businesses and stores not owned by stockholders in the Fairbanks Airplane Company, everywhere letting it be known that the Wien brothers wanted to go into the airplane business and would welcome investors. Two men volunteered.

Gene Miller was a thirty-year-old Oregonian who had worked as a photographer in Hollywood. He had come to Alaska with a film crew, succumbed to its pull, and remained. His own dream was to photograph the wonders of the Great Land and to sell post cards and educational films. A bachelor, he was making a meager living from prints and post cards. Filming Alaska from the air would be an exclusive, he thought. Noel had earlier found Miller to be friendly and he liked and trusted him. It was agreed that the photographer and Noel would each invest three hundred dollars, Ralph would invest his time and skills, and each would have a one-third interest in the venture. Miller would accompany Noel on flights when there was room, making his films, and Noel would fly him on special hops in between working flights.

The second volunteer was Harry Phillips, owner of the cigar store, "a fine fellow" who in old-timer fashion handed Noel three hundred dollars without asking him to sign a note. Six hundred dollars was accepted as down payment on the Standard, and Wien, Wien, and Miller owned an airplane, the value of which was about to be tested.

After a thorough examination, Ralph decided that the Hisso needed only a top overhaul, but that the plane must have a new radiator. The old one had been pinched and soldered beyond endurance and leaked like a fountain. They bought a spare from Fairbanks Airplane, a brass-sided oval model wider than the old rectangular one. Ralph finished the overhaul in a month, working steadily at nights while keeping his powerhouse job, for he could not forgo the wages.

Ralph was a worn-out but proud man when finally Noel bounced the old craft off Rickert's on its first test-hop. Compression was low, revolutions were low, and the dirty old fabric luffed through the air like a drained sail. But the Standard flew and Noel bravely assessed it as airworthy. He did no stunts. The old fabric later became covered with names and messages written on it by Eskimos and Indians in the bush. They would come out when the plane landed to see if there were any "letters" for them, and to inscribe notes to friends and relatives on this flying post card.

On the nineteenth of June, 1927, a few days more than two years since making the first flight to Nome, Noel raised the Standard from Fairbanks, and he and Miller set out to establish their company at the Bering Sea village. At Fairbanks, among the Swallows and the Waco, Noel thought the ancient Standard was a "forgotten has-been," and he wondered if it would get them to Nome. It did, in the fine flying time of 7:05, after a fuel stop at Ruby. If only the old Hisso will hold out for about one hundred hours, Noel thought, we can service the Seward mining camps and make enough to buy a better airplane. The Standard will look a lot better in Nome than it did in Fairbanks. There was no other airplane west of Fairbanks.

Noel and Miller landed at the Bessie Creek airfield at three o'clock in the morning of June 20, 1927, a few hours after the biggest annual event in Nome life, arrival of the first boat to get through the ice from Seattle. Among its passengers returning from school Outside was Ada Bering Arthurs, a few days short of her twentieth birthday anniversary, reluctant to return to dreary Nome.

23. AT THE ARTHURS'

Everybody turned out a few days later for the Cheechako Ball, Nome's most exciting social event of the year. The ball was held as soon as possible after the unpredictable arrival of the first boat through the ice in June. Old friends returned from Outside were welcomed home, newcomers greeted and appraised. Women who had remained in Nome through the eight-month winter had need to examine the new styles worn by those fortunate enough to have spent the winter Outside. The farsighted few who had remained in Nome but who had ordered new gowns from Seattle on the first boat required an occasion to display the finery. The ball provided for this and more. The grip of Nome's winter relaxes so suddenly as to be breath-taking, and each year there came an explosion of good cheer that simply had to be enjoyed en masse and memorialized with a public rite.

The larger of two Eagles halls, the Big Eagles Hall, was opened and aired. It was one of six fraternal palaces built during Nome's main boom between 1900 and 1910. Some were three stories tall, and most had bay windows from which the three-block length of Front Street could be viewed. Front was the only street with wooden planking atop its mud. Inside, the Eagles Hall had an expensive hardwood dance floor. Tin sheets stamped with curlicues and painted green, now faded, covered the walls as well as the ceiling. A balcony perched around both sides and across the rear of the hall. There were no wallflowers at the ball: men and boys outnumbered females three to one, and males of all ages lined the sides of the hall waiting their chance. On the floor a mass of dancers in evening gowns, flapper skirts, satins, ginghams, summer parkas, tuxedos, blue serge, miners' flannels, overalls, dancing pumps, mukluks, oxfords, and clodhopper boots swirled, dipped, pumped, and stomped to "Three O'Clock in the Morning," "My Buddy," "Yes, We Have No Bananas," and "Ain't We Got Fun?" played on a piano, a drum, and two violins from a dais at center front.

Ada Arthurs came to the 1927 Cheechako Ball with a neighbor couple and was soon caught up in the warm tribal contentment that linked the whites of Nome at these ritual events. Tom Jensen, a bachelor who had escorted the two newly arrived schoolteachers to the ball, asked Ada while they danced, "Have you met the aviators yet?" When she said she had not, Jensen pointed them out on the balcony. Ada did not think it proper that she should go to the balcony to meet the men; they should come down to meet her. Jensen insisted it was her "civic duty" to welcome the men to Nome. "After all," Jensen explained, "they're here to start our first airplane service and you can't count what that will mean to our city. Everybody must make them feel welcome."

Ada went with Jensen to the balcony and was introduced to the new men as "a native daughter, a true and beautiful Nome nugget." The aviators bowed. Gene Miller was short, fair, and thirtyish, Ada noted. The other man, Noel Wien, was taller, thinner, had thick brown hair and a dimpled, shy smile. The lower part of his face was covered with large brown spots and scabs. Oh, dear, Ada thought, oil from his airplane motor has spattered out and burned him. She learned later that he had contracted what was known unprofessionally as "barbershop crud." He was embarrassed by it.

"Miss Arthurs and I want to invite you down to the floor to join the dance," Jensen told the men. They refused politely, pleading fatigue and their inappropriate clothing. Both wore leather jackets, breeches, and high-laced boots. Well, Ada thought, they are better dressed than half the dancers, and, anyway, what difference does dress make in Nome? But I won't beg them. While Jensen attempted to cajole them into joining the dance, Ada said good night and expressed her pleasure in having met them—but not very sincerely. She took Jensen's arm and turned to leave.

"When is the next dance?" Wien called.

"We always have a real big one on the Fourth of July," Jensen told him.

The pilot looked at Ada. "Will you be there?"

"Yes," she said.

"Then I'll be there too."

Ada and Jensen returned to the dance floor. At mention of Wien's name Ada had recognized it as that of the Fokker pilot with whom she had taken a short hop in 1925 after he had made the first commercial airplane flight to Nome. After that flight in the old Fokker, during which she had peeped at the back of the aviator's head, Ada had gone to the pilot and thanked him. "He grinned," she said, "and there were these very deep dimples in his cheeks. He had blue-gray eyes, very wide, open, and innocent-looking, completely unsophisticated and natural. He seemed such a nice-looking, pleasant young man."

At their second meeting two years later at the 1927 ball, Ada was less interested in the pilot than in the fact that his airplane was to be Nome-based and perhaps her summer need not be so dull after all.

About two weeks later, the aviator did show up at the Fourth of July Ball in the Arctic Brotherhood Hall. He had made a few flights and had collected some money and was dressed in new gray herringbone trousers and a blue blazer, with white shirt and brown, low-quarter shoes. "He looked neat," Ada said, "but he always looked neat and clean no matter what he wore." Pink tinges marked the remains of the "oil burns" on his face.

"May I have this dance?" he asked Ada. Ada noted the boyish, appealing grin. She accepted, and danced with him two more times that evening. During the last whirl he asked, "Would you like to go for an airplane ride?"

"Oh, yes, yes, I would," Ada replied quickly, pleased that she had not had to direct the conversation to the airplane and cast hints for a sample.

"Have you ever been up?"

"Yes."

"Oh? Where was that?"

"Right here in Nome, and you were the pilot." She told him she had been "quite the thing" at college in California because none of her school friends had ever been flying. He did not remember the seventeen-year-old girl among his passengers two years before, but he showed no embarrassment and made no excuses. There was a pause while Ada gave her partner a chance to make a date for the airplane ride, but he did not. Finally she asked him, "Would you like to come to dinner?"

"Yes. When?" he accepted eagerly.

So now it was to be dinner before flying. "Well, uh, how about day after tomorrow, about seven o'clock?" The pilot said he would be there.

People have always talked about Noel's bashfulness, Ada said, but he never seemed bashful with me. He asked me right out, "When?" Right from the start I felt comfortable with him, and apparently he did with me. Some young men made me uncomfortable. They were too pushy or too boring. Noel treated everyone with respect, and even when we had nothing to say for long periods, we weren't bored or uncomfortable.

The food in Nome restaurants was just terrible then, so I can understand his eagerness to get a home-cooked meal. My mother was working and I was doing all the cooking at home that summer while my dad worked at Little Creek as a blacksmith on the dredges.

About six o'clock two days later the Standard flew over the house and Noel gunned the motor. He was coming back from a flight to Deering and was letting me know he would be to dinner on time. I had fixed a pork roast with mashed potatoes and made a lemon pie. My dad carved the roast and served. He always piled the plates so high that when you went to get a bite you didn't know where to take it for fear the whole thing would come tumbling off.

Noel ate very slowly. When he finished his plate, my father asked if he would have some more and Noel said, "I would like some more." My dad filled up his plate again, just heaping it like before. When he finished that plate, my dad asked if he wanted some more and Noel said, "Yes, I would like some more," and my dad filled up a third helping just as tall as the other two. Very slowly Noel ate all of that.

The others had stopped after one plate, but I took something and pretended to nibble to keep him company. He was not embarrassed, just natural and relaxed. After he finished the third plate, I served the pie. Noel ate his piece and I asked him, "Do you like the pie?"

and he said, "That is very good pie," so I gave him another piece and he ate it.

My dad got a great kick out of this. After Noel left he said, "It's a lucky thing that young fellow came to dinner and not to breakfast, because with what he eats he couldn't have gotten the load off the ground to fly to Deering this morning."

It turned out that Noel had not eaten at all that day, as was his habit. He would get up and fly all day and then eat all three meals in one huge meal. I don't know how he did it.

Before he left that first night Noel said he had a few flights lined up and he would call me the next time he got back to Nome to set a date for the hop in his Standard. Gene Miller, Noel's partner, got Emily Polet and we four went up. Gene and Emily sat in the front cockpit, which was made for two, but Noel and I had to squeeze into the back cockpit, which was made for one person. We flew over Nome for about fifteen minutes, making big, slow turns. He didn't try to show off or to frighten us, as so many other men would have.

Noel was flying everywhere that anybody wanted him to, provided he could land there. I don't know how it happened, because we did not arrange it, but every time he would arrive back in Nome he would fly over, gun his motor, and then call. I would invite him to dinner, if we had not eaten and if there was time to prepare. Soon he was spending every evening with us when he was in Nome.

I was having dates with other men in Nome when Noel was out of town, and he had dates in Fairbanks, too. He showed me pictures he made of Fairbanks girls, but he never asked me about my dates. It was understood after a while that if Noel showed up unexpectedly in Nome, I would break any date to spend the evening with him.

My dad and Noel were alike in one thing, neatness. Even when he had on working clothes, there was a neatness about my dad. I remember one boy friend I had was a college graduate and I enjoyed him very much. But he came to Nome as a mining engineer with the idea that when you were out in the sticks it did not matter how you looked. He would come to the house in dirty work clothes, with his shirt unbuttoned. Why, my dad couldn't stand that man. But he liked Noel right away and I think a lot of it was because no matter what Noel had on, he looked fastidious.

And my mother just fell for Noel right away. She never once told me, "You can do better than that," as she told me about so many other men. The remarkable thing about this was that although my mother was born in Minnesota, she was not of Scandinavian parents, and I've never known anyone with a stronger racial prejudice. I remember when I was just a little girl she made the remark that "it will be just my luck to have you marry one of those Norwegians or Swedes." Noel was Norwegian *and* Swedish.

I think it must have been Noel's open, natural honesty and the fact that she felt no worries about her daughter when I was with him. It even got so that she would make lunches for him to take on flights between Nome and Fairbanks, not only for himself but for his passengers, too. It was her idea. Noel never had to pay for it. Often, when he came back from Fairbanks, which had railroad connection with the coast, he would bring my mother lettuce, tomatoes, and other fresh things we didn't have in Nome.

She must have been attracted, as I was, by Noel's good looks, his even disposition, his soft voice that never got harsh or loud, his steady eyes that looked right at you. His manner never changed, and for a long time I thought that maybe he never got worried or excited at all. It was many years later before I learned that he did worry.

Over the next two years my parents got to know Noel better than any parents usually know the man their daughter marries.

Whenever there was room in the Standard, and later in the Stinson that he bought from Wilkins, I would fly with Noel on his hops. I worked in the post office during the summer of 1927, Noel's first in Nome. That fall I became court reporter for Judge G. J. Lomen. In later years Noel would come into the office and say he had room for me on a trip, and Judge Lomen would let me go if we were not actually in court. One time in the Stinson cabin plane, Noel asked me to hold the plane straight and steady while he took some pictures. He had taught me to do this. He climbed in the back seat and I flew the plane and did a pretty good job. I fixed my hair and straightened up my collar and posed while he made the pictures. When the prints came back I looked at them and asked, "What happened to the pictures of me?" There weren't any pictures of me. He had taken photographs of the instrument panel.

We did not talk much on these trips. It was too noisy. Noel would point to something and tip the airplane up so I could see it. He brought aviation magazines to the house and after dinner we would talk for hours. I read the magazines so I could talk with him about flying and airplanes.

Noel told me about his childhood and his flying circus days. I talked about myself. Noel was very natural, with no unnecessary talk. He never talked about building up the business. It just grew incidentally to his flying. He knew nothing about business, and I did not think in terms of worldly goods either. If I had, Noel would not have been the man for me. Although the company grew and became very large and successful, all Noel wanted was just to fly in Alaska.

Only one time do I recall him ever saying anything about his hopes and dreams. He said someday he wanted to fly over the pole to Norway, to the home of his people. It was not an obsession, and he never did more than mention it.

On Noel's part, his relationship with Ada and the Arthurs family was the most comfortable of his life. Mr. Arthurs was a "fine gentleman" who told hilarious dialect stories, not sparing the Irish. In the quiet aviator he found the perfect noncompetitive audience. Noel listened to his tales, laughed at the proper places, and immediately forgot them. He and Billy Arthurs played a duet at the table, the host piling high his guest's plate and Noel accepting and eating every crumb.

Noel thought Mrs. Arthurs was "nice at all times" but rather "stern" with her daughter. After dinner, Mr. Arthurs (and Mrs. Arthurs, when she was not at work) would withdraw to their bedroom. No matter how late Noel stayed, never in the months that followed did either call down to inform the young people of the time. That may be something of a parental record for any latitude.

Noel thought Ada was "intelligent, attractive, and a good cook." He remembers that first meal at the Arthurs' home. He thought Ada looked like Gloria Swanson. During their times together she spoke of many things that the farm boy aviator did not know, things she had learned during a year at Mills College in Oakland and at business school in Seattle. She told him of the old sourdoughs she knew so well and he laughed at the ingenuity of Peter X. Petersen, one of maybe a dozen Peter Petersens out on the creeks and the only one of them who regularly received the mail intended for him, only because he had inserted the "X" into his name. She told him of seeing Amundsen, Ellsworth, Nobile, Knud Rasmussen, and other great explorers who came through Nome, of her sled dogs, and of her rich girlhood in Nome. She worked in the post office and she knew everybody. She was interesting. She was comfortable to be with.

24. COURTSHIP

Nome watched the relationship between its new aviator and its favorite belle as closely as it oversaw the growth of its new airplane service.

No citizen attended to the former with more dedication than did Dan Camp, an old sourdough bachelor who lived in a cabin next to the Arthurs' house. Dan's one-room frame home was crammed like a rat's nest with everything portable that he had ever found in his nugget sniping along the creeks. There were two paths through this treasure dump. One path led from the door to the two-burner cooking and heating stove that kept the cabin temperature at a steady ninety degrees. The other path led from the stove to Dan's bunk, which looked like an explosion in progress.

No female entered Dan's nest. Dan never washed a plate or a pan. He ate from the same crusted plate every meal, his grub warmed in the same grimy frying pan. Surprisingly, his person was always neat, so he was a not unwelcome visitor in the Arthurs' home next door. Ada thought Dan "a precious old fellow," and Dan loved Ada as all the Nome old-timers did, remarking on the beauty of her black hair and black eyes.

Dan's cabin, like all buildings this far north in Alaska, had a storm porch, an appendage somewhat like a telephone booth attached outside the door. In winter, a person entered the storm porch, closed its door, then opened the inner door and entered the house, leaving the blowing snow and some of the cold behind. There was one small dirty window in Dan's cabin, unsuitable for observation, but through a knothole in a storm porch's wooden door facing the Arthurs' home the sourdough kept up with the courtship—or what the village hoped was a courtship—of Ada by Noel. Let there come a sound from the Arthurs', and Dan would zip through the paths in his junk trove, out onto the storm porch, and up to the knothole.

"Noel stayed pretty late last night, didn't he?" Dan liked to ask Ada.

"Oh, no," Ada would reply. "He left about midnight."

"No he didn't," Dan would snap. "He left at eleven minutes after one." Dan had sharp ears and a good clock.

While Dan kept an eye on the courtship, Noel's development of the airplane business was keenly watched by the merchants of Nome and the miners, trappers, and traders strung out along the dog trails of the Seward Peninsula. Despite its years of rough use, the old Hisso Standard hung together, and despite the fierce winds and impenetrable summer fogs of Nome that kept him grounded often, Wien flew 108:05 hours in his first six weeks, taking aviation deep into the treeless Arctic to such places as Candle, Deering, Kotzebue, and Point Hope.

A familiar saying by people who know Nome is, "I've never been in Nome when the sun was shining." There are a few bright blue days in the spring and summer after breakup and when the ground has thawed enough for the winter's accumulation of dead to be buried. Summer's average temperature is fifty. A chill wind blows in from the Bering toward the strangely desertlike beige mountains behind the village; and when the wind stops, there usually is fog, rain, or mist.

Snow arrives in September. It does not fall; it whistles in on the wind, driving horizontally. One notable difference between Nome and Fairbanks is the gentle fall of tiny snow crystals that float straight down upon Fairbanks in a windless quiet, so in contrast to Nome, where almost any snowfall is a blizzard. Sometimes it snows until June in Nome.

With the coming of the airplane Nome witnessed a new

stampede. Businessmen clamored to get into the air. People wanting to fly crowded around the Standard at the Bessie Creek landing field and waited for its pilot to show up. Often, after having chatted with Ada until 1:11 A.M. (Dan Camp time), Noel would get out of bed at six to find the weather not to his liking and would go back to sleep. Insistent passengers sometimes went to the Golden Gate Hotel, where he and Gene Miller lived, and threw stones against the side of their room until Wien looked out and told them they would have to wait until another day.

Like the stockholders of the Fairbanks Airplane Company, some thwarted customers grew peeved and spread a story that Wien was afraid or, at best, a lazy slugabed. Word got around that he spent most of the night sparking Ada Arthurs and had to sleep all day. Noel was merely exercising his habitual caution, and most Nome people gradually came to respect it. He had no crashes, he never hurt a passenger.

His returns to Nome—particularly after he began landing on the Snake River ice right in town—invariably drew a crowd. By the time he taxied to shore, twenty-five or so people would be waiting. "He had passengers and freight to unload," Ada said, "but I could see him smiling with the dimple in his cheek and he would shake hands with everybody, careful not to overlook anyone."

Departures also became a leading spectator sport. There are people in Nome today who relish the memory of the shy pilot loading a Lapp woman aboard a cabin Stinson later that year. In an attempt to assist the Native economy, reindeer were imported into Alaska in 1891 and Lapp herdsmen came to instruct the Eskimos. Some brought their women. This woman was going to Unalakleet and would be first off the airplane, so she was the last aboard after the cabin had already been stuffed.

"She was stocky like all Lapps," said a witness, "and she was dressed like an Eskimo with two parkas, one with the fur turned inside against the skin and the other with the fur outside. And mukluks. She was as wide as she was tall and too wide for the cabin door. It was a good thing there was a crowd waiting to see Wien take off, because it took a good many of them to help Wien shove this woman through the door while the people inside pulled. I don't know how they ever got her out at Unalakleet."

Soon there was so much flying that Noel worried more than ever about the precarious health of the old Standard. Rather than remain in Fairbanks while Ralph worked on the craft, Noel began bringing Ralph back to Nome whenever there appeared need for work. For clean-living young men, Nome offered no evening diversion. The Glue Pot was a small cigar store with a card room in the back. Ralph did not play cards or smoke cigars. There were the saloons and the fancy women behind the fence. Ralph patronized neither. So he would go with Noel to the Arthurs' house, eat a meal that stupefied even Billy Arthurs, accustomed by now to serving Noel, and sit up with Noel and Ada. Sometimes when Mrs. Arthurs was home, he would play cribbage or checkers with her.

The largest of the Wien brothers was a sociable person, somewhat of a tease, the only Wien with a store of small talk, and he usually had a comeback for Billy Arthurs' sallies. Ralph had a sense of time like Dan Camp, and it was he who usually brought the evening to a close with the suggestion that Noel get to bed. "Both of them became like sons to my parents," Ada said. Ralph spent his evenings with the family even when Noel was not in Nome.

Noel flew mail, groceries, clothing, small machinery parts, and passengers into the bush from Nome. Mail was not payload at first, but was carried as a favor to potential customers. Errands were run for the same purpose. Mrs. Nielsen at Shishmaref wanted a message delivered to Mrs. Smith at Shaktoolik; Mrs. Smith wanted a swatch delivered to the dressmaker at Nome and wanted the pilot to pick up some thread and bias tape for her and bring it the next time he came to Shaktoolik. There were no charges for these services, just repayment for out-of-pocket expenditures and, of course, the freight charge.

By the time the second summer had ended, Ada was an experienced flyer, although she was never to land an airplane. She wanted to learn and to solo. "It probably was a good thing I did not take real instruction from Noel," she said, "because I would have been too impatient with him. He tried to teach me to drive a gear shift automobile. Instead of telling me what to do, he told me what was happening when I pushed in the clutch, how fast the motor was running, what happened when you moved the shift lever.

"He does that to this day and it is one thing I get very irritated over. I want to know *what* to do and *how* to do it and I don't care about all the background. When it comes to a machine, Noel is really talkative. He was a good instructor. He taught four men to fly that summer, with just the single controls in the Standard. They had to jam themselves in the back cockpit with him. But you ask him a question that he could answer with 'yes' or 'no' and he will take ten minutes leading up to the answer. If he had started to teach me to fly, I never would have made it."

When Ada did not fly with Noel, she often had long and painful waits; but she had been born into a time when and at a place where women were accustomed to waiting. Fathers and husbands were weeks and months at their diggings, or days and weeks on the trail through blizzards, and there was no way to send messages of assurance. In the absence of word to the contrary, women assumed continued survival.

One beautiful clear day, Ada said, Noel flew the Standard north and was expected to return the same day. Suddenly a fog came in over Nome from the sea so thick you couldn't see more than a block. A few hours later we heard the plane up above us and rushed out of doors to listen. The sound seemed to go out to sea and gradually diminished until there was no more sound. I knew Noel was almost at the limit of his gas, and he had gone out over the Bering Sea.

For about three hours we sat, my parents and Ralph and I, talking foolishness. Every now and then somebody would say, "Well, it's time we heard something from Noel." Then the phone rang. It was Noel. He had turned around above the fog out of earshot and had crossed the coast well to the east of Nome and landed on a river bar. He walked down to a trail, got a ride at a roadhouse, and came to Nome.

Another time Noel failed to come back from Shishmaref, off the northern shore of the Seward Peninsula. Ralph came to the house very disturbed. I was worried, too, but Ralph made me more uneasy. Finally he left and we went to bed, all of us with Noel on our minds. The next morning he still had not returned, but when my mother got up she told me: "Don't worry. Noel's all right. He'll come home this afternoon when the sun is about there" (she pointed) "and the smoke is blowing that way. I dreamed it." That is just the way it happened. At three o'clock I was looking out the window, the sun was in the spot she had indicated, smoke was blowing the way she said it would, and there came Noel's airplane, just like in the dream.

Noel went to Candle one time and did not return for six days, although he had expected to come right back. During this time the weather was beautiful in Nome. But no Noel. I thought for six days that something dreadful had happened to him. But I was not a pessimist, and I never thought, "Oh, goodness, Noel is dead." My dad always said, "The Lord has his arm around Noel." I thought that he could be in trouble, but that things would always work out. If I had not thought this way, I would have been hysterical once a month even before we were married. Indeed, when he came back, he explained that it had snowed for six days in Candle and had blown so hard that he could not even take off.

The first Christmas Noel spent in Alaska he was expected to come from Fairbanks bringing Nome the first "fresh" Christmas mail it had ever received. But he was missing then too and did not arrive until January. I had bought him a gift, a belt with a sterling buckle engraved with the letter "W." When he came in January he had not brought me a gift, so I just did not give him the belt. You see, he would bring the gifts of food, the practical gifts, but he had not been trained to give personal gifts. The next Christmas he bought me a camera and I gave him the belt that had been put away. He chuckled years later when I told him about this. He still wears that belt and buckle.

I did not think of marriage while Noel was flying from Nome in 1927 and 1928. Noel was just a nice, interesting person to be with. Gene Miller was the first to mention marriage. He told me, "Don't ever think you'll marry Noel. He knows his work is too dangerous. He'll never marry you."

Ada and Noel were married on May 19, 1929, in the first church wedding Nome had seen in years, ending a two-year courtship that had left many residents exasperated at Noel's slowness. Many more rugged miles were to pass beneath his wings, though, before that wedding day.

25. MOOSE PTARMIGAN

The airplane business at Nome had been an immediate success. Noel and Miller arrived at the Bering Sea village on June 20, 1927, without benefit of advance promotion. Their first customer walked in the next day and ordered a flight presaging the imaginative use to which the isolated residents of Nome were to put the Standard. Wien was hired to fly what probably was history's first aerial reindeer roundup. He took businessman Ralph Lomen and his foreman Dan Crowley seventy-two air miles east to Golovin, an ancient Eskimo coastal village that since 1898 had supplied the gold fields inland along the Niukluk River.

Wien landed the Standard on a creek sand bar. Lomen and Crowley consulted their herdsmen, who wintered at Golovin, as to where the reindeer bands might have roamed. Then Noel, with the Eskimo chief herder in the front cockpit, took off to find them. The grazing herds, undulating darkly over the still snowy, treeless hills, were easy to spot from the air. In less than three hours all were located and their whereabouts marked on a map.

Lomen's herdsmen now knew where to find their twenty thousand charges in order to bring them in for the annual slaughter. Weeks of work had been saved. The Fairbanks newspaper recognized the economic significance of the flight when it reported a month later that the Standard had covered "an immense area . . . to locate straggling herds . . . without the arduous task of locating them by walking through the hills." For these and other flights Wien charged one dollar a mile, using the ground mileage that the dog sleds covered or whatever he could estimate from maps.

Next there were two miners bound for Deering, a village of 100 inhabitants on the northern shore of the Seward Peninsula, 135 miles north of Nome. Gene Miller jammed himself and his cameras into the rear cockpit with Noel. With their passengers as guides, they flew the old railroad pass through the mountains north of Nome to the Kuzitrin flats, followed the Goodhope River through another ridge to the coast, then turned east to Deering.

There were splendid landmarks in this country. The pilot was happy to note that hills, ridges, flats, and rivers did not blur together as did those in the Interior. "I could remember them after I had seen them once," Wien said. "It seemed to come naturally, same as I can remember faces. If I've seen a man's face once, I can remember it when I see him many years later."

At Deering, he landed on a six-hundred-foot strip of smooth beach west of the village. As at almost all of his stops, Wien offered the Standard for joyhops. Miller photographed. They flew twenty-five miles southeast to the mining camp of Candle, landing on a seven-hundred-foot sand bar in the Kiwalik River and introducing themselves to the excited citzens. Among the joyhoppers here were a Mrs. Ausley and her ten-year-old son Robert, who fell so in love with flying that he had to be pulled howling from the cockpit at the end of the flight. As soon as he was old enough, Robert Ausley went to Fairbanks, learned to fly, flew the bush for several years, and eventually became a Northwest Orient captain.

On the flight from Deering to Candle, Wien noticed in the distance a strange strip of land that looked somewhat like a turkey neck, running out of sight into the sea toward the northwest. After his last joyhop at Candle, he turned the Standard's nose north toward this strip of land. He crossed the Arctic Circle forty-five miles north of Candle and flew on toward the end of the peninsula which now broadened out at its end like a gobbler's head. On the way, at Miller's insistence, he landed on a beach near a gigantic herd of reindeer which his partner photographed. Miller was to make hundreds of exposures during the several months of their association, but Wien said he never did see a print.

At the tip of the thin peninsula, at the gobbler's head, was Kotzebue, originally an Eskimo summer fishing site, now a reindeer station and large permanent village of 250 residents. Tents and sod

houses clustered on the khaki-colored sand along the shore of
Kotzebue Sound, its edges crusted with the remnants of winter's
ice.

There seemed to be no place to land the Standard. Wien circled
and studied the surface. He flew about for half an hour and all he
could see was uninviting ridges, swampy-looking flats, and stretches
of niggerheads. The only flat, solid-appearing terrain was immediately along the shore, and that was dotted with huts.

Joe Crosson, who had joined Fairbanks Airplane at the end of the
1925 season, had landed near here in 1926 while on a Wilkins
expedition flight in a Hisso Swallow from Barrow to Fairbanks. He
did not want to risk the long, dangerous nonstop direct to Fairbanks
over the Brooks Range. Crosson's landing had been on skis, which
make almost any landing possible so long as there is snow or ice.
Noel was on wheels, at the ends of rigid struts, that would dig into
snow or marsh and flip the airplane.

He must land, however. He needed fuel and Kotzebue was the
only place within range where there was a gasoline supply. The
cautious Wien picked out what appeared to be the smoothest and
hardest spot within sight, about three miles south of the village,
approached hanging on the propeller, and stopped the Standard
into the wind in a full stall, as expertly and abruptly as a fly lights on
a caribou ear.

He and Miller walked toward the town. Just at its southern edge,
near the Signal Corps radio shack, Wien found that what had
appeared from the air to be a swamp was a solid, smooth stretch of
gravel covered with a thin layer of moss, an ideal landing site. On
this spot is now Wien Memorial Airport, named for Ralph Wien,
who died here.

Among Kotzebue joyhoppers was one Archie Ferguson, about
thirty years old, whose parents ran a trading post there. Ferguson
demanded that the pilot "pour it on and give me my money's
worth." Wien put on a mild show that was more than Archie's
money's worth. He had sunk out of sight into the front cockpit by
the time Noel returned him to earth. But he recovered. Two years
later he learned to fly in Fairbanks and became an Arctic bush flyer
known as "the world's craziest pilot." Until his death in Mexico in
1967, Ferguson often told of his first hop with Noel Wien and how

he had held on so tightly that his "fingers made dents" in the Standard's hardwood longerons.

Almost without plan, a sort of regular circuit evolved—Nome, Deering, Candle, Kotzebue, Candle, Deering, Nome—covering an air distance of about 450 miles. There always were customers ready to fly from one village to another, and at each stop the joyhoppers lined up for a thrill. New camps were added to the list as the demand arose. One day an Eskimo woman asked Wien to take her to her husband, a white man who was mining out in the bush. She would show him the way. There was a "good" landing place there, she was certain, on a smooth dome.

Domes had no lure for Wien, and he had long since lost faith in groundlings' ratings of landing spots. A Nome miner told him that the woman's husband was out on a creek near Granite Mountain, a 2,800-foot prominence 140 miles northeast of Nome. Nobody knew anything about a landing place there. The woman became teary. She wept at Noel's refusal to take her and continued to weep, remaining by his side. This universal ploy succeeded, for finally Noel agreed to fly to the camp; but he would decide only on arrival if it was safe to land. The tears ceased instantly.

Noel checked the spare propeller lashed to the outside of the fuselage. Domes and noseovers were inseparable. With the beaming Eskimo woman in the front cockpit, the Standard headed out over the hills, passing the Niukluk, Etchepuk, Arathlatuluk, Omilak, and Tubutulik rivers, picking up Granite Mountain while still sixty miles away.

Wien was mildly surprised to find that there was indeed a smooth stretch atop the dome. But it ended too soon. It was only about three hundred feet long. Circling, he studied the dome. It sloped steeply, and at one end there was a bulge with a still steeper slope. If the wind held right, maybe he could safely land uphill into the slope and safely take off downhill, although downwind.

He circled lower, feeling the wind. He made an approach to the upslope, noting the blur of the ground under the craft, judging his speed. A safe landing seemed possible, but he pulled up. The Eskimo woman wailed and waved an arm. Noel took the Standard around again and set up a long final approach. His careful preparation made the landing easy. The Standard lit three point at the edge of the smooth stretch, ran uphill to the bulge, and stopped halfway up after rolling only 270 feet.

Three miners, nearly hysterical at the sudden appearance of an airplane at their remote diggings, scrambled breathlessly up the fifteen-hundred-foot dome from the creek below, waving shovels and bellowing greetings. One of them was the woman's husband; she leaped from the plane to join him. Noel put the men to work hauling the Standard to the top of the bulge and turning it around. As they held the wings, he ran the motor to full revs, signaled a release, and the Standard took off almost as if from a catapult.

At each of these places, Wien was the first aviator to land. Early in August he made the first flight to Point Hope, an old Eskimo village 280 miles north of Nome across Kotzebue Sound. Called Tikiqaq by its inhabitants, the settlement sits at the end of a finger of sand that points into the Chukchi Sea and beckons to the whales that pass close ashore. Hunting is easy here. Wien's passengers were Bishop Peter Trimble Rowe of the Episcopal church and a Major Ian Simpson of British Columbia. Rowe, a hale and intrepid man, was Alaska's first Episcopal bishop, serving from 1895 for more than forty years, traveling his half-million-square-mile diocese by snowshoe and ski, dog sled and pole boat, rail car and steamboat, tractor and gas boat. Now with the arrival of Noel Wien he took to wings.

Bishop Rowe reached Nome intending to take passage to Point Hope aboard a revenue cutter. But he discovered that he was too late. His disappointment changed to delight when he learned that Nome now had airplane service. He was no happier than Noel Wien, however, for this would be Wien's longest flight beyond the Arctic Circle. Each new adventure meant the opening of more territory and additions to his unique store of experience in and knowledge of Alaska flying.

A nonstop flight to Point Hope was not possible, so Wien took off for Kotzebue, where the three men would spend a night and refuel. Fifty miles out from Nome, a change in the sound of the old Hisso told the pilot that there was trouble. Oil drops spattered back against the windscreens. The motor began to overheat. Below was the Kuzitrin River, just north of its junction with the Kougarok.

From his previous flights over this area, Noel was familiar with the Kuzitrin sand bars. He chose a long, solid one and landed the Standard. Too much oil, he found, had been put into the crankcase.

The surplus was bubbling from the breather atop the motor and the Hisso responded by overheating. Wien drained a little oil and took off from the same long bar without turning and taxiing back. It was only a routine crisis. Serious trouble would have stranded the trio miles from the nearest cabin, with the marshy, pond-filled Kuzitrin flats somehow to be traversed.

Early the next morning the Standard rose from Kotzebue, crossed the sound to the village of Sheshalik, and then followed the coast in its northwest sweep, 150 miles to Point Hope at 68°21′ north latitude. Along the way, dozens of rivers and creeks curled down to the sea between ridges of bleak, low hills. The sandy finger of Point Hope was unmistakable to Rowe and Simpson even though they had never before seen it from the air. They waved and pointed excitedly. Noel glided down and banked for an inspection.

Even at one hundred feet the signs of habitation were difficult to make out. Sod igloos seemed to melt into the barren flats. Only the graveyard, outlined with its fence of white whalebone, stood out. Wien flew up and back above the sand, and up and back again, studying the land. Finally, just inland from the graveyard, he found an inviting strip of moss through which a base of white gravel gleamed. It made a perfect airport.

The village was as it had been for hundreds of years, the most primitive Wien had seen. There was no swarm of joyhoppers. "Eskimo people afraid," said Chester Sevek, a resident. Years afterward, a woman told Ada Wien that she was a little girl out picking blueberries on the tundra the day the airplane flew over. "I fell on the ground and put my hands over my ears and my head between the niggerheads," she said. "I thought a monster bird was coming to destroy me." The few natives who did not hide concluded that they were witnessing a miracle and were not at all surprised when it was the revered Bishop Rowe who climbed down from the back of the big bird.

After a few hours some of the braver Eskimos appeared and approached the Standard. When they found it to be a peaceful beast, they felt it, patted it. Never having heard of such a thing, they referred to it in Eskimo words that Wien later learned meant "moose ptarmigan"—a flying creature huge beyond belief. Archdeacon Goodman was the only joyhopper that trip. Bishop Rowe confirmed thirty youngsters at special services, and that night the three flew back to Kotzebue for refueling and then on to Nome. The bishop had spent less than three days on a visit that in the past had required six weeks. From then on he gradually lost his identity as the mushing missionary and became the flying bishop.

Wien had cause that first Nome summer to abandon his habitual caution and stake his life on his ability to complete an "impossible" flight. His motivation was the saving of another man's life. He arrived in Kotzebue one evening to find a radio message awaiting him. It was from Ralph Lomen at Nome. "Bookkeeper dying. Must get to boat at Seward. Please come immediately."

Wien refueled and flew to Nome. George Treacy, a large, affable man, did the accounts for the Lomen family interests. From a sore on his foot he had developed septicemia, the dreaded "blood poisoning" that until the development of antibiotics was often fatal. Lomen thought there was gangrene in the foot. Days could be saved in getting Treacy to medical help in Seattle by flying him to Anchorage and putting him aboard the Alaska Railroad for Seward, where he could catch a boat.

No one had ever made the flight from Nome to Anchorage. It was a distance of 560 straight-line miles barred by three mountain systems, the Kaiyuh, the Kuskokwim, and the towering Alaska Range. There was no compass in the Standard; the pocket compass Noel carried was of little use so far north where there was considerable ground magnetic disturbance. Navigation would be by hunch.

An overcast at about two thousand feet enclosed Nome in a murky summer night. Bits of lower cloud scud whipped by overhead on a fresh wind blowing from the direction of the proposed flight. All in all, Noel's bones told him this was no night for flying, certainly not into the face of what could become a gale.

Noel had met Treacy. He liked the man. He pictured him waiting in pain, confident that the pilot would take him to where his life might be saved. Noel did not hesitate. He fueled the Standard and checked over the creaking old craft.

Treacy was carried out on a stretcher. His ashen face, lips pulled back from his teeth, told of his agony. Carefully he was placed in the front cockpit. Hoarsely he told his friends that he could not stand the pain of his leg in a downward position. They moved him to one side of the cockpit and slowly raised the leg until it

Ada, Noel, and Merrill, dressed in Arctic-hare outfit, in Fairbanks, 1931. Behind them is the 220-horsepower, four-place Stinson Jr., J5, which Noel flew from the Midwest to Nome in December 1930. Courtesy of Noel Wien

Excited residents gather around Ford Tri-Motor after its landing in Barrow in 1938, as part of Wien's regular continuing flight from Fairbanks to Nome, Kotzebue, Wainwright, and Barrow. Unusually high pressure ridge is visible behind plane. Courtesy of Noel Wien

The Ford Tri-Motor down to its wings in Harding Lake on May 2, 1939. Courtesy of Noel Wien

Five days later the Tri-Motor has been hoisted from the lake by A-frames attached to its skis. In front of Ada and Noel, water seeping through honeycomb ice 3½ feet thick attests to the rotten state of the ice on the lake. Courtesy of Noel Wien

protruded from the cockpit and rested against the other edge. In this unnatural position, Treacy was tied into the seat.

The sight of the poor fellow, his leg sticking up like a mast, made Noel ache in sympathy. He eased into the gentlest of takeoffs, leaving Nome without waiting to obtain weather reports from the McGrath-Takotna area that lay about halfway along the direct route to Anchorage. Noel was committed to this flight, good weather or bad, and he did not want to waste time waiting for information that would not alter his decision.

To save time and fuel, Wien decided not to fly the coastline eastward. Instead he took up a course east by south that gradually took the Standard about 25 miles out over the Bering Sea. A straight-line flight to Unalakleet, a distance of 150 miles, would save nearly 100 miles. By the time they reached Golovin Bay, and started over the 55-mile stretch of open water of Norton Sound, they had been forced down to one thousand feet by the lowering overcast. Noel realized that his southeast course would have been necessary in any event: with the restricted ceiling, he could not have topped the Nulato hills or Notakok Mountain had he followed the coast and then held eastward toward Nulato or Kaltag.

The Standard bored in and out of scud, giving Noel sufficient glimpses of the white-capped sea below to allow him to maintain contact. He wondered if the scud would turn solid. He concentrated on keeping straight and level, catching an occasional reference sight of the coastline to his left, and on listening to the Hisso. The old motor had been working heroically under almost continual use during the summer. If it quit now over water beyond gliding distance of land, there would be no chance of survival.

When he reached the eastern coast of Norton Sound south of Unalakleet, Wien felt a thrill of hope at noticing that the overcast was somewhat higher, obscuring the hilltops but leaving clear holes above the river canyons. Fear followed right behind, however. In checking his map he calculated that he had made good a ground speed of only 50 miles an hour. He was losing about 15 miles to a headwind. His rule of thumb for the Standard's range was six hours. Six hours at 50 would take them only 300 miles. The McGrath-Takotna area toward which he was striving was 335. In the Kuskokwim country, there was no other place to land and refuel.

There was no thought of turning back or diverting. Without

making a conscious decision, Noel had staked his life; he would get the dying man to medical help or die with him out here in the wilds. He followed the Anvik River for a while, then found an open creek valley that took him eastward to a huge, surging river. The Yukon! From here on, his rudimentary map showed that most of the streams lay generally north-south on the land. If he cut them at about a seventy-degree angle, he estimated, he should reach the Takotna River near McGrath.

IIe would have to hold that seventy-degree angle without the aid of a good compass. If he missed the Takotna, which was hardly more than a creek, he would soon reach the Kuskokwim, a mighty stream, and could turn back knowing that the Takotna was behind him; that is, he could do this if he reached the Kuskokwim at a point far enough south, where it was a mighty stream, and not too far north, where it also was only a scratch on the crinkly surface.

We ran into some heavy rain. This was new and wild country to me. I kept studying my map, trying to identify the rivers and hills and to keep cutting them at what I thought was the angle to get us to McGrath.

Pretty soon we'd been in the air for four hours and we had only two more before we would be out of gas. The rain was steady and heavy, but the overcast didn't come any closer down and that was a help. I crossed river after river, went up and over range after range, and found that I couldn't identify any of them. The map was just no good, or else I was a long way off from where I thought I was.

After five hours, I was still flying without knowing if we'd ever get where we wanted. All we could do was keep flying until we ran out of gas. Treacy couldn't move, of course, tied in with his leg sticking out. I didn't even know if he was still alive. When we ran out of gas and went down, though, he would soon die anyway, and maybe I would also.

I didn't hit any checkpoints at all. Nothing below tied together with anything on the map. I couldn't see ahead very well. I kept maybe too much right rudder, because I didn't want to miss McGrath-Takotna-Ophir to the north where there was nothing at all, but wanted to miss them to the south, if I was going to miss them at all. Iditarod and Flat were to the south.

Five hours of flying like this are very tiring to a man. I kept looking down and hoping to see the trail from Flat to McGrath. I throttled back, which cost us some speed but saved some on gas. I guess it really didn't matter much, because you lost one and gained another.

Six hours now we'd been in the air. I kept the nose of the Standard up almost into the wind, counting on the wind staying the same, because there was nothing else to do. I didn't know where we were and couldn't find out. With six hours gone we couldn't have but a few more minutes to fly.

Twenty minutes later I saw that trail below, crossing us at ninety degrees. I can't describe what a thrill that was, the first sign of man in hours. But which way should I turn? Right or left? If I'd been right in favoring right rudder a bit, we were somewhere south of McGrath. I gambled and turned left to the north and flew down over the trail, which was a light streak through the brownish land.

The gas gauge was just about empty. Somehow we flew for fifteen minutes and then we topped some hills and saw a village. What a wonderful feeling! There was a gravel road there, just a track, a bad landing place, and there weren't any fields at all in that rough country.

I figured that this must be Ophir and the track was the road to Takotna. They had that very short airfield at Takotna, the one I couldn't land the Fokker on to pick up the postmaster's corpse. I thought I would fly over the trail the twenty-five or so miles to Takotna and land there. If we ran out of gas, I could put down on the trail and we wouldn't be too far from help in either direction.

That bad, short field at Takotna would be the most welcome sight I ever saw. I hadn't ever been so anxious before in my life. The gas gauge was on empty now. We'd flown for 6:35 and that seemed a miracle. We couldn't go much longer. I followed the trail, as high as I could without losing sight of it through the scud and fog that was forming, ready at any second to nose down and land when the motor quit.

I saw the high hills around Takotna ahead of us. We had been flying seven hours and should have been on the ground, but the Hisso kept turning. I saw that little airfield up on the hill, but half of it was covered by fog. The spruce trees were right on the edge of the field and at each end.

There was no way to tell how low the fog was. If it was on the ground over half the field, we were in for a bad landing, because the way the wind was blowing we had to approach from the foggy end. That meant I had to go down into the fog and hope to break down through it in time to see to land.

I made a turn, expecting the Hisso to conk out, and glided down into the wind. Just as I was ready to go down into the fog, the wind blew it all back toward us and the whole landing field opened up and we made a perfect landing. I wished I could have thanked that Road Commission fellow who built the field and who felt so bad when I wouldn't land the Fokker there. That day it was a perfect airport.

When I measured the gas with a stick, there was about three-quarters of a gallon left, enough for one more turn around the field. That was a miracle, for we'd flown for 7:30 and I never figured the outside limit at more than 6:30. I still can't explain this.

After all he had been through, all those hours tied into the cockpit with his leg sticking up so uncomfortably, rain beating in on him, George Treacy was still cheerful. In a little while some men came up to the airfield and several of us got George out and carefully carried him down the steep hill. We had food and warmth and rest there in the roadhouse.

The next morning the rain was just as heavy, the ceiling was only a few hundred feet, and I couldn't see from one end of the field to the other because of the fog. We couldn't take off in that.

By the next day we knew the weekly boat had already pulled out of Seward, so there was no rush trying to get there. We couldn't have gotten through the Alaska Range to Anchorage anyway, because the ceiling was still very low.

I decided to make a try for Fairbanks, where Treacy could get some kind of medical help and then decide what to do after that. I couldn't take off from Takotna with a full eighty-gallon load, so I took on a few gallons and flew the eighteen miles to McGrath and topped off there. Besides, gas was cheaper at McGrath, only one dollar a gallon, because it was on the main Kuskokwim River.

From McGrath to Fairbanks was familiar ground for me. The flight was easy, even though we flew through solid rain and had to keep low under a ceiling.

The doctor at Fairbanks decided to amputate George Treacy's leg at the knee immediately to save his life. They said that even if we had gotten him to the boat, he probably would have died on the way to Seattle. So it was a good thing that we had had all our troubles on the flight and were delayed. They sent Treacy to Seattle and some more of his leg was cut off. I never did see him again. It was a great relief to me to get him to the hospital in Fairbanks. The trip was one of great discomfort and suffering for him. He was a brave man.

26. WINTER

As the short northern summer neared its end, Wien began wondering what he would do when, inevitably, winter grounded him. He probably would have to go Outside to try to find work. There were few laboring jobs available in Fairbanks, none at all in winter-fast Nome. Anyway, he wanted to fly, not to drive steam points. Perhaps there was a barnstorming outfit in the States that could use him.

In 1925 he had flown into the beginning of the Alaska winter and had discovered that a Standard was, as everyone had suspected, no plane for winter work there. Even if pilot and passengers could bundle up sufficiently against sixty-mile-an-hour blasts of forty-below air into the open cockpits, the old liquid-cooled Hisso could never work efficiently in such conditions. And when the temperature reached sixty below and colder, as it did in the Interior, then what?

The Nome winter would be "mild" enough by comparison, but many of the bread-and-butter hops from Nome to the Seward Peninsula mining camps would cease after freeze-up. The main prospect for heavy winter work would be in maintaining mail and freight communications between Nome and Fairbanks, and Fairbanks was in the gelid Interior. A Hisso Standard was as useful in an Interior winter as a bathing suit.

As Wien luck so often had it, however, something turned up. This time it was an airplane perfectly suited for flying the Interior winter. Wien would become the first aviator to maintain service through an entire Interior winter, and he would do it flying not for someone else, or as the partner of another, but as president and pilot of Wien Alaska Airways.

The plane was a four-place cabin biplane, the fifth Stinson built, which had been bought for Captain Wilkins by the Detroit *News*, a major sponsor of his early transpolar attempts, and christened the *Detroiter II*. It was powered by a 220-horsepower, air-cooled Wright J4B Whirlwind, direct antecedent of the reliable J5 that had taken Lindbergh across the Atlantic that summer of 1927. The *Detroiter I*, a sister ship, had been abandoned on the Arctic ice 125 miles north of Barrow where Wilkins and Eielson were forced down in 1926.

Cabin accouterments in the *Detroiter* were strange. There were no seats, even for the pilot. Where front seats would have been was a forty-gallon fuel tank. Behind that in the cabin was just open space. Two cushions were placed atop the fuel tank, a wooden backrest was attached to a tubing frame, and on this the pilot and front passenger rode. Rear passengers made do by perching on their luggage or whatever freight was aboard. No one was ever known to complain. For people who had made the four- to six-week dog team trip from Nome to Fairbanks, transportation comfort was a faint if not forgotten memory. Most of them slipped into their sleeping bags and flew as cozy as snowed-over malemutes. Behind the cabin was a small baggage compartment. In there Noel was to store the canvas motor covers, the fire pot, a five-gallon can of emergency rations, and ropes. The ropes were used for tie-downs, for throwing over the wings, and for "sawing" off frost and snow.

There was a thirty-five-gallon fuel tank in the wings on each side, giving the craft a total of 110 gallons. At a cruise speed of ninety, the *Detroiter* had a range of about nine hours, or 800 miles with no wind factor. And there were luxuries, life-saving luxuries: two Pioneer compasses, an airspeed indicator, a turn-and-bank indicator, an adjustable stabilizer for trimming and reducing pilot work, and, best of all, brakes. Air-cooled motor, enclosed cabin, speed, phenomenal range, instruments, brakes: the perfect Alaska aircraft.

Noel had never before flown an airplane with these wonders aboard. They were to enable him to put in 280 hours of money-making time during the six months of winter between October and May, averaging one round trip a week between Nome and Fairbanks, with dozens of shorter hops interspersed. He carried as many as six passengers, if some were children, and once hoisted a payload of eighteen hundred pounds. He reduced the Nome-Fairbanks fare to three hundred dollars, maintaining the freight rate at seventy-five cents a pound.

An opportunity to buy the Stinson from Wilkins came in August while Wien spent a month flying out of Fairbanks for his old employer, Fairbanks Airplane Company. Joe Crosson had gone Outside to vacation, and the owners pleaded with Noel to come from Nome and fill in. He did so as a favor. His own business was thriving, so he did not need a job. Noel arrived in Fairbanks August 18 to take over for Crosson, bringing the Standard stuffed with Gene Miller and his equipment; Mrs. Ross Kinney; seventy-five pounds of mail; 150 pounds of freight; and Lindy, a German shepherd. Lindy was a notable Alaska citizen, the son of a pair that had flown across the pole to Teller with Amundsen, Ellsworth, and Nobile in. the airship *Norge*. Noel flew the Fairbanks Airplane Company's Hisso Swallow and, glory be, the comfortable old Fokker F. III, toasting beside the roaring BMW and recalling early history-making days as he again flew to familiar Livengood and Circle Hot Springs. Despite its lack of use and care, the old craft still could do a job.

By midsummer, Nome businessmen also had begun to anticipate a winter shutdown of their airplane service. Some had approached Noel and offered to invest enough funds to buy a suitable airplane. But Noel recalled too well the frustrations of working for a panel of nonflying owners. He would, however, consider taking a loan from these men if he could find the right plane. At Fairbanks he found it.

Noel did not know that Wilkins was near the end of his string. Two seasons of failures had dried up his resources and made it almost impossible for him to raise money from new donors. The *Detroiter II*, brand new that spring, was for sale. Price, ten thousand dollars. Noel had looked at the aircraft longingly during his flights to Fairbanks that summer, and when Wilkins told him he was trying to sell it, Wien thought he had found rainbow's end.

Charley Milot, "the Scrap Iron Kid," who rounded up abandoned metal objects in the North and shipped them to the States; the Lomen brothers, Alfred and Ralph and the others; and Dan Crowley, who worked for Lomen Brothers, headed a group of Nome men that went from door to door soliciting loan money. They raised $6,000 and turned it over to Noel and Ralph. Gene Miller decided that the airplane business was not bringing him what he had hoped it would, and sold out his share of the Standard. As was customary among many nonbusiness people in Alaska in those days, he asked only what he had put into the venture, $300. He had, of course, drawn living expenses from the operation. After buying out Miller, Noel and Ralph had $3,500 to show for their summer's work. They took the $9,500 to Wilkins.

"I will accept it," the Australian told the brothers. "If you make a success with the plane, you may pay me the remaining $500. If affairs do not work out for you, then you owe me nothing more." Nothing was put into writing. The next spring when Wilkins returned to Alaska—with a sleek Lockheed Vega in which he and Eielson finally realized his dream of flying from America to Europe via the Arctic—the Wien brothers handed over the $500. They had been so successful that they had also repaid the borrowed $6,000 early in 1928.

Nearly thirty years later, Wilkins, by then Sir Hubert, received an honorary degree from the University of Alaska. He saw his old friend Noel Wien in the audience and interrupted his address to remark that it was the purchase of the Stinson by Wien, "the dean of Alaskan aviators," that allowed his project to go forward. "I had scraped the bottom of the barrel," he confessed. "Without the money from the sale of the Stinson, I could not have returned to Alaska the next year and made the flight."

The first flight by the new Wien Alaska Airways was an emergency round trip from Fairbanks to Deering, a total distance of 900 miles, to bring to Fairbanks an ailing Mrs. Sam Magids. Noel flew both ways nonstop, taking 6:00 over on September 8 and 6:15 back on September 11, into the wind both ways.

That winter Noel maintained the schedule of one flight to and from Fairbanks each week. There was work at each end of the line. Ralph stayed in Fairbanks permanently. The Seward Peninsula and Arctic coast links were flown out of Nome as often as there was a demand and as winter fogs permitted.

It was a proud day when Ralph and I flew the Stinson to Nome for the first time, flying at least thirty miles an hour faster than we had in the Standard. For the first time in the history of Nome and the Peninsula, the last boat leaving in October didn't mean isolation from the States until the first boat in the next June. For the first time ever, Nome got mail and fresh foods for Thanksgiving, and everybody looked forward to getting Christmas mail and foods, although they were disappointed there—I was down on a lake in a blizzard Christmas Day and for a while thought I'd lost the new airplane.

My main principle of flying that winter was to keep flying. To do this we changed the oil at the end of every flight between Nome and Fairbanks, about every five to seven hours. Ralph kept the motor looking like new, and there was always a film of new oil on the pistons.

I turned back whenever things didn't look just exactly right, or went on to the following stop if a scheduled landing looked bad. It really paid off, to go back, because the next day would often be a good one and the Stinson was undamaged and ready to go. So many of the new pilots coming into Alaska later in the thirties didn't realize this. They would go on in where they shouldn't and then be out of service for a while or maybe forever.

It kept me humping to get back to Nome from Fairbanks within a week. The weather stopped me cold sometimes. Fog and blizzards came in and I'd have to wait part way back to Nome or out of Nome. It was specially bad at the head of Norton Bay when I was trying to get to the Yukon when going east or from the Yukon when coming west. Many times I had to go down the coast to Unalakleet, like on the flight with Treacy, and fly under a low ceiling up the Unalakleet River.

The Interior weather could be real bad also. There were snowstorms so thick you couldn't see one bend of the river from another. Either you had to turn back or try to sneak through just over the river and below the treetops to the next village, or else plump down on the river if you were sure it was smooth ice.

Yukon River ice is usually very rough, but there are occasional smooth spots; however, the sun has to be shining before you can pick out those smooth places. There have to be shadows on the rough spots, you see.

The Yukon is so wide in some places that it is hard to pick it out from the rest of the land when the river and everything else is white. You have to fly right along the shore where you can see the trees every now and then. On a cloudy day, if you fly low over the middle, you can get into a whiteout, where everything is white and you can't tell the surface from the sky. You don't have a horizon and you can crash into the Yukon.

That really keeps you guessing. The thing to do is not to gamble. The easiest way to live through this is to go back, which is hard to do when you've gone part way and it's getting dark and you need to get to a town before dark.

This was the first winter flying, so we had many problems we had to work out. We had to make skis; we had to keep the oil and motor warm on the ground; and we later found in flying at forty and fifty below zero that we even had to do something about keeping the oil and motor warm even when we were flying. That really was something new.

We'd had some experience with skis, of course, living in Minnesota, and Dad was a very fine carpenter and made fine skis. We modeled the Stinson skis after the ones he used to make.

Ralph did the designing. We had to make them limber enough and strong enough in front to stand all the bending that would come from running over drifts and rough places. We got good hickory wood eight feet long and one foot wide and had a Fairbanks carpenter shape them the way Ralph said. At first, we didn't put metal on the bottom, but smoothed, waxed, and oiled them. That worked fine until I got to the Nome area, where I had to land on pure ice because the winds blew all the snow off. This wore them out too quickly, so we later put metal coverings on the bottom.

Ralph knew what we needed for stands, so he designed a tube-braced-type pedestal with three tubes in front—one as a cross brace and two under the center of the axle—and then three more in the back, one of them a cross brace. The bottoms of the tubes were welded to a flat piece of metal that could be bolted to the top of the skis.

The hard part was finding just the right balance, the right place to fit the ski under the airplane. It had to be the spot that would let the front of the skis tilt upward when the airplane speeded over snow and let the load ride on the back half of the skis and not the front. Later we found out that we had to tip the rear end of the skis upward a bit so the plane could be dragged backward over the snow at the airports. And we found that one foot was not quite wide enough for real deep snow.

I soon learned that I couldn't hop out of the airplane and leave it for any time sitting on the snow or ice. If I did, the skis would freeze to the surface and it was a tough job getting them free. I began taxiing onto poles or logs or anything that would keep part of the skis up off the ground.

When it was fifty-five to sixty-five below zero, I found I could make a sort of runway by pouring gasoline onto the snow so the airplane could slip easily and pick up enough speed to take off. I learned by doing things wrong, but I learned most from the kind old sourdoughs at the camps and roadhouses.

Early in the fall, before it got very cold, we could heat the motor enough to start it by using a small blowtorch to heat each cylinder one by one. When the days got colder, we tried a flat, two-burner camp stove. With a long canvas cover over the motor, hanging down to the ground like a tent, and the camp stove suspended on wires just under the motor, this device worked well.

When it was forty below and colder—that was only in the Interior—there usually wasn't any wind. But the wind blew on Seward Peninsula and in the Arctic and you had a real problem keeping the motor cover from flapping into the fire. You had to stay right there, get under the cover, and use your hands to keep it from the pot. We had more than one cover catch on fire before we realized we had to do this. In later days we even lost a couple of airplanes when pilots we'd hired let the cover catch on fire.

I'd drain the oil while it was hot, as soon as I could after landing, and take it inside the roadhouse or cabin where I stopped overnight. In the morning I'd heat the oil on a stove inside and try to rush it to the airplane before it got cold.

Sometimes it was so cold that I had to reheat it on the motor pot before it could be poured into the motor. At Nome, after freeze-up, I used to land on the Snake River. There was usually a long stretch of snow on the river that gave us plenty of room for takeoff even with an overload. After drawing the oil out, I'd put the pan on a small sled and pull it up to the home of Carrie McLain on the shore. Before I took off, I'd call Mrs. McLain and she'd put the cans of oil on her cook stove and heat them slowly. I would go by, wrap the cans in canvas, and pull them down to the airplane on the sled. I'd pour the oil into the motor just before takeoff, after everything else was ready.

After we got the oil problem licked, we found we needed to do something about keeping the motor warm in the air. It would get cold even while running when the temperature was forty below or colder. Ralph and I wrapped the oil lines with asbestos, but that wasn't enough.

As the days got colder and colder in the Interior, we wrapped more and more of the motor. Next thing we did was wrap the rear of the motor with sheet asbestos, in and around all the parts. This was hard to do because of the many corners and hollows and edges. Later we tried using water glass, mixing it with water and plastering it on the front and rear of the crankcase. This was much more successful. It was fireproof and covered all the hollows and corners.

The cowling around the air-cooled motor had been designed to cool the motor, and this was just what we were trying to retard a little. Ralph attached some shaped pieces of tin baffles to the front of each of the nine cylinders. On the first test hop we found the air was being directed too far from the cylinders. They ran hot and the smell of paint filled the cabin. So we clipped pieces off the baffles and kept testing and clipping until we had a warm running motor with enough cooling for each cylinder.

We kept in mind always that we had only one airplane and no spare parts at all. Besides changing the oil every seven hours, Ralph greased the rocker arms after each flight. Because he was so careful, we put over one thousand hours on the Whirlwind with only one top overhaul—grinding the valves and putting in new piston rings.

The Stinson needed to be outfitted properly to meet the rigors of the Alaskan winter, and so did pilot Wien. A costume of Outside-type clothing—wool shirts, mackinaw, hunting boots—of no matter how many layers, would not keep a man alive in country where gasoline could freeze, where panting men and dogs could freeze their lungs if they inhaled too lustily, where boiling water tossed suddenly into the air would freeze with an exploding crackle.

Noel picked and chose from among sourdough and Eskimo items until he had a comfortable ensemble. First he donned a suit of heavy cotton long underwear, then a cotton dress shirt to keep the next layer, a heavy wool flannel shirt, from touching his easily irritated skin. Over the shirt went a sleeveless, hand-knit woolen sweater and on top of that a Filson outdoorsman wool jacket.

When the weather dictated, Wien wore an additional jacket, a double-thick canvas slipover parka, knee-length, the uniform of the early sourdough. This had a full hood, wolverine-ruffed, that could be pulled forward of the face and tightened to make an opening of about four inches, allowing its wearer to see somewhat and furnishing a tunnel to warm the air before it reached the tender lungs. Unlike other furs, wolverine hairs will not break off easily when frosted and thus are most desirable for Arctic apparel.

Wien had another jacket to wear when he was on the ground and not working around the plane. This one was made of Australian wombat fur with a wolfskin collar that, when turned up, covered the ears and left only the top of the head bare. The only discernible sign of vanity in Wien concerned his hair, which he began losing in his twenties. He blamed tight flying helmets for the loss. In the belief that it would help in rethatching, he went bareheaded down to the lowest temperature he could stand. Then he donned a cloth cap with muskrat-lined ear and forehead flaps.

On his hands Noel put woolen gloves and, over these, fur mitts. The mitts were attached to a simple yarn harness hanging around his neck so that when he needed to use his gloved fingers briefly, he would not lose the mittens. One might remove mitts for a short time, but no one removed gloves in the bitter Interior cold that could inflict instant frostbite.

For the feet there were first cotton socks, then one or two long, woolen socks, and heavy felt innersoles. All this was then stuffed into Eskimo mukluks with caribou uppers and seal soles of wondrous slipperiness. In later years Noel discarded the two layers of woolen socks in favor of Eskimo socks of caribou hide with the fur turned inside. This was no country for the ticklish. In the spring when water was overflowing onto the melting ice on which he landed, Noel adopted waterproof walrus-skin mukluks that reached to the hip.

Dressed in full regalia of the north, many a person walked stiff-armed and stiff-legged like a penguin. In the murky darkness of a winter's day, intently watching their footing through the tiny opening in their hoods, old friends could pass each other within touching distance without knowing it.

27. BLUE CHRISTMAS

"I often guessed wrong on the weather out of Nome," Wien admitted. One of his memorable wrong guesses was in October, when he was hired to fly the skipper and engineer of a beached ship from Teller to Nome, and then to take the captain and a Nome businessman to Fairbanks. The *Silver Wave* had been trapped in heavy ice near Teller. Unable to turn back or to proceed, it languished until a gale blew it onto the beach amid crushing ice. Only the captain and engineer had the money and desire to fly out; the rest of the crew stayed behind.

There were no signs of bad weather when Noel, Captain Strand, and Billy Cameron took off from Nome for Fairbanks, but when the Stinson reached the mountainous stretch between Norton Sound and the Yukon, its ground speed suddenly dropped to that of a moose on glare ice—almost zero. A fierce headwind had been encountered.

Just as this became apparent to the pilot, the air was pulled from under the Stinson and it dropped like a stone toward the mountain tops. Wien reacted instinctively to maintain attitude and air speed. As suddenly as it had hit, the downdraft released the plane.

How could there be such a draft, Wien thought, over mountains that reach only four thousand feet above sea level? He associated such a condition with the Sierra and the Rockies. Cautiously he turned twenty degrees to the right to take him toward still lower hills, and turned east again when he reached the narrow Nulato River valley.

Again the Stinson was seized and flung downward. This time there was no quick release. Fighting the urge to haul back on the stick and risk stalling out, Wien began a flat turn to take the craft away from danger.

By the time he had completed a 180-degree turn, the plane had dropped two thousand feet and his seadog passenger, dearly wishing he had never left his gale-battered ship, could almost touch the dwarf willows on the mountainsides.

Flipping and fluttering in the severe turbulence, with loose articles crashing about in the cabin, the Stinson flew before the wind back to the coast. Wien then turned farther south, entered the Unalakleet River canyon, and flew through it to the Yukon on one of the roughest flights he can remember. (It did not sell Captain Strand on the preferability of air travel over sea travel.)

December 1927 was a harrowing month. On the sixteenth, returning to Fairbanks from a side flight to Wiseman Noel ran into thick snow and building fog banks south of the Yukon. At this time of the year in the Interior there are fewer than four hours between sunrise and sunset. The darkness is not total: it is more a deep twilight, as the white-covered surface usually reflects a sky glow. But any diversion of a planned flight in bad weather can be fatal.

Wien could not fly into the blinding snowstorm, so he turned away from it toward the west over Minto Flats. His thought was to fly south from the flats to the railroad and then up to Fairbanks, or south to the Tanana and then up the river to Fairbanks.

He could do neither. By the time he reached the flats the snow was so thick, the light fading so rapidly, that he landed on the first lake he came to. There was no time to fly around and find a cabin, a trail, a way out. Besides, he was not going to take any chances of ending up out over the Toklat, where his first Alaska ordeal had originated.

The lake he picked turned out to be a tight fit, only about 650 feet at its widest. He sat down along what he judged to be the shore to avoid possible wind-piled rough ice in the middle. He turned the engine off. He could see nothing but swirling white a few feet beyond the Stinson's nose.

His best shelter, he thought, was the airplane itself. It would be too dangerous to leave it to search for something better. He had no sleeping bag, but he wore the canvas parka and mukluks, which were warm enough, he thought, as he settled down to wait out the storm.

Within a few minutes he began to shiver. The temperature was on its way down to forty below zero. He could not stay still; he would freeze to death. He decided to walk around the plane. This he did, off and on, with brief rests inside the cabin (by now hardly warmer than the outside), for the next eighteen hours.

When the gloomy winter daylight came sometime after ten the next morning, he saw that he had cut a circle around the plane three feet deep into the old and new snow. He was exhausted.

The storm still raged, but the feeble light let him see to the edge of the lake. He would try to find a trail, but would venture only a short distance from the airplane. If he could not, he would return.

Struggling through the deep snow, he reached the lake shore and immediately found a trail, its sled-smoothed surface cutting through the snow and snaking out of sight. He turned left and slipped and slid down the trail.

Within a quarter mile two cabins appeared through the curtain of snow. Dogs were staked outside the larger cabin and smoke spewed from its chimney into the wind. As the Fairbanks newspaper reported, he had walked around his downed aircraft for eighteen hours almost within sight of habitation. He was at a place called Crossroad, where the dog trail crossed the Chatanika River. But his decision to remain with the plane was the correct one. Had he left it and found the trail, he could have walked down it to his death, unable to see the cabins in the nighttime blizzard.

Dogs barked. Two men came from the larger cabin. They welcomed Noel, took him in, and fed him. They had heard the Stinson the day before, but assumed it had flown on.

The storm continued and Noel slept briefly and warmly. About noon the snow stopped. When Noel awakened, he returned to the plane, lighted the Coleman stove to warm the motor and the oil, began trying to scrape the skis clean. He had not been able to find poles or boughs to slip under them after he landed. Knots of hard snow could not be removed.

Noel taxied the plane rapidly, trying to knock the snow off and make a track for takeoff. He would need a quick takeoff to get out of the tiny lake, but he thought he could just make it. There was almost no load of gasoline left.

He barely did make it, estimating that if the lake had been ten feet shorter he would not have. Airborne, he throttled back to 1250 r.p.m. from the normal cruise of 1650, found the Alaska Railroad, and followed it to Fairbanks. He had one gallon of fuel remaining when he landed.

The significant year of 1927 ended with a disappointment. Influential citizens of Nome had arranged for first-class mail coming in from Outside during December to be flown by Noel from Fairbanks to Nome. For the first time in history there would be fresh mail for the holidays, gifts and news from the Outside, and fresh foods.

On December 18 Noel flew 950 pounds of freight from Fairbanks to Nulato, returning on the twenty-second with freight for Ruby and Fairbanks and a sick Native for Tanana. On the twenty-third he hopped to the Kuskokwim with a passenger and freight, intending to return to Fairbanks the same day and start his Santa Claus flight to Nome.

Housewives at Nome were preparing for a new kind of Christmas dinner. The pièce de résistance would not be meat, but a fresh salad. In the past, holiday salad was homemade cranberry jelly cut into the shape of flowers with green mint jelly forming the leaves. This year, however, everyone looked forward to fresh tomatoes and cucumbers and apples, delicacies shipped from Seattle no more than two weeks before.

Darkness caught Noel on his flight back to Fairbanks on December 23 and he landed on Lake Minchumina, a nine-mile-long body along the Fairbanks-McGrath dog trail sixty-five miles northwest of Mount McKinley. As the last light faded, he taxied the Stinson over soft snow into a cove sheltered by spruce and birch. He stopped at the edge of the lake, dismounted, and climbed about two hundred feet up a gentle slope to Kammisgaard's Roadhouse. He enjoyed a supper of moose roast, and relaxed before the fire. Ed Kammisgaard was not his usual yarn-spinning self, complaining of a bad cold.

I really learned something about Alaska in the next few days. There was no wind when I landed and I thought the ship was safe in the cove, so I didn't even tie it to a tree.

During supper and afterward we could hear a little wind in the trees. It was from the northeast and I remembered the terrible northeast winds that had blown me down on the Toklat and had caused me so much trouble also on the Treacy and the ship captain flights. But I wasn't worried, because the Stinson was down in that cove.

About eight o'clock, though, the wind picked up. I could see snow flying around and hear the wind moaning and whistling around the heavy log roadhouse. It seemed to be getting worse, so about eleven I decided to go down to the ship and tie a wing to the trees.

When I got to the cove, I couldn't believe it for a minute. The ship was gone. I couldn't see it anywhere. It simply wasn't in the cove.

I stepped out on the lake and went down flat on my back. The wind had blown the two feet of snow away from the surface and there was just the glare ice.

I got up and started more carefully out onto the ice to try to find the Stinson. The wind was howling around me, and I went down flat again. So I started crawling on my hands and knees.

I had to find the ship. It was my whole life and wasn't paid for yet. But I couldn't make any headway into the wind, even crawling. It blew me back. I couldn't see the ship. The wind was blowing about fifty miles an hour, and I knew I couldn't stay out in it even in my parky. I crawled back to the cove and went up the rise and tried to see the ship from there. It was just gone.

There was nothing more to do that night but wait for morning. About eleven the next morning, when it finally got lighter, Kammisgaard and I saw the plane from the roadhouse. It was about a mile out, almost in the middle of the lake. The wind was still blowing—it blew for three straight days—and I couldn't tell if the ship was a wreck or not. The snow was blowing over the ice so you couldn't see too well.

I crawled out to look it over and found some damage to the flippers and the bottom ailerons, but otherwise it was in unbelievably good shape for having been in such a wind.

There was a drift of solid snow around the ship up to the lower wing. I made a bad guess then. I thought the snow was packed so hard under the wing that the airplane would never move from that spot, particularly since it had headed itself into the wind like a weathercock. I should have chopped a stake hole into the ice and tied the wings, but I didn't. It took a long time to crawl back over the ice to the roadhouse.

The next day was Christmas, my first in Alaska. When it got light enough to see, about eleven, the Stinson didn't seem to be out there. As hard as I looked, I couldn't see it. The wind was still blowing and the snow was swirling, so I thought maybe it was still there but had just been drifted over.

I knew it was no use going out in that weather. I couldn't stay warm in that wind and there was nothing I could do if I went out and found the ship.

It sure was a blue Christmas. I thought of the folks in Nome and in Fairbanks. They couldn't know where I was or if I was still alive. And all the people in Nome waiting for their Christmas mail and food.

The wind stopped on my third morning at Kammisgaard's. When it got light, we could see a dark spot in the snow two miles away on the other side of the lake. The ship must have been blown another mile.

Kammisgaard was real sick by now, with a terrible sore throat, so he couldn't help. A sourdough whose cabin was nearby went out with me. We followed the zigzag trail made by the plane as it had been blown away and it led to the black spot we'd seen. It was the Stinson, and it was a pretty sad mess.

The ailerons and flippers were bent much more. One ski was bent up forward so that the toe was on top of the lower wing. The other ski was pushed up in back. When we got the ship dug out of the snow, I saw that the ski stands weren't busted, but both of the flipper control rods were. That was serious.

We didn't have any special tools to work with. The sourdough and I hammered and pried and managed to straighten the skis and the flippers and ailerons. We made splints for the control rods with some strips from gas cans, and punched holes with an awl and managed to bolt the rods together. I had plenty of doubts about trying to fly with them like that, but I knew I was going to try it anyway. If they let loose in the air, that would be the end.

Kammisgaard was in very bad shape now, so he wanted to go to Fairbanks with me. I told him chances were we wouldn't make it, that we would crack up, because the patching job couldn't stand the strain of carrying both of us. But he said he had to get some help for his throat.

I walked all over the lake trying to find a good place to take off from. There were small drifts everywhere, and they were so hard now that I couldn't even kick a dent into them. I finally picked out what I thought would give me a good enough clear run.

The sourdough and I helped Kammisgaard into the cabin and I started up. But the drifts were too much for the weakened skis. We reached full run and I thought we had it made when suddenly a ski stand let loose where it had been weakened and we went up on the nose in a big cloud of snow.

We weren't hurt, but it looked like the Stinson would never fly again. The ski was broken off at the stand and, worst of all, both tips of the Hamilton metal propeller were bent backward.

We were 160 miles from Fairbanks and the nearest mechanic. We had sustained damage only a trained mechanic could fix with special tools on a bench. But I had to get out of there—I already had been missing four days—so I had to try to do what seemed impossible, to straighten that propeller and fix the ski back on the pedestal.

First we nailed a board on top of the ski and nailed it back on the stand. It seemed strong enough for one takeoff anyway. It didn't give way when I taxied the Stinson back near the roadhouse. The propeller tips were bent exactly alike, so perfect that the motor didn't overvibrate.

Kammisgaard had a Lambert hand blowtorch. For two solid days the sourdough and I worked to straighten the propeller. I would heat the blade all around as evenly as possible with the blowtorch and then with a big monkey wrench bend the blade slowly.

For the first time in my life I felt impatient and had to make myself take it slow. If I'd twisted too hard, the metal would have cracked, or I could have broken it clean off. Then it would have been June before I could get back to Fairbanks, because Kammisgaard and the sourdough couldn't spare me their dogs to get out with.

I pulled just a tiny bit at a time, so slowly that you could hardly see it. Then I'd heat the blade again and twist some more. It took one whole day to bend each tip back into pretty good shape. Nobody Stateside would fly a blade that had been bent that far. It would have gone to the junk heap. But it was all I had and I wanted to get to Nome at least before New Year's. I had already disappointed those people enough.

I picked out another place for a takeoff attempt and we started again. In my mind were all the things that could go wrong. The ski could break again. The other ski could hit a hard drift and break. The propeller tips could fly off and shake the motor out of the ship. The patched flipper controls could break and we would go straight down into the trees.

But everything held together somehow and we got into the air. It was the hardest flying I ever did. The lumpy fabric where the flippers were damaged kept pulling the tail down. I had to push hard on the wheel to keep the nose level. And, when we'd bent the propeller tips back, we'd taken out some of the pitch. We turned about two hundred r.p.m. faster than normal and so we cruised much slower. It was a long hop to Nenana, where I had to land and rest my arms.

We gassed up and I looked over the ship. I still couldn't believe that it was flying. It was the most patched-up ship I ever tried to fly home. We got to Fairbanks and Kammisgaard got well, but it was six days before the ship was properly repaired. That made me two weeks late, and I got the Christmas mail to Nome on January 5, 1928.

Noel did not know at the time that Nome spirits had already suffered a major dampening besides failure of the Christmas mail to arrive. The movie theater burned down on Christmas Eve and both projectors were destroyed, meaning, as Ada Arthurs reported sadly, "no more shows this winter."

In February, in one tour-de-force demonstration, Alaska showed Wien a catalogue of other impediments it would place before winter aviation. A one-day flight turned into eight days of crises. Nome was unusually clear when Noel took off in the Stinson with three passengers. At Candle, however, a northwest wind was blowing and yet the village was obscured by fog. Wind and fog are not often companions.

Cautiously Noel nosed the Stinson down, peering from side to side to catch intermittent glimpses of the river bank, and discovered that the "fog" was snow, blowing snow swirling to a height of two hundred feet. The thirty-m.p.h. wind was creating a surface blizzard under blue skies. Noel's landing was not picturebook. Later, unwilling to try to take off in the unusual storm, Noel snugged the aircraft to the bank (remembering Minchumina), drained the oil, and covered the motor. It was five below zero.

The next morning's wind howled even louder. Those who went outside Tom Roust's roadhouse found they could not stand up against the gale. There was no way to get word of their predicament back to Nome. Noel listened to Roust's sourdough stories, his passengers played cards. There was no change the next day. Nor the day after that. For six days they waited.

The seventh day was calm, but the temperature had dropped to forty below. When he went out to the Stinson, Noel found that, even though he had covered the motor, every crack and indentation of it was packed hard with snow, as if the entire machine had been frozen into a block of it. Noel picked and scraped, with his passengers helping to remove as much snow as possible. He replaced the canvas motor cover and lit the pot.

Gradually the packed snow melted and dripped to the ground. Noel asked one of his companions to begin warming the oil in the roadhouse. When finally he was able to pull the propeller through a full turn, he told his passengers to load aboard. He retrieved the oil from the roadhouse stove, ran back to the plane. They took off for Elephant Point, named by a British Royal Navy captain who found fossil elephant bones here in 1826. In 1928 it was a reindeer station.

We weren't in the air very long before the motor began cutting up, missing and jerking and losing power. I had to advance the throttle more and more, until I had it wide open and we were still losing altitude.

There were no decent landings along the Eschscholtz Bay coast this side of Elephant Point, so I had to keep going. Finally I could see the village beyond some low hills. The motor was shaking and it seemed like the spark plugs were going out one after the other. We just barely cleared the two-hundred-foot hills with full power and landed straight in on the bay ice.

Two of the passengers got off here. I went to work taking out the plugs and found them badly carboned and wet with gas. I spent a couple of hours cleaning all eighteen of them. The motor seemed to run normal again, so I took off with Alfred Lomen, my remaining passenger, and headed northwest for Kotzebue. I was anxious to send a message to let the Nome people know we were safe. We'd been gone eight days now.

After just a few miles, the motor began to shake and vibrate again. I turned back to Elephant Point immediately and just made it. I knew then that something other than spark plugs was the problem. After looking for some time I found what it was. There was ice around the needle valve stem of the mixture control, meaning the mixture stayed rich and caused the motor to run rough at altitude. When we had heated the motor at Candle, some of the melted snow had run down on the top of the carburetor and then frozen there.

We had to stay the night at Elephant Point and it was a bad one for me. We had reindeer for supper and it must have been bad. I was up all night with diarrhea and terrible stomach pains. But when it got light, we went on. Kotzebue was fifty-five miles away and I wanted to get the message off to Nome. We got there all right, and sent the message and started back.

Twenty miles south of Candle we ran into thick weather, heavy snow blowing in from the Bering Sea, and I decided to go back to Candle. We stayed there two more nights, with the people in Nome wondering what had happened to us now. I finally got back to Nome on February 15, having left on the sixth for a one-day flight.

28. VANISHED

The first licensed aircraft that Wien flew was a Waco 9 equipped with a 100-horsepower OXX-6 (twin magnetos) owned by his Fairbanks archrivals, Bennett-Rodebaugh. Its registration number was 2775.

Noel flew the two-cockpit biplane with the thought of buying it. Business for Wien Alaska Airways was thriving. With the arrival of longer days in the spring of 1928, Noel found himself flying eleven hours a day, making as many as four trips a day out of Fairbanks or Nome. He took prospectors and their season's provisions into the Kobuk and up into the Brooks Range to Walker Lake, the Coleen River, and the Chandalar. The Territorial Legislature had made funds available for three proposed mail flights from Fairbanks to Nome during breakup, and the United States Post Office Department approved. The flights, each carrying 500 pounds of mail, were scheduled for April 16, May 2, and May 23.

Springtime was the most profitable time of the year for bush flying, Noel discovered. Weather was good. The land from Fairbanks north was still snow-covered, and skis allowed airplanes to land almost anywhere, greatly increasing utility. Wien Alaska found itself unable to meet half the demand for its services. Another airplane and another pilot seemed to be the answer.

Although the Waco was a year old and had not been well maintained by Bennett-Rodebaugh, the Wien brothers agreed to pay thirty-five hundred dollars, almost the new price. Their plan was for Noel to teach Ralph to fly in it—and later to teach Fritz, when business increased enough to warrant a third pilot—and to use it for shorter hops and those into shorter fields. Fritz was then working for Fairbanks Exploration out at its Chatanika camp.

Ralph was an apt pupil, despite a certain impatience with himself and his machine. What with instructing Ralph and three or four other students who showed up, Noel did not exactly cut down on his flying hours; but his sturdy body and placid nature carried the burden.

In April Wien Alaska won a contract to fly a Fox Film expedition from Fairbanks to Point Barrow, substantially underbidding Bennett-Rodebaugh and increasing the competitive bitterness. Two aircraft making two flights each would be needed to move five men and twenty-eight hundred pounds of movie-making equipment. The Wien bid was for six thousand dollars; Bennett-Rodebaugh asked ten thousand. Headed by business manager Virgil Hart and director Ewing Scott, the Fox crew planned to film Eskimo and animal scenes.

The Waco was useless for the job, so Noel hired quiet, competent Russel Merrill of Anchorage Air Transport and his Travel Air biplane. This craft, with a four-place cabin forward and an open pilot cockpit aft, was powered by a Wright J4 Whirlwind of 220 horsepower. Navy-trained, Merrill had first come to Alaska in 1925. With a Curtiss F boat, he and the owner R. J. Davis tried to establish an air service at Seward. The plane was wrecked in a storm, and Merrill went Outside. He came back in February 1927 and went to work for Anchorage Air Transport, established in 1926 by Art Shonbeck, an oil products distributor.

Merrill was Wien's kind of man, soft-spoken, always smiling, always agreeable. He was eager to make the Arctic flights and flew to Fairbanks on May 12. Noel had completed his second mail run to Nome ten days before, and accepted no jobs but the Fox flights after that.

On May 13 the first stage of the Fox expedition was mounted. Neither pilot had ever before flown to Barrow, at 71°18′ the northernmost settlement in the United States. Snow had almost disappeared south of the Brooks Range, so Noel's Stinson and Merrill's Travel Air had already been fitted with wheels for bush hopping. But on the Arctic Slope and beyond on the Arctic Plain, the land was still frozen.° They would need a refueling stop where

° The Arctic Slope, or North Slope, is the north descending slope of the Brooks Range. The

they could make wheel landings, and then they would make a nonstop leg to Barrow. Noel chose Wiseman as the refueling stop. It was 200 miles from Fairbanks and boasted the hard-packed bar where Noel had made the historic first Arctic landing several years before. From Wiseman, Barrow was a straight-line distance of 315 miles.

Before the takeoff at Fairbanks photographs were taken of the two airplanes and the entire party, which included Charles G. Clarke, chief cameraman; Captain Jack Robertson, a bow-and-arrow marksman and showman; and Ray Wise, cameraman. Business manager Hart and a planeload of photography gear were loaded aboard Noel's Stinson. Merrill carried Robertson and Clarke and a load of baggage. The plan was for the planes to return to Fairbanks the following day and fly back to Barrow with their second loads the day after that.

Although Barrow was quite a large settlement, there was no communication from it; but Wiseman radio reported sunny and clear at Wiseman. The two heavily loaded planes took off about 9:30 in the morning. They landed safely on the Wiseman river bar, gassed up, and took off again.

"You go ahead," Russ Merrill had told Noel, "and I'll follow. You know a lot more about this country than I do." Neither pilot had ever flown beyond the Brooks Range. Prospectors told them that the North Fork of the Koyukuk wound through a fine open pass, so Noel turned the Stinson westerly from Wiseman to pick up the river. The Travel Air fell in behind.

Neither plane could climb high enough to top the Brooks peaks, so they flew through canyons below the tops. This is risky business. Unlucky pilots have nosed into box canyons that end suddenly at heights above the climbing capability of their planes and are too narrow for turning back in.

All the land beneath the two planes was still gripped by winter. Noel counted himself lucky, however, to have hit upon one of the Arctic's unusually good days in May. Above, there was only a high, thin overcast. Visibility was unlimited. He found the North Fork, flew up it through Anaktuvuk Pass, picked up the Anaktuvuk River, and followed it down the North Slope to where it met the Colville,

---

slope flattens out to become the Arctic Plain or North Plain. Oil discoveries of the late 1960s were on the North Plain, not the North Slope, but the misnomer became current.

the Alaskan Arctic's mightiest stream, about 160 miles north of Wiseman.

Here Wien and Merrill came upon a fantastic land in which for the next month they would live a nightmare. Noel's map showed nothing beyond the Brooks Range but the Colville River and the Arctic coast, roughly sketched in, and a notation that there were lakes and other rivers in the area. The notation was an understatement. The 130-by-130-mile expanse of tundra between the Colville and Barrow was like a sponge, dotted by at least fifteen thousand lakes of a bewildering sameness in size and shape.

On a clear day the flyers could have taken up a course down the Colville to its mouth, then westward along the Arctic coast to Barrow, a distance of about 150 miles. This was a sure navigational plan, because it did not depend upon the unreliable compass needle that in these parts swung thirty degrees away from true north. Almost as easy would have been a rough compass course northwest to pick up either the coast or two dependable landmarks between, the giant Teshekpuk Lake, twenty-one by twenty-eight miles in size, or Admiralty Bay, some thirty-five miles southeast of Barrow.

But suddenly the day was not clear, and neither of these courses could be taken up.

On beyond the Colville we met a fog bank which was hitting us from the side, coming in from the northeast. It laid right on the ground and reached up to five thousand feet or better. We were over the Colville at about sixty-five hundred.

When we turned to a north-northwest heading, we began skirting this bank, as it paralleled us for a ways and then covered over our course ahead.

We'd been in the air for maybe three hours from Wiseman and I began worrying about our gas running low. We could have continued along the fog bank as long as we could and then turned west and gone to the coast near Wainwright if possible. But I thought it best that we save gas and put down and wait for the fog to lift. We had enough provisions for a few days.

I waggled my wings to Russ Merrill, banked, and started a glide. Everything was white below. There was snow all over and it looked deep. I spotted a lake—there were lots of them—that seemed big enough and I went down. Russ Merrill started a descent behind me.

It turned out there was about sixteen inches of fairly well-packed snow, and with the eight-inch tires on the Stinson I landed well and didn't sink in too much. The Stinson was light on the nose, also, and that helped.

Russ Merrill landed and he didn't do too well. His six-inch tires sunk in deeper and stopped him very short, but he didn't nose over. The fog soon rolled in over us and we waited it out comfortably enough, although the temperature got down about zero.

The next morning it cleared nicely. The frost on the snow from the fog stood up a half inch, showing that the fog had been solid down to the ground.

Russ Merrill and I talked it over. We both knew he couldn't take off with his small tires, so he didn't even try. I would go on to Barrow, we decided, with Hart and a couple of hundred pounds of film that Hart didn't want to leave out in the cold. We would unload everything else from my Stinson.

From Barrow I would bring food and shovels and other equipment back for getting Russ Merrill out. We needed other food, because we found out the two men in Merrill's ship had trouble digesting the chocolate that we had for emergency rations.

I was able to take off easily. There's always a wind on the Arctic and it was blowing from the northeast toward Barrow. It was hard to keep any kind of a compass course, so the compass was no use to me in figuring out my course back to the lake where we landed.

Barrow was easy to find on the clear day, but it was much further from where I left Russ Merrill than we had figured, about 130 miles. When I took off from Barrow with the equipment and flew back to where I thought he was, I couldn't find the lake.

It seemed an easy thing to do on such a clear day. But I didn't have a compass course, and I realized I should have done things differently the day before. I should have flown on to the west along the edge of the fog bank as far as I could, instead of landing when the fog closed in to the north. When I did decide to land, I should have landed on a lake near a river so that I could use it to find the lake again.

I flew up and down over the tundra, five hundred to one thousand feet up. There were just thousands of lakes. The tundra was perfectly flat. The ground and the sky were all the same color. I thought I would have to be no farther than two miles away to see the little dark spot on the lake I was looking for.

I simply couldn't find the lake, and I was just sick about it. I flew around for five hours and had to go back to Barrow. There was no way to send a message from Barrow. The closest wireless was at Kotzebue, about 350 miles southwest.

The next day was foggy. In the springtime the fog rolls in and sometimes lasts for two, three days before clearing. Whenever I could get under the fog, I took off. Sometimes I had to come right back and other times I was able to make it to where I thought the lake was. There were no landmarks at all.

I wish I could have carried a passenger with field glasses to help look through the whiteness, but I thought I couldn't take more weight than was absolutely necessary, because when I found the Merrill party there would be a heavy load to bring in. I was certain I would find them, every time I took off.

Later I began to feel so helpless, but I couldn't give up. I flew out every day I could. One time the fog came in again from the north and it stormed and snowed for six days and never did clear up in that time.

Wilkins had busted some metal skis and left them at Barrow. I repaired them enough to get by with and put them on the Stinson. The weather stayed bad and I decided to fly out eastward along the coast as far as I could and land and wait out the weather as close to the missing lake as possible.

About sixty miles east of Barrow, not too far in from the coast, I spotted a reindeer herd and landed near it on a little lake. I stayed there four days. The first night I slept in the tent with the Eskimo herdsman and his wife. But I started coughing and itching so much that the other nights I stayed in the Stinson in my sleeping bag. I think the air in the tent was filled with reindeer hair from their clothes and bedding. I got a mouthful every time somebody moved.

On the sixth morning I tried to take off, as the weather didn't look too bad. But soon as I got off the ground, I realized I'd made a mistake. I was in a whiteout. I couldn't see a thing, just white. There wasn't any ground or sky or horizon.

Real easy, I turned and landed with the wind, anything to get back down. I was lucky that time. The edge of the little lake I had been on was about ten feet above the surface, and after I turned back I was able to catch a glimpse of dark slope where the snow had blown away. That gave me some depth perception and I could land. If I hadn't spotted that, I might have crashed.

To keep warm and to cook with, the Eskimo was burning hunks of dark stuff he just picked up on the ground all around his tent. This was oil from seepage under the tundra. The Eskimos had always known about the oil, long before there was any drilling for it.

The sixth night I was able to get away. I made another attempt to find the lake, but it was no use. I decided to go back to Barrow and see if any news had come in. Low cumulus clouds were rolling close to the ground and I flew low between them.

When I got near Barrow, I saw an airplane on the ground there. I knew it had to have something to do with the search for Merrill and the others. As I got closer, I recognized it was a Travel Air 2000 from the Anchorage Air Transport, the company that owned Russ Merrill's ship.

It was now two weeks since Wien, Merrill, and the Fox Film party had left Fairbanks. The last genuine word about them had been a message from Wiseman radio that they had taken off from there on schedule and that the weather to the north was good. After that there was only silence. And then the rumors, all bad, started. In Nome Ada Arthurs, and in Anchorage the wife of Russ Merrill, and in Fairbanks Ralph Wien waited. In Fairbanks also, Fox director Scott, with his equipment, his friends, and his co-workers having vanished from the face of the earth, frantically tried to get reassurance from somewhere. The others were used to waiting. He was not.

There was nothing anyone could do, Ada said. During the first few days there was speculation about what could have happened. We thought the possibility that serious accident had come to both planes was slight. Every day one, if not both, of the planes was expected to return. Ralph was to wire me from Fairbanks as soon as this happened.

As more days passed, though, rumors and sad predictions started going around, reaching from Fairbanks to Nome. About a week after the disappearance, Bennett returned to Fairbanks from a flight to Wiseman.

"One of the airplanes definitely crashed," he told everybody. "A prospector came into Wiseman while I was there and said he saw the two ships heading over the range on May thirteenth. The biggest plane—that would have been Wien's—was really in trouble, the sourdough said. The motor was missing and it barely skimmed the mountaintops. The other plane was much higher, the old-timer said."

A few days after that story reached Nome, Bennett flew into town. I rushed out to meet him, hoping he had some word. Or that he could give me some pilot's ideas of what could have happened.

"There's no chance for them," he told me flatly. "They haven't a prayer."

I was shocked by this conviction and by the way he told it, as if he were glad about it. He told me all the horrible things that could have happened to Noel and Russel. I was young then, not yet married to Noel, and I didn't really know what to make of this man's lack of compassion.

Back in Fairbanks, Ralph and Scott, the film director, were also having sad experiences with this pilot. The competitor company had two pilots and two cabin planes, both suitable for a search. Either could have gone along Noel's route to Wiseman and Anaktuvuk. Or if they wanted to be safe, they could go to Barrow by way of Kotzebue and Wainwright. This would have been over ground that airplanes had been flying since Noel started the routes. And at least we would have known if Noel and Russel had reached Barrow.

But these men seemed to be sulking because the Wien brothers had made a lower bid for the flights than they had. They absolutely refused to make any kind of a search.

Soon Scott was being pushed by his Hollywood superiors to do something. People did not just disappear down in the States, and they could not understand why we would not go out and find the expedition. People in Fairbanks began talking and asking why a search was not started when there were airplanes and pilots to make it.

After days of pleading by Scott and angry remarks by Fairbanks people, the flying company finally agreed to go on a search. But they demanded five thousand dollars for it, for one flight. This was half what they had bid for the original two flights. These men further demanded that the full amount be deposited in the bank before they took off. And they also stipulated that if for any reason whatsoever they had to return to Fairbanks—weather, mechanical trouble, whim of the pilot even—they would get fifteen hundred dollars. For just taking off they would get fifteen hundred dollars!

Even after the Fox people agreed to all this, the plane did not take off. It just sat there. The pilots waited around for days, and nobody seemed to know what they were waiting for.

Finally, in desperation Ralph and Shonbeck of the Anchorage Air Transport decided that Shonbeck's only other plane would have to go out. Matt Nieminen, the other Anchorage pilot, would fly to Barrow and see if he could get some word on the missing men. Matt had come to Anchorage about the time Russ Merrill had. He was another Minnesotan.

It was decided that Matt would take a Signal Corps wireless operator, Dick Hyser, and a key transmitter and receiver with him so that he could send back whatever news they could find. Matt took off from Anchorage to pick up Hyser in Fairbanks, from where he would fly the Yukon to Ruby, then north to Kotzebue and on to Barrow. It was thought safer for them to follow the ground trail. Dog teams took the mail along the coast four times during the winter. And Eskimo hunters followed the caribou up and down. Maybe Matt could get some news from them.

Nieminen's en route time was calculated and it was decided that five hours after the time he was scheduled to arrive at Barrow, all radio stations would be listening for his signal. Five hours would give Hyser time to set up his equipment and start sending.

They took off from Kotzebue and the word was flashed to Fairbanks. We waited for the flight time and then for five more hours. And we waited and waited and waited. Every wireless in Alaska was waiting for Hyser's code to start. We messaged to ask if Wiseman or Kotzebue had heard anything. There was no message at all from Nieminen and Hyser.

Now there were three planes and seven men missing in the Arctic. We waited and prayed, and hope started to fail.

All that was left now was the faint possibility that Bennett would

Wien Alaska Airways hangar at Fairbanks in 1929. Courtesy of Noel Wien

Weeks Field, Fairbanks, in 1934, with Wien hangar in center. Courtesy of Noel Wien

The Fairbanks International Airport, newly opened in 1951. The terminal in the foreground was greatly enlarged in 1969–71. Courtesy of Noel Wien

Noel, Fritz, and Sig at Boeing Field, Seattle, in April 1974, taking delivery of Wien Air Alaska's fifth Boeing 737. Courtesy of the Boeing Commercial Airplane Company

take off on his five-thousand-dollar one-flight search. The closest he ever came to it was on June 6, three and a half weeks after Noel and Russel had left Fairbanks. Bennett actually got into his airplane.

But first he had to wait for a storm to pass over the Fairbanks airport. Then he thought of one thing after another that he had forgotten and called out to the ground crew to do this and that.

For once, all his delaying backfired on him, for suddenly the old seven-passenger Lincoln, Fairbanks' only taxi, came dashing up to the airport and ran right out on the field. Ewing Scott jumped out of it and ran in front of Bennett's plane waving his arms and shouting, "Stop, stop!" A message had suddenly come through from Nieminen at Kotzebue. Nobody asked what he was doing back at Kotzebue, because the message was that the missing men had been found.

Scott said he almost broke the taxi driver's back pounding on it trying to get him to go faster on the way to the airport. After all the painful waiting and pleading, he certainly did not want to pay five thousand dollars for a flight that no longer was needed.

He got to the plane just as a mechanic was ready to spin the prop.

---

29. RESCUE

The Travel Air that Noel saw on the ground when he returned to Barrow was Nieminen's. The Anchorage pilot and the wireless operator Hyser had arrived that day and gone immediately into Charley Brower's roadhouse, where Hyser began assembling his wireless set.

Exactly at the appointed time, Hyser began sending. First he keyed out the call letters of Wiseman, pausing for a reply. There was none. He tried again. No answer. Then he sent the call letters of Kotzebue and waited for an answer to come back. Silence. For five minutes he alternately called Wiseman and Kotzebue, waiting hopefully after keying each call group.

He checked the set. It seemed to be in perfect condition. He was certain his calls were going out. Again and again the letters clocked out. There was no response. He tried the Fairbanks call and, wild hope, Fort Yukon, even farther away. Silence. They were beyond contact with the world. Two days later newspaper headlines in the States announced, "3 Planes, 7 Men Now Lost in Arctic."

I was certainly glad to find Nieminen at Barrow. The Merrill plane and those men were at least one hundred miles out from Barrow, where, not even they knew. Finding them out on that flat country with thousands of lakes would be like flying over one hundred miles of water in a crosswind and navigating directly to a two-mile-wide spot of land with a poor compass. It was mighty hard to navigate even by following the coast eastward and then going straight inland. Having an experienced pilot along to help would make a big difference, even if he didn't know the Arctic.

With Nieminen flying a couple of miles to one side, just within sight, I took a new course farther to the east. And we found the Travel Air. Just like that. Just flew right to it, both of us turning and heading for the little black speck at the same time. It was 115 miles from Barrow, about twenty-five miles south of Teshekpuk Lake.

I had the Wilkins skis, so I landed on the snow right beside Russ Merrill's ship. We had put my big eight-inch tires on Nieminen's ship, and he landed up on the bank on a thawed area; but even so, he nosed over and bent the propeller a little. We were able to straighten it without much trouble.

There was nobody at Merrill's ship. It was a forlorn sight. Wind had drifted the snow over part of the ship, and all the camera equipment was stacked outside with the big black photochanging cover over it and a tripod sticking up above it like a signal. There were no tracks anywhere in the snow.

Inside the Travel Air Wien found a fragmentary diary kept by Merrill and labeled by the old Navy flyer, "Ship's Log." Noel read it.

May 14. Noel Wien and Hart left for Barrow to bring shovels, gas and some oil. Was to return same day so we could shovel out runway and take his baggage and my full load to Barrow. Did not return although weather fine except for stiff breeze.

May 15. Weather foggy parts of day but good for considerable period in morning. No Noel.

May 16. Low clouds and low visibility or foggy all day. Tried snowshoeing down a runway.

May 17. Low clouds and fog. Snowshoed runway did not harden at all.

May 18. Started to clear runway 1:15 a.m. I worked until 2 p.m. Others probably four hours each. Decided impractical to do.

May 19. Practically clear midnight. Sunset 11:45 rose 1. Blowing hard all day. Snow blowing badly.

Sun 20. Blowing hard all day. Wind ENE as usual. Compass variation seems to be not over 15 degrees E.

May 21. Foggy and blowing snow all day until about 1 p.m. Could see N horizon then.

May 22. Cleared some in a.m. and more in p.m. Tried to get off but no chance—even alone. No wind. Robertson and Clark decide to walk for Barrow. Would follow course of about 315 degrees Mag. I decide to take my chance with the ship. They left at 11 p.m. Have very little grub. Weather is calm and while overcast is not snowing. According to suncompass they went a little east of north. Doubt whether I could make it to Barrow on foot.

May 23. Cleared about 30 ft. in front of ship. Foggy in morning (after 3) but cleared. Wind changed and it became foggy again. Found doughnut in tail of ship! Will probably cook all rice and hit the trail myself.

May 24. Flying condition 1 a.m. seemed favorable so tried to take off ship in spite of no wind. Nosed her up bending propeller. Pulled her tail down, tied her down, drained oil. No damage whatever except to prop. Leaving at 9:45 p.m. Wearing Robertson's fur lined jacket and undershirt of Clark's. Also taking Clark's sleeping bag and a thermos bottle—owner unknown. Will follow compass course of 315 degrees (mag) unless same proves to be too far from true north. Will follow this until I reach river going in approximately same direction and will follow river to coast. Have enough rice cooked with me to last four days anyway. Hope to make Barrow or a native home, but rather doubt whether I can. Dearest love to my wife, boys and fine two brothers.

R. H. Merrill

Had to return as could get nowhere necking the sleeping bag, etc. So am leaving same and thermos bottle. Again love to my dear wife. Leaving at midnight this time.

R. H. Merrill

Merrill, Robertson, and Clarke had stayed with the downed aircraft for a week after the landing in the fog. Each had subsisted on a half cup of rice a day. On the ninth day, Noel learned from Merrill's log, Robertson and Clarke had left to try to walk to the coast. He thought that they must have perished. During their wait on the lake, the men had heard no airplane motors, no Eskimo hunters had mushed by. They were lost and, they thought, hopelessly abandoned. Wien must have crashed and never reached Barrow. No one knew where they were, there could be no search. They must walk out. Merrill estimated that they were sixty miles from the coast. He gave the two men a small pocket compass. They left the remainder of the rice with him.

It was two days later that Merrill decided he had long enough observed the downed aviator's safety rule of staying with his craft. He too struck out on foot over the rotting snow of the tundra.

Eight days later Noel and Nieminen found the lost and now abandoned airplane.

During his weeks of searching, Wien had landed whenever he saw people on the ground. They were hunters or reindeer herders. He asked them if they had seen the downed airplane or its occupants, and enlisted their help in the search. After finding the aircraft without its occupants, Noel and Nieminen continued this strategy. It paid off immediately.

Leaving the downed Travel Air, Wien and Nieminen flew different courses northward in search of the missing men. They planned to rendezvous back at Barrow. Fifty miles east of Barrow Nieminen saw two persons on the icy coast below and landed to ask their help. They were Clarke and Robertson! For eleven days they had stumbled and crawled through the crusted snow. They had come seventy miles. Clarke could no longer move his feet. His Achilles' tendons had ceased to function and his feet were fixed in a toe-up position like airplane skis with broken rear cables. He had been dragging himself along by his elbows and hands and with help from Robertson.

Their faces were black from exposure, their lips swollen to twice the normal size, cracked open and oozing blood. Their toes were frozen. They told Nieminen that they had vowed that day would be their last. If they had not reached Barrow, they told him, they would simply have stopped moving, lain where they were, and died, ending their suffering. Clarke had lost forty pounds, Robertson thirty. After Nieminen picked them up in his arms and put them into the cabin of his plane, both men began shaking with silent weeping.

Noel's search was futile. Before returning to Barrow, he landed at Cape Halkett on the Arctic, 110 miles east by south of Barrow. "There was a white man running a trading post there, name of John Hegness, a good dog team man," Noel said. "He was the winner of the long race, the Nome Sweepstakes from Nome to Candle and back. The people at Barrow said he would be a good man to go along the coast looking for the three missing men."

Two days later, on June 1, Hegness was traveling the dog trail to Barrow near Cape Simpson, not far from where Clarke and Robertson had been found by Nieminen.

"I was going at a good clip with my dogs," Hegness said, "when I spotted a polar bear about three hundred yards ahead. They look kind of dark at a distance. It dropped from sight. I unslung my rifle and went on very slowly and carefully.

"When I got about twenty yards away, I saw it was a man. He was lying crumbled up in the trail. I didn't know whether he was dead or what.

"I went up to him and turned him over. He looked awful, his face swollen, black, cracked, and bleeding. I shook him a little and he opened his eyes.

"He said to me, 'You wouldn't be going to Barrow, would you, and could give me a lift?' "

Hegness was known as a jokester and even now he could not resist a macabre jibe. "Why, no," he told the wretched man at his feet, "I've already got too big a load."

He said later that he thought the man would know he was joking. Instead, the resolute Merrill—for it was Merrill—lurched to his feet and without a word resumed reeling down the trail toward Barrow still fifty miles away.

Hegness realized the cruelty of his misfired joke, took the half-conscious flyer by the arm, and sat him on the sled.

"Look, you are Merrill, aren't you?" he asked.

Merrill nodded and fell back against the skins on the sled.

"I'll take you to Barrow," Hegness said. "I've been out looking for you." Then he fired his camp stove and heated some stew. Merrill ate a few spoonfuls and threw up. Hegness tucked him in aboard the sled, started the dogs moving.

Merrill had been able to trudge about eighty miles from where his plane had gone down. He had shot some lemmings with his Luger and eaten them. Once he found a cache of whale and reindeer meat and ate it ravenously, although it was foul with rot.

When Hegness found him he was more than half dead, forcing himself along the trail with instinctive courage. In a little while, after Hegness had started up for Barrow, Merrill began moaning. The musher checked and decided Merrill was suffering also from snow blindness, an agonizing and dreaded Arctic affliction. Hegness pushed himself and his dogs, racing them the thirty miles to Barrow in one day. Merrill, Clarke, and Robertson received treatment from the experienced Arctic hands there.°

Nieminen left for Anchorage on June 6, stopping at Kotzebue to send the message ahead that all the men were safe. They had been unreported for twenty-four days. Most Alaskans had been convinced they were dead.

Once he had found the Travel Air, Wien knew exactly how to return to it. He marked in his memory the small lake on which the plane sat. It was shaped like a backward letter L, just east of two lakes that formed an exclamation point, just south of a larger lake shaped like a sitting frog, all about seven miles from where Inigok Creek made a pronounced bend eastward.

The day after Hegness brought Merrill in, Wien and Hart flew out to the Travel Air and brought back the remaining equipment. Four days later Merrill was on his feet, wobbling a bit, and demanding to be taken out to the plane. He said he would fly it back to Barrow himself.

With misgivings, because Merrill still looked ill, Noel piloted him out to find his craft. Their old nemesis fog was waiting again, covering much of the Arctic Plain with patches of dense white. Noel could not locate the lake in the fog, and after a five-hour search they returned to Barrow.

Their failure was fortunate, for after their return to Barrow Merrill became acutely ill, developed a high fever, and for several days writhed in delirium. He might have been stricken while flying his airplane, had they been able to find it, and he could hardly have survived another period of wandering the tundra.

Matt Nieminen returned to Barrow on June 12, bringing Fox

° The Hegness episode is reconstructed from various contemporary newspaper reports.

Film director Scott and cameraman Ray Wise up from Fairbanks. Determined that the party would not again be without communications with the Interior, Scott brought a powerful radio set. Nieminen and Wien flew out to the lake the next day and returned to Barrow with Nieminen flying the Travel Air. It had been on the elusive lake exactly one month.

On the fourteenth, the two airplanes, two pilots, five Fox Film personnel, and their equipment started back to Fairbanks. The whaling and polar bear seasons were over. There was no filming to be done. They took the long but safe way, around by Wainwright, Kotzebue, and Ruby. Merrill, still gravely ill, was left at Barrow.

Newspapers back in the States continued to headline the story. Fox Films had ballyhooed its expedition, and public interest in the apparent tragedy and the dramatic rescues was high. Unnoticed except by Alaskans, another classic of Arctic aviation had taken place during the month-long continuing story. Ralph Wien was the hero.

After Noel and the other four men disappeared into the Arctic, all that remained of Wien Alaska Airways was Ralph and the open-cockpit Waco 9. But there was the commitment for the third and final mail run from Fairbanks to Nome. The flight was scheduled for May 23, ten days after Noel had flown into the void.

In the building of the West, each new mode of transport was put to the test by the postal service. Solitary rider, oxcart, stagecoach, railroad—each in its turn bid for mail contracts and was required to deliver trial runs on schedule or lose out. Second chances were rare, and even acts of God seldom excused failure. The airplane and Wien Airways were now at their moment of truth in Alaska bidding to join the river boat and dog sled as mail couriers. Ben Ei 'son had nosed over in 1924 and his contract had been canceled befoi 2 it was completed. Before he disappeared, Noel had made the first two runs to Nome and on to Kotzebue and Candle. At one dollar a pound, the 500-pound load to Nome brought in welcome revenue. A permanent contract would mean additional money for the new airline, which made the flight anyway and could accommodate mail sacks at little extra expense in the hefty Stinson.

The Waco 9 perhaps was equal to the task, although it was a short-range craft. But could Ralph Wien do the job? The older brother had had only eight hours of dual instruction time, only two hours of solo. All of his flying had been at Fairbanks, where he landed on the comparatively grand airfield with its smooth surface and long, clear approaches. He had never piloted cross-country, had never been required to do the simplest navigation. He had never landed on a short, rough bush field. For meeting the challenge of Alaska flying, he was dangerously unprepared.

Besides, Ralph had a heavy cold verging on pneumonia. But he knew that if Wien Airways failed to make the run, it might never again have a chance at a mail contract and competitors might be awarded the Nome and Seward routes. He could not allow this to happen. Without telling his wife Julia, Ralph decided that if Noel were still missing when May 23 arrived, he would attempt the flight.

May 23 came. The first-class mail for Seward Peninsula, up from Seattle by boat and the Alaska Railroad, was at Fairbanks. Ralph told Julia what he had decided to do. She was aghast, pleaded with him, accompanied him to the Fairbanks airport still trying to dissuade him. Wheezing from his cold, Ralph loaded the Waco's front cockpit with the mail bags, checked over the aircraft, and wearily climbed into the rear cockpit. Worn out, he rested for a long moment. When he took off, Julia fainted.

Eleven days later the Fairbanks *News-Miner* reported: "Last week a student flyer who only a short time before had made his first flight alone, Ralph Wien returned to Fairbanks Tuesday evening after having accomplished safely the longest trip in the itinerary of Alaskan airmen—the flight to Nome and Kotzebue and return. Wien says the trip was made without the slightest trouble."

Ralph's refusal to acknowledge "trouble" was typically Wien. Of trouble there was plenty, not even to mention his illness.

It was an incredible feat for a beginner airman. He made all eleven landings perfectly. He piloted and navigated masterfully, meeting his schedule in what Noel and Bob Reeve have called one of the greatest flights ever made in Alaska. After his return to Fairbanks, he did not stop to doctor his illness but continued to fly until Noel returned.

Noel came back to Fairbanks from the Arctic on June 16. A reflective man, having experienced what he had during the previous month, might have taken a few days off to sort out, analyze, and catalogue the hectic events. Almost any man might have wanted to rest awhile after putting in sixty hours of flying under such stress.

Not Noel Wien. It was flying as usual. Within two days of his return he had taken the Waco to Chena Springs, flown four joyhops, and made two charters to Nenana. Then he flew the regular run to Nome, Deering, Kotzebue, and Candle. Just as he regarded his years of trail blazing in the North as only an aviator's workaday activities, he shrugged off his missing month as routine. He was surprised by the clamor of newsmen for stories and, as always, frustrated them by his inability to see drama in his experiences and to communicate it.

On July 4 the powerful radio set that Scott had taken to Barrow crackled out an urgent message to Noel at Nome. Russ Merrill had taken a turn for the worse. Would Noel fly in and take him to the hospital at Fairbanks or Anchorage? Noel and Ralph left that day, flying the Stinson over almost unbroken fog to Wainwright and then to Barrow. The flight took nine hours.

A litter was fixed above the cabin fuel tank in the Stinson, and Merrill was loaded aboard in it. Miss Morgan, the government nurse at Barrow, was sent to attend the gravely ill man. The intrepid Ralph, still with only a few hours flying time, piloted Merrill's Travel Air, a type of craft he had never been in before. The brothers battled fog all the way to Kotzebue, spent a night, then skirted and topped and ducked fog to Nome.

The weather east of Nome closed in and for two weeks the Wiens were unable to attempt a flight to either Fairbanks or Anchorage. But the hard-working Noel was able to get through to the north and, while Merrill rested in the Nome hospital, he made pay hops to Teller, Cape Prince of Wales, and Deering.

On July 20, with Ralph piloting the Travel Air and Merrill and Nurse Morgan aboard the Stinson with Noel, the group flew to Fairbanks. Merrill spent a few days in the hospital there, and on July 26 Noel flew him down to Anchorage. Merrill's wife and two sons met the plane. He had been gone two and a half months. The citizens of Anchorage gave Noel an inscribed pocket watch in thanks for his rescue of their aviator.

30. SMALLPOX

WHAT WILL YOUR TERMS BE PARTICIPATE
IN BYRD EXPEDITION STOP BEST REGARDS
BALCHEN

The skill, courage, and persistence that Noel displayed during the Fox Film searches and rescues had attracted more than passing attention. Three days after he flew Russ Merrill home to Anchorage, Noel received the above message from New York via the Washington-Alaska military cable and telegraph system. A glittering opportunity was being offered the Alaska aviator.

"Cmdr. Richard E. Byrd is looking to Alaska to furnish him a pilot for the proposed Antarctic expedition," a *News-Miner* story reported. "Through Bernt Balchen, his chief pilot, he has tendered an offer to Noel Wien, Fairbanks and Nome flyer, to join him in his dash to the South Pole.

"Wien said today that if he goes he will engage another flyer to pilot the Stinson plane of the Wien Alaska Airways. Balchen and Wien became good friends while the latter was in New York in 1926. At that time, the local flyer also met Cmdr. Byrd and Floyd Bennett, who contracted a fatal illness while flying in aid of the Bremen crew." °

Noel had told the reporter that he guessed he would have to hire another pilot if he went with Byrd; however, he knew even then that he would not accept. By joining the highly publicized Byrd

---

° Bennett had died in 1928 of pneumonia developed while searching for the crew of the German airship *Bremen* lost over Newfoundland. On November 28, 1929, Balchen piloted the Byrd Ford Tri-Motor named for Bennett over the South Pole from the expedition's base at Little America. Balchen died in 1973.

project, Noel could have made his name even more familiar worldwide; but he was not a man to be influenced by such a consideration, or even to be aware of it. The business is really going well now, he thought, and if I leave, Ralph and I may lose out. More and more pilots are coming up to Alaska. We can't let them take over what we've built up. Besides, there's Ada. Recently he had begun thinking of Ada Arthurs in other than culinary terms.

He messaged Balchen that he could not accept the job, and with never a regret over the decision continued flying. During the second six months of 1928 he flew 310:30 hours, tending the old routes and opening up new areas of the Great Land. In August he made the first flight to the Koyukuk, flying four miners from Alatna on the Koyukuk north to the headwaters of the Koyuk in the Endicott Mountains.

Often, now, when he arrived at Nome he was asked to spend the night in the sumptuous apartment of Granville (Grant) R. Jackson, president of the Miners and Merchants Bank. He always accepted, for Jackson stocked food delicacies and Noel discovered breakfast: fruitcake and ice cream, which he ate every morning to the accompaniment of Jackson's laughter.

For some time Noel's gaze had lingered on photographs and drawings in aviation magazines of the beautiful new Hamilton Metalplane. This craft was to the Stinson as the Stinson was to the Waco. "Man, oh, man," he thought, "this must be the world's finest airplane." Northwest Airways at Minneapolis had ordered ten of them with which to expand its routes. The high-winged, all-metal beauty had a forward cabin cockpit with positions for a pilot and a copilot, seats for six passengers in the after cabin, and a baggage compartment behind that. It weighed 3,100 pounds and could hoist a maximum load of 2,300. It was powered by a 420-horsepower Pratt and Whitney air-cooled Wasp that cruised her at 120 m.p.h. and gave her a high speed of 140. Her ceiling at gross was a remarkable eighteen thousand feet. Noel wrote the Milwaukee factory and learned to his disappointment that the Metalplane cost twenty-six thousand dollars, a fortune.

By September 1928 Noel and Ralph had ten thousand dollars in the bank. Both were flying almost daily. Looking ahead, Noel had begun giving flight instruction to younger brother Fritz during stopovers at Fairbanks. The third Wien brother soloed, put in thirty hours, but did not develop the need for flying that distinguished the other Wiens. Fritz's main flying experience came in the thirties as copilot with Noel in a Ford Tri-Motor.

Over ice cream and cake Noel told Grant Jackson of the great all-metal flying machine, and the banker, of course, produced a financing plan. They would incorporate as Wien Alaska Airways, Inc., with Noel as president, Ralph as vice-president, and Jackson as secretary. Jackson would invest $6,500 in cash for a one-third interest. With this added to the company's $10,000 bank account, $10,000 would remain to be borrowed in order to buy a Hamilton and have it shipped to Alaska. On October 20, 1928, two hundred shares each in the new company were issued to Noel, Ralph, and Jackson. The loan was arranged, the order was placed for one Hamilton Metalplane.

From time to time during the next two months impatience gripped Noel Wien as it rarely had before. Like a child waiting for a promised toy, he yearned to see the glistening metal beauty of the Hamilton, hear the roar of the Wasp, and feel the great machine react to his touch. To protect men and the new machine from the Fairbanks winter, the brothers began erecting the first Wien-built hangar at Weeks Field. They devised new skis. Noel had discovered that one foot was not wide enough for deep snow work even in the lighter Stinson. They would try eighteen inches for the Hamilton. Three hickory boards were joined together to achieve this width. Thick in the mid-length section, they thinned toward the front and had only a gentle upsweep. Noel had learned that too sharp an upsweep necessitated placing a plane's weight too far aft, making takeoff difficult. The taper in thickness toward the nose made for a limber ski far more efficient than a stiff one. Noel proved these theories later. In side-by-side contests with aircraft identical except for the skis, he could be airborne two hundred feet before the others.

Smallpox, a perennial scourge of the Native villages, swept parts of Alaska in the late fall. Kotzebue reported 150 cases, nearly half its population; Unalakleet, 46. There was no telling how many were stricken in other settlements. One of the three physicians in the Interior was Dr. J. A. Sutherland at Fairbanks. Alaska's governor asked him to go to the lower Yukon to investigate and give what treatment he could. Sutherland chose Noel to pilot him. They left

Fairbanks in eighteen-below-zero weather the morning of November 22, flying in the Stinson. By 2:30 P.M. darkness was closing in and Noel landed at Ruby, where it was twenty below. Sutherland kept a diary.°

We drained oil from the crankcase, covered the motor with canvas, took the mail to town and hunted up lodging and a good dinner.

Fri Nov 23 1928. Temperature 12 below zero. Visibility good. Up at 6 a. m., had breakfast and took off. Took our warmed Mobiloil B Across the river to the plane and started to warm the motor. Mr. Wien has a rather novel method of warming up his engine. He has a blowtorch and a camp cookstove. He gets these started and places them on a couple of gasoline cases and other articles (we used mail sacks one time), then he puts them under the engine. The canvas that we had covering the engine is draped so that the ends drop nearly to the ground. They are pinned so that it forms a sort of tent over the airplane engine and around the boxes carrying the stove and blowtorch. He then puts his five gallon can of oil on the stove and warms both the oil and engine.

This morning there was a slight wind and that coupled with the low temperature made the warming up a slow work. In fact it was so slow that I had both cheeks slightly frozen before we finished. Then we put in three cases of gasoline, put the warmed oil in the engine and took to the air.

Noel decided to shortcut the sweeping southward bend that the Yukon makes seventy-five miles west of Ruby. He flew the streams through the Iditarod basin, coming again to the Yukon at Holy Cross, a Jesuit mission superimposed on an Eskimo village 275 miles from Ruby. Below the village the Yukon turns west to the sea. "Evidently the school was let out for the children to see us," Sutherland wrote. "They streamed out and waved at us."

Sutherland wanted to land and check for smallpox, but after dragging the river and shorelines Noel decided that there was no safe landing. He banked south again and headed toward Marshall, their primary goal, 130 miles downstream around the westward bend, leaving the Holy Cross children heartbroken. Yukon fog closed in below the Stinson and, after flying what Noel judged was long enough to reach Marshall, they spotted a village through a hole and Noel put down. They were at Russian Mission, 50 miles short of Marshall. Sutherland wrote:

None of the people at Russian Mission had ever seen an airplane before and it was quite an object of interest and a great curiosity and treat for them. We left shortly, flying in light snowfall which we ran out of in a few minutes.

° The Noel Wiens have a copy, given to them by Dr. Sutherland.

At Marshall a landing place had been marked on a slough. There were brush fires burning and a pennant had been placed at each end. Men were standing along the edges and waving. We landed at dark at 3 p. m. after five hours of flying. I found five cases of smallpox and five others coming down. I vaccinated 49 natives.

The next day Sutherland found six smallpox victims at Mountain Village. He did what he could for them, vaccinating others, and then took off with Noel for Unalakleet, their next scheduled stop. Sutherland's account continued:

When we were about 10 miles past St. Michael we ran into a heavy snowstorm and had to turn around as we could not see 50 feet ahead. We turned east and then north trying to get around the storm. We dodged and circled and turned, but could not find any breaks, so flew northeast by east until we got over a lot of mountains from 2500 to 3000 feet high where we were lost for about an hour and a half.

Mr. Wien decided the best thing to do was to find a river and follow it to its mouth. We flew probably 30 miles farther and found a river and began to follow its course. The sensation of being lost over a lot of mountains with no landing spot in sight for a hundred miles or so was not a comfortable feeling. Everywhere you looked you would be above spruce timber or jagged rocks. Of course, one knows that he will come down, but one does not know how nor when nor where.

Eventually however about 10 miles away we caught sight of the Yukon River and a more welcome sight is hard to imagine.° After getting over the big river we followed its course northward until 3:30 p. m. without seeing any known mark or village so it was necessary to land before it got any darker as it was then hard to see to land.

We landed near the river's edge and taxied close to the bank, expecting to "siwash" it, or in other words, camp out for the night. While we were draining the lubricating oil and covering the engine, an Indian came up and told us we were 22 miles below Kaltag. When we asked about shelter he told us there was a white man's cabin in a slough three miles below.

The aviator then took a long rope and tied his plane to some fallen timber on the bank. We then hiked down the river to the slough and cabin. The owner of the cabin was away on a trip to Nulato, so we preempted his abode. After lighting a fire and the candles from which we were to get our light, we melted some snow for drinking water.

We found a pot of beans already cooked and warmed up a mess of them that combined with a can of smoked salmon which Mrs. Petric had given us at Mountain Village, one sandwich left over from lunch and some sweet chocolate we brought with us, made up a very good meal.

The only meat there was was some fresh lynx, which the Indians think was fine but we were not hungry enough to tackle that. There was an old spring cot and

° Sutherland, who did not know the land, was of course more excited than his pilot. Wien knew all along where he was in relation to the Yukon, but had not wanted to retrace his course so far back from Unalakleet. The Yukon flowed southward a bit more than 50 miles east of Unalakleet.

mattress with two quilts, so I took the cot and Mr. Wien the mattress and after washing the dishes we turned in and spent a fairly comfortable night.

They arose at 5:00 A.M. to view a cold, moonlit Yukon scene. After cleaning the cabin—a rule of the bush—they walked the three miles to the Stinson. It took two hours to warm the engine sufficiently to start it. They reached Kaltag with twenty gallons of fuel remaining, refueled, and took off, flying under a low overcast above the dog trail to Unalakleet. Sutherland administered to the victims there, left a supply of vaccine, and the Stinson then droned westward to Nome. Flying time Fairbanks to Nome was 16:45.

While Sutherland worked with disease victims in Nome, Noel put in nearly two weeks of work, flying to Council and Teller and making another aerial reindeer roundup for the Lomen brothers. He started back to Fairbanks with Sutherland on December 13, fighting bad weather that held up their arrival until December 17. Five days later, Noel overloaded the Stinson with freight and Christmas mail, packages and foodstuffs, and took off for his second Yule flight to Nome. He battled foul weather all the way, landing at Ruby, Nulato, Kaltag, and Unalakleet, with visions not of sugarplums but of a second consecutive failure working in his head. But just at dark on Christmas Eve, the Stinson droned over Nome and joyous residents streamed out of their homes and up to the Snake River to welcome their private bush Santa Claus.

Noel closed out 1928 with 1940:30 hours of command time in his logs, 1290:35 of it in Alaska, making him, it was said, the most experienced northern aviator in the world. He returned to Fairbanks January 8, 1929, to find that his own best Christmas present was on hand. The Hamilton Metalplane had arrived.

I walked into our new hangar, and man, oh, man, I saw this beautiful, shining, corrugated metal airplane. It had come in by railroad about five days before, and Ralph and two or three helpers had taken it off the flatcars and attached the metal wings to the fuselage.

It had that brand new P&W 420-horsepower Wasp engine, considered the finest in the world, the second P&W model-B engine with Zerk fittings on the rocker arms same as the A, but with improvements. It *was* the finest engine in the world. It didn't have too many accessories on it to go wrong. It had an electric inertia starter that never gave any trouble.

Here in our hangar was Alaska's largest airplane, eight-place with a baggage compartment too and a door between the pilot compartment and the cabin. We could have had a small toilet in the back, but we needed the baggage and freight space. We just landed more often, if it was necessary, for people to go. Most of the time we carried cartons made out of ice cream paper with a tight cover to relieve the passengers. It worked quite well.

The space where the toilet would have been we used for baggage. The Hamilton was a very fine load packer. We never had any trouble with getting out of balance.

The Hamilton had a large wingspread, more than fifty-four feet. It didn't have a high lift curve, but even so I could get out of an eight-hundred-foot field, pulling out of four feet of snow without any trouble. This was because of the really fine ten-foot propeller, also built by Hamilton. It made that ship the perfect one for Alaska—high load and quick takeoff. It cruised very nicely, also. I turned it at 1650 to 1700 and cruised along at 110.

When I would drain the oil after flying from Fairbanks to Nome, about five hours, you couldn't tell it had been used. It was the same green Mobiloil A or B that I'd put in it. I would put in only five gallons of oil, although the tank held ten. Changing the oil that often kept the engine new even after 425 hours, when it was overhauled by the new company we sold it to. They found no carbon and said the motor was just like new. That's the way we kept it running all the time.

Hamilton NC10002 became one of the most famous airplanes in Alaska history. In it Noel Wien made the first round trip between North America and Asia, the first flight by an American into Soviet Russia since the Bolsheviks had seized power, the first aerial crossing of the Bering Strait. In it Ben Eielson crashed and died.

PART IV

31. SIBERIA

In 1924, Noel Wien's first year as an Alaska bush pilot, the Army's around-the-world flyers hopped three massive Douglas biplanes down the Aleutian Chain to Japan. It was the first trans-Pacific flight. But by 1929 no man had yet flown across the Bering Strait. None had flown nonstop from America to Asia or joined the continents in the other direction. Nor had man flown from North America to Russia. And with the xenophobic Communists in power in Moscow, their government officially shunned by the United States, it was unlikely in 1929 that an American would be allowed to accomplish those aviation firsts.

Early in February 1929, however, motivated by who knows what, the Russians suddenly agreed to allow such flights. Wien Alaska Airways at Fairbanks received a query from Swenson Herskovitz Trading Company, the New York fur dealer that held the exclusive right to trade for furs in Siberia: would Wien consider flying to the ice somewhere off Siberia to the icebound Greenland fur ship, *Elisif*, and rescue its $600,000 cargo of white fox pelts?* In addition, the company had eight thousand pounds of furs at a Siberian village farther west that it wanted flown to market later, if the first four flights were successful. Pay for the first round trip would be forty-five hundred dollars; for subsequent trips, four thousand.

These were enticing terms—about two dollars a mile—but there were minuses to be considered. The endangered ship was about 1,150 miles from Fairbanks, off the rugged coast of Siberia. During

* The ship was identified in some news stories as the *Ellis F.* The name on her bow, however, was *Elisif*, and she was so identified by the *National Aeronautical Association Review* in its story of Wien's great flight.

233

most of the flight emergency landing spots would be extremely scarce, if not nonexistent. Beyond Nome Noel would be flying over completely unfamiliar territory. Wien Airways, having recently undergone incorporation, had been using the Hamilton Metalplane for only two months. The plane was not paid for. Should the company risk its immense investment and its only full-time pilot on such a flight? Swenson Herskovitz messaged that insurance could be bought. Grant Jackson, the Wiens' Nome associate, by coincidence in New York on a visit, voted his approval of the venture and said he would arrange for insurance. The unknown itself was not among the minuses, for Noel had no fear of that. With the project appearing to be economically sound, Noel and Ralph accepted the assignment.

Noel made the regular run from Fairbanks to Nome, ready to take off into the Siberian unknown as soon as weather permitted. Although the Nome temperature was a mild ten below, the weather westward remained closed in for a week. The Nome *Nugget* reported: "A trip that is unique and dangerous and which will tax the flying abilities of Noel Wien will be attempted in a few days when he will hop off from Nome over a route which a plane has never traversed. The route will lead from Nome to Cape Prince of Wales thence across the Bering Strait over the Diomede Islands to East Cape, Siberia, and thence along the Siberian Coast to North Cape."

The trapped ship made wireless contacts daily with the Nome Signal Corps station of the U.S. Army. Noel messaged asking that the furs be prepared and ready to go, so that he would lose no time waiting in Siberia, that is, if he found the *Elisif.* An R. S. Pollister, a representative of the trading company who was aboard the *Elisif,* promised that all would be ready for the aviator. The United Press reported in the States that Wien expected to make the trip in six hours each way. One story had it that he would make the round trip in one day. But this was early March, when days were still short, and even the intrepid Noel Wien would not attempt nighttime dead reckoning through this unknown.

Word came from New York that Jackson was having trouble finding an insurance underwriter to cover the plane, cargo, and pilot. Swenson Herskovitz tried to find coverage in Europe and failed. The trading company finally approached Lloyds and, to the shock of the supplicants, was turned down by a group that traditionally bets on anything. There would be no insurance. But Noel had by now mentally made his commitment and he would attempt the flight, staking not only his but the company's future.

Measuring with a ruler on his map, Noel figured that he had six hundred miles to go between Nome and North Cape. Weather reporting between Nome and the *Elisif*, of course, was nonexistent. There were no cities or stations between. He could see what the Nome weather was; he could peer westward and guess what waited beyond. The *Elisif* could radio what the weather was at North Cape and what it seemed to be to its east. Grant Jackson was quoted in the New York press as saying: "If Wien went down, his troubles will only be starting. There is no one who could go looking for him. Chances are nine to one he would never be heard from again."

Ralph could not make the Siberian flight. He was needed to fly the Wien routes in Alaska. But Noel would not fly alone. Calvin (Doc) Cripe, an auto mechanic, was hired to accompany Noel. He would be the aviator's only "insurance." Doc Cripe was in his mid-thirties, a short-legged man who kept up with taller companions by running. He was almost always at a trot. In his early days in Alaska he drove stages along the Valdez trail from Fairbanks; he later drove trucks and tinkered with them until he became an expert mechanic. He was so good at repairing equipment battered on the rocky Fairbanks-Valdez trail that the nickname "Doc" was bestowed upon him like a knighthood. Cripe wore a perpetual smile and was widely regarded as an all-round good fellow. He had never worked on an airplane before his trip with Noel to Nome, and here he was about to set forth on a flight that would write history.

Early on March 7, 1929, Pollister radioed from Siberia that weather was fine at the *Elisif* and looked equally good to the east. Noel noted that the skies seemed to be clear westward from Nome. The Hamilton had been preflighted before Pollister's word arrived. Noel had been assured that there was a supply of aviation fuel at North Cape, enough for his return flight. Noel had learned also that the *Elisif* crew had been without fresh meat for months. He stowed a whole hog and a quarter of beef in the Hamilton. He and Doc Cripe took off on skis at 7:20 A.M.

The Associated Press reported that there was a haze to the north of Wien's course, "which undoubtedly would delay the return of the Arctic Ace, as Wien is known throughout the Northland." Noel was known as no such thing, but no matter. In Fairbanks, the *News-Miner* said: "The trip is a remarkable one and will go down in records as the first of its kind ever attempted in the north country, especially taking place in the dead of winter with the thermometer ranging to 50 below zero on the Siberian coast." Evidently the *News-Miner* knew something that Noel did not; Pollister had wirelessed Noel that the temperature was forty below at North Cape.

Wien set his cruise r.p.m. at 1650, scanned the instruments to note that all were within safe readings, set a course west by north to take him the 110 miles to land's end at Cape Prince of Wales. He knew this country, so it was easy for him to judge drift by noting his heading and track. There was very little wind at six thousand feet where the Hamilton leveled off to cruise.

In a few minutes more than an hour, the plane droned over Wales. From their altitude, Wien and Cripe saw the full curve of the sand spit that arched northeastward there like a giant plume gracefully bending before the wind.

The North American continent fell behind them. Noel took up a course of 293° true (277° magnetic). In fourteen minutes the Hamilton was over Little Diomede Island, a pebble lying just off the larger pebble of Big Diomede. Between them ran the international date line, over which they passed from March 7 to March 8. Little Diomede is American, Big Diomede Russian, but in the 1920s the Soviets had not yet erected their frost curtain that stopped the exchange of trading and ritual visits between Eskimos living on the two islands. In fact, visits by the cousins even from the two mainlands across the Strait were not terminated until the 1930s.

Now the silver monoplane turned right to 310° true (295° magnetic), which Noel calculated would take them to East Cape. Involuntarily the pilot kept in a toe's weight more left rudder. He did not know how clear the demarcation between sea ice and shore ice would be on the Siberian coast. He wanted to fly over East Cape, not skirt it to the northeast.

In seventeen minutes the plane reached the Asian continent and droned over its eastern extremity, which from the air looked like a bison head. Noel made out the village of Naukan. He was happy to find that there was a textural difference between the whiteness of

the sea and the whiteness of the land: the coastline would be easy
enough to follow, without the peril of wandering out to sea. Noel
was 165 miles from Nome. He estimated that North Cape and the
Elisif were about 440 miles west by north. "All" he had to do was
follow the coast. His map showed an almost featureless coastline.
Only a few of the many promontories and indentations were
marked. This was Sibir' or "the sleeping land," aptly named, for all
that was in view was dormant whiteness. Noel calculated that if the
windless condition held, the Hamilton should be at North Cape in
four hours and ten minutes. If after that time it was not, then he
might worry.

I had hoped that when we got across the Bering Strait there
would be good emergency landing places, but that was not so. The
sea ice was very rough, with many pressure ridges and cakes so big
we could easily see them from six thousand feet.

On shore there was something I'd never seen along the Alaska
Arctic coast: two- and three-hundred-foot-long snowdrifts, very
high, one after the other, very close together. That meant that a
high wind usually blew from the northwest down that coast. We
never could have landed safely.

Things were going along all right when suddenly I noticed the oil
pressure had gone up from eighty pounds to 120. This was very
dangerous. It could bust the oil tank and that would be that.

It had happened before. For some reason the Hamilton people
had put the oil tank vent right out in the open on the leading edge
of the right wing. When I tested the new ship in Fairbanks, it was
twenty below and the little vent tube froze up with frost mixed with
oil and busted the tank. Ralph fixed the tank and we decided to put
a tin can over the little tube. We welded a can over it.

In the Interior there usually was an inversion and the temperature was higher at altitude. The can worked to keep the vent
unfrozen. But along the Siberian coast the temperature was steadily
between ten and fifteen below. The oil frost had started to form,
and the can had filled up with it and then the vent clogged.

I told Cripe he had to do something, he had to get at that vent
and open it or we would go down and crash. He tried to open the
emergency hatch above our heads, but it opened forward and we

couldn't get it open into the windstream. The pressure was holding at 120, but I knew in just a few seconds more the oil tank would bust and we would go down.

Cripe pulled out his long knife and opened the wing window on his side and reached out as far as he could. By stretching out of the window, sticking out his arm as far as it would go and pointing the knife, he could just reach the can. Then he scraped out the oil frost and that relieved the pressure.

But it didn't last long. In about fifteen minutes the pressure started up again and Cripe had to reach out the window into that below-zero wind blast and scrape the can. I don't know how many times he did it, but it was a real show of toughness.

We both watched the pressure gauge. Going down in Siberia would be something. I later found out those drifts were so hard you couldn't dent them with your heel. And there were hard clumps of ice between them that the dog sleds slid sideways over.

We never could have made a landing, and nobody would have come looking. We just had to keep some venting going into the oil tank. This was a new airplane that had cost us more than a little money. That was on my mind. It was a wonderful airplane, but I didn't know why they hadn't put the oil tank behind the motor like all other airplanes. Bad engineering, I guess.

From East Cape to Cape Serdze, about eighty miles, was known to be reindeer country, but we didn't see any. I didn't look inland much, but kept my eyes on the coastline so I wouldn't lose it. After a while there were mountains coming down almost to the coast. About 150 miles from East Cape there was a big bay [Kolyuchin-skaya Bay] cutting southeast. After that the mountains pulled back about forty miles from the coast and there was tundra under us, all snow-covered and drifted. We didn't see any sign of life or people for four hours. Doc kept opening the oil vent and after a while was just about exhausted.

About an hour west of the big bay was a large river [the Amgyuna]. Off the coast there were still the jagged ridges. After we'd been flying six hours—at about 1:20 P.M. Nome time—I started looking for a ridge that came down from the inland mountains almost to the coast. My map showed a ridge like this east of North Cape. I saw it, and then ten minutes later we came to the cape. Three miles offshore I saw a black speck and I glided down toward it and saw the three masts of the schooner sticking up. That must be the *Elisif.*

The thermometer out on my strut read forty below. I learned that this was fairly warm compared to what it had been. About a mile out from shore I spotted the landing place they had prepared. It was a two-thousand-foot-long depression in the ice. This is the way a lead that has frozen over again looks. They had a fire going at each end of the lead. I glided down and banked to set up an approach.

It was one of the roughest landings I ever made. The *Elisif* crew and some cape natives working under the Russian governor had tried hard to chop down the hard drifts on top of the frozen lead. But it was still mighty rough.

I came in at about sixty, about five miles over stall, and put down real easy. But we banged into the ground so hard that Doc and I both bounced off our seats with the terrific jolt. I thought of pushing the throttle in and going around, but we had slowed up enough so I hauled back on the stick and stalled it down. What had happened, I realized, was the shock absorbers had frozen. The oil in them wouldn't take forty below.

I was scared stiff. We banged down that lead hitting clump after clump of small, hard drifts. I thought that the fittings on the ends of the struts would pop loose, because I'd never banged down so hard on a landing. If one of them had let go, we would've lost the airplane and Doc and I would've been icebound with the furs. There aren't any brakes with skis, and I just kept trying to steer as long as I had rudder control.

We finally stopped and I jumped out right away to check over the damage. The ship had taken all that pounding and thumping without damage. The struts were all right and so were the ski stands. They had taken enough of a beating to be completely busted, but nothing was knocked off.

A crowd of about forty people surged around the aircraft and shook hands with Wien and his mechanic. The greeting party consisted of about ten to fifteen crew members from the *Elisif,* all Norwegians, and two dozen Siberian Eskimos who had come from their village three miles inland via dog sleds. The loudest roar ever heard in northeast Siberia echoed over the bleak scene when the men spotted the pig and beef quarter in the airplane. The meat was unloaded with reverence. Pollister, the American trading company representative, introduced himself and the Russian who was head of what government there was at the cape.

"Pretty rough landing spot," Noel told Pollister. "My shocks are frozen and we nearly cracked up."

"The weather has been like this for the past month," the fur trader responded. "We've had fifty below with a fifty-mile-an-hour wind blowing constantly till now."

Other supplies brought by Noel were unloaded from the plane, and men and goods were hauled the two miles to the icebound schooner by dog sled. When Noel reached the top of the ice from the bottom of the trenchlike lead where the plane had landed, he could see only the tops of the *Elisif* masts sticking above the jagged piles of sea ice that held it captive. When Noel and Cripe arrived at the ship, they found a feast already under preparation in the galley.

Wien asked Pollister to load the furs aboard the Hamilton immediately. There were, he learned, 6,400 fox pelts weighing 4,400 pounds and worth, on the New York market, about $600,000. These Noel was to transport to Alaska in four flights. In addition, there were 60,000 sable and 80,000 squirrel pelts stored five hundred miles away at Nizhne Kolymsk on the Kolyma River.

The Russian governor was most friendly to Noel, even allowing the American aviator to take photographs of him with the ship and members of the ice-locked party. The natives of the coast are Eskimos and Chukchi, speaking tongues different from those of American Eskimos. Noel thought that they looked distinctly different, too: their faces were rounder, skins darker; they walked differently; and they dressed entirely in reindeer skins.

The ship's wireless messaged to Nome for Noel:

ARRIVED ELISIF SIX HOURS RETURN TOMORROW
GOOD WEATHER TOUGH LANDING.

An Associated Press story datelined Fairbanks went around the world: "Noel Wien, Alaska aviator, landed at the fur ship frozen in the ice at North Cape, Siberia, six hours after taking off from Nome, the aviator's dispatches from the vessel revealed today. The trip was over ice that had been traversed but once before and that by dog team."

There were toasts and much hilarity aboard the *Elisif* that night. Noel and Cripe were heroes, the first new faces the men had looked upon, the first break in their melancholy routine during their seven months as prisoners of the ice.

Through Pollister, who spoke Russian, the governor told Noel a rambling story about how his government had established a colony on Ostrov Vrangelya (Wrangel Island), about one hundred miles due north of where the *Elisif* sat. Thirty men and two women had been isolated there for three full years. No word had come out, and attempts to send a ship through the ice to Wrangel had failed for two successive summers. Moscow was concerned for the welfare of these colonists.

"He wants you to fly there and bring out the furs," Pollister told Noel. "And also to take supplies and medicine to the unfortunate colonists." Perhaps here was an explanation for the Soviet government's surprising authorization of Noel's invasion of Siberia. The Russians wanted to re-establish contact with their lost colony, and there was also the matter of three years' catch of furs that could bring Moscow hundreds of thousands.

The aviator considered the proposal for a few seconds and then said he would make the flight for five hundred dollars.

"It's a good thing he didn't take me up on it," Noel said. "I found out that the 'aviation' gas they said they had ashore at North Cape was about ten years old. It had been left there for a flying boat that was supposed to fly along Siberia but never did. It was very poor grade gas and very old.

"I had to use about seventy gallons of this stuff mixed with what I had left in the Hamilton tanks and in the five cases (fifty gallons) I had brought to get us back to America. It ran very poorly. If I had used up all my American gas going to Wrangel and back, we never would have made it home. That Russian gas couldn't have got us back to Alaska."

The American press clamored for more news. During the night Noel received a full-page wireless message from North American Newspaper Alliance offering him one hundred fifty dollars each for five, one-thousand-word accounts of his flight. Once again the reticent aviator disappointed the newsgatherers. He did not file the stories.

The temperature at the *Elisif* the next morning was forty below and by 10:00 A.M. had risen to thirty-eight below. The Hamilton had already been stuffed with 2,000 fox furs weighing 1,370 pounds, baled by a machine that pressed them almost solid. Ten to fifteen bales nearly filled the cabin, and a left-over batch was placed in the baggage compartment. Pollister had hoped to fly out with Wien, but decided to send furs instead. He had to wait a few months longer for rescue. The engine was warm under its heated canvas tent, the oil warmed and poured. The fire pot had loosened the frozen shocks.

At 2:00 P.M. a message from Siberia reported to Nome that Wien had taken off at 12:15. No other information was given. The world then entered that trancelike state (so familiar to groundlings of the twenties and thirties) into which it sank after aviators were reported off into the void and before they were reported safely arrived or hopelessly overdue.

We put seventy gallons of the old Russian gas in the tanks, giving us half old gas and half gas I had brought from Nome. I started the Wasp motor and gave it a long warm-up. It never got to running real smooth. The Russian gas was just no good.

About eleven o'clock I decided to take off. I gave it full power and we started bouncing down that runway full of hard-packed snowdrifts. I kept hoping that one of them wouldn't break the landing gear.

About a third of the way down, the skis hit a big bump and kicked us into the air. I knew we didn't have flying speed and I could feel something even more dangerous—the tail wouldn't come up at all. We were too heavily loaded. I cut the power and stalled back down onto the bumps and we stopped before crashing into the end.

When Pollister and some crewmen came running up to find out what was wrong, I told them we had to take out some of the furs. Pollister didn't like this at all, but I said it had to be done. We took the 280 pounds—about 375 skins—out of the baggage compartment. The crewmen picked up the Hamilton's tail and turned us around and I taxied back to the end of the lead. They turned us around again.

Even with the load lightened this much we had a time getting off. I figured that bad Russian gas let the Wasp develop only about three-quarters of its power. We roared off again and got the tail up about halfway down the runway. I took her off and then held the nose down to get some speed and then hauled back and cleared the ice wall at the end by about ten feet. I circled back over the *Elisif* and dipped the wings and could see the men waving.

It was pretty hair-raising getting home. The motor was missing just a little from the Russian gas and then the tin can on the wing started frosting. Cripe again had to reach out and clean the frost off so the oil tank would be vented. He did this all the way back, every fifteen minutes or so, for a little over six hours, and it must have been real torture for him in that below-zero slip stream.

I expected the motor to start coughing or running rougher any minute, but it just kept turning over with that little bit of roughness. Cripe kept stretching out into the cold, the white coast rolled past underneath. On the flight over I kept expecting safe landing spots to appear under us, but going back I knew there weren't any. It was a strain on both Cripe and me.

Noel put the fur-laden Hamilton down at 6:10 P.M. on a field northeast of Nome, next to the U.S. Signal Corps station. He found that the tail skid had been knocked loose by the first takeoff attempt and the damage had gone unnoticed before the second try. A day was spent on repairs before he flew the furs on to Fairbanks, with a fuel stop at Nulato.

An exultant Grant Jackson was quoted in the New York papers hailing the successful mission. One story ended with his statement that "Wien was armed with a revolver and a telegram in Russian from the Moscow government authorizing the flight, issued for what it was worth. The revolver would probably be more useful in case of need." Jackson said he made no such statement. In a wireless to Noel from Washington, the assistant secretary of commerce for aeronautics termed the feat "a most worthy pioneering effort." Editorials soon replaced news stories, hailing the flight for its implications for the future as well as its technical accomplishment. The *News-Miner* wrote that the "history making first commercial flight from North America to Asia has excited the interest of both Alaskans and those in the States." The Seattle *Times* speculated, "Perhaps Arctic voyages by air soon will be a facile proposition."

As usual, Noel paid little attention to the sensation he had caused.

He returned to the daily grind, awaiting word from Siberia for the second trip to begin. Instead, a message came from Khabarovsk, thousands of miles south of North Cape:

PLEASE STOP SENDING YOUR PLANES TO NORTH CAPE
UNTIL YOU RECEIVE OUR ADDITIONAL SPECIAL PERMISSION.

It was signed by A. Shvorsoff, "authorized agent for the State Trade Authority." The reason for this temporary change in policy was never made clear. Perhaps the Russians were displeased because Noel had not donated the Wrangel flight. Noel and Grant Jackson° thought it was because offense had been taken at the news story's erroneous remarks about the relative usefulness of a revolver and a letter from Moscow.

32. SEARCH

Wien Alaska bought its third aircraft in March 1929. For thirty-five hundred dollars Noel and Ralph took over a Stearman that had made only one flight. But it was no bargain. At the time of purchase the three-place biplane was under six feet of snow on a Brooks Range lake where it had crashed on landing. The Arctic Prospecting and Development Company, hoping to save money on hauling supplies and men to its outpost on Walker Lake, eighty miles west by north of Bettles, had bought the Wright Whirlwind-powered airplane in the States and had it shipped to Fairbanks, where it was assembled and flown out by its newly hired pilot. End of Arctic Prospecting and Development Company aviation department.

After buying the craft, Noel flew Ralph and Earl Borland, a new

° Grant Jackson died on July 26, 1973, in Santa Barbara, Calif., at the age of ninety.

mechanic, to the site. They dug to the surface around the plane, erected poles, stretched a canvas, lit fire pots, and waited for the snow to melt inside the shelter. Then they assessed the damage. With the tools they had brought with them they could straighten this and that, including a bent motor mount. But an entire new lower wing would be needed.

Ralph noted down measurements of the spar and ribs, and hacked off samples of each. Noel flew these to Fairbanks and Fritz took them to a cabinetmaker. Yes, he thought he could duplicate the wing frame. Fritz, who had just started to work for his brothers, bought spruce for the spar, quarter-inch plywood for the ribs, linen for the cover, and watched over the work. Holes were drilled for assembly, and the first prefab wing built in Alaska was then flown to Walker Lake where Fritz and Borland painstakingly put it together and bolted it to the fuselage. It was a perfect fit. The job had taken three weeks, during which the men had lived under conditions of daytime thaw and nighttime freeze that made the walk between the wreck and their camp ashore a hiker's hell. The toes of their snowshoes, even though they turned up in the Alaska fashion, broke through the crusty surface of the snow at every other step.

All of it nearly went for naught anyway. The Stearman finally sat on its skis apparently as good as new, and Noel mounted for a test hop. "Just as he took off," Fritz said, "the left wing got lower and lower and the plane went into a partial turn, but before it crashed Noel throttled back and landed."

The plane had been saved by the flying sense of a master aviator. While the wing was being replaced, the aileron control wires had been crossed so that the pilot attempting to bank right banked left. When the left wing dipped, Noel instinctively cut power. Many a pilot has died in a crossed controls accident. In trying to right his craft his instinct works only to compound his peril and in a second or two it is all over. In the few seconds allowed him, Noel sensed the fatal error, cut power, and landed.

It was in the Stearman that Ralph was lost in May, eight days before Noel's and Ada's wedding. On May 11, Fritz telegraphed Noel at Nome:

RALPH NOT HEARD FROM SINCE HE LEFT.

The older brother had left Fairbanks to haul mail and freight to Alatna, a tiny Eskimo village on the north bank of the Koyukuk across from Allakaket, thence to Bettles, Wiseman, and back to Fairbanks, a circuit of about five hundred miles over terrain now as familiar to the Wiens as the environs of Fairbanks and Nome. When Ralph did not return to Fairbanks the second day, Fritz messaged Wiseman and learned that he had not arrived there.

From Nome, Noel set out to find his brother. He saw marks on the snowy landing field at Alatna and, assuming that Ralph had reached that far, he continued on to Bettles, forty miles up the Koyukuk. Yes, he was told, Ralph had arrived at Bettles and had nosed over on landing in deep snow on wheels. The surface snow had melted at Fairbanks and Ralph had taken off from there on wheels. "This was always a tough decision to make at that time of the year," Noel said. "We went to wheels from skis usually in May. Some places would have snow still, and others wouldn't, and it wasn't easy to figure whether to try to land on bare ground with skis or on snow with wheels."

The Stearman had flipped onto its back at Bettles, and the people there had helped Ralph turn the airplane right side up. Before he took off, he drained the fuel tanks to separate the water that had seeped into them. With great thoroughness and Wien caution, he and several villagers shook the Stearman violently to squeeze every last drop of water from the fuel lines. Then he refilled the tanks and took off on the short hop to Wiseman, forty-five miles northeast into the mountains. Villagers gave Noel an ominous report: the mountains were visible when Ralph took off, but shortly afterward they became obscured by clouds.

"Extended Search Fails To Reveal Fate of Aviator," a *News-Miner* headline read. The story said that Noel Wien had flown up the Koyukuk in a vain search for his brother Ralph and that he would take off again after a short rest. Noel flew the route from Bettles to Wiseman and back again, scanning every foot of the white surface but failing to find a trace of the aircraft or its pilot. He returned to Fairbanks, arriving at 12:30 A.M. on May 15.

"He's not down along the route," he told Fritz. "That means bad weather pushed him to one side or the other before he went down." Fritz did not have to be told what that meant. Ralph had fueled at Bettles, so he could have gone down anywhere within a range of one hundred miles. Noel fell asleep with this gloomy thought on his mind, rising after three hours and taking off again for Wiseman.

From Wiseman he flew a wide zigzag course down to Bettles. No luck. He returned to Fairbanks with another sad report for Fritz. It was impossible for a man to disappear along so well known a route, they reasoned; therefore, Ralph must be down a long way from the Bettles-Wiseman line.

But the north country is a strange country, someone said, and on that same day, four days after he had begun the flight in Fairbanks, Ralph walked into Bettles. He lugged on his back the sack of first-class mail that had been entrusted to Wien Airways. "I suppose we just didn't rock the airplane enough," he explained to Noel, who flew to Bettles to get him. "Thirty miles out, water hit the carburetor and the Whirlwind stopped."

He had landed dead stick on tundra lichens amid stunted willows that freakishly broke up the outline of the Stearman as seen from the air and made it impossible for Noel to identify from above, although he had flown within sight several times. Nor had he seen his brother sliding and slipping down the dog trail carrying the mail sack. Ralph had walked for three days unobserved from above by Noel.

And Ralph had experienced the very same craving his brother had felt during his epic walk from the Toklat in 1925. "All I could think of was ham and eggs," Ralph said.

Noel telegraphed Ada at Nome four days before their wedding:

RALPH WALKED INTO BETTLES YESTERDAY PICKED HIM UP WATER IN GAS FORCED DOWN IN BRUSH LITTLE DAMAGE HAD TOUGH WALK OUT BUT FEELING FINE BEST WISHES EVER NOEL.

After their marriage, at which Fritz replaced Ralph as best man, Noel moved his company headquarters to Fairbanks, and he and Ada bought a log house on Fourth Avenue. Noel and Ralph took only five hundred dollars a month each in salary, a practice Noel continued into the 1940s when pilots working for him were making 20 percent of what they grossed, often more than two thousand dollars a month in pay.

Ada said: Noel tried to keep the once-a-week round trip between Fairbanks and Nome, and his load factor was 100 percent both ways. The plane was always loaded when he left Fairbanks and at

Nome there always were men waiting to come to Fairbanks—often they had to draw straws to see who would get aboard.

In between these trips Noel would fly out of Nome and out of Fairbanks to the camps in the areas. These trips were made when and if he could. He couldn't keep a schedule because of the weather and the winds. Noel was his own weatherman. He could look at the clouds and the wind direction and tell what was coming. He got a little Taylor barometer and could predict from that. I got so I could, too, and even after a weatherman came to Fairbanks we found that we could sometimes predict better than he could.

When Noel would return to Fairbanks he would fly over the house and gun the motor. I would blink the kitchen lights to let him know I heard him and would be coming to the airport to meet him. We would take the passengers to the hotel or wherever they were going and deliver the smaller freight.

Ben Eielson returned to Alaska during that summer of 1929. It was in August. He had flown with Wilkins to Barrow in 1926 and 1927, and in 1928 they made the flight to Spitsbergen. That winter he went to the Antarctic with Wilkins. He came back in 1929 representing The Aviation Corporation, which was buying up flying services all over the country.

Noel flew to Nenana to get Ben off the train and fly him to Fairbanks. We had him to dinner that night. Ben was a mild-mannered gentleman, soft-spoken like Noel but firmer, more positive, yet not so relaxed. He admitted that he was afraid to fly and would stay up and walk the floor the night before a flight. But he was a man who had a vision right from the start of what aviation would mean in dollars and cents to Alaska.

After dinner Noel took us to a movie. There were seven of us, and Ralph drove and I sat in the back on Noel's lap with Ben next to us. On the way I reached down and pinched Noel's leg. He did not move. What nerve, I thought, not to acknowledge my love pinch. So I reached down and gave him a hard pinch I knew it hurt him, but he didn't move. So I looked down, ready to pinch again, and I saw some gray-striped pants that I knew were not Noel's.

"Oh, Ben," I said, "I'm so sorry. I thought it was Noel."

"I know you did," Ben replied.

For a long time I worried for fear that Ben would think I had deliberately pinched him. I was so embarrassed I can still feel my hot face.

Eielson was reliable and well liked. Some of the other pilots were a fast-living bunch—heavy drinkers, card players, gamblers. When it was time to take off, they would go into the hangar and use the oxygen to try to sober up and cure their headaches and then jump in and take off. They were so different from Noel, yet they knew they couldn't change him. At a banquet given for Noel in 1964 one of these men—one who tried to run roughshod over Noel and me—came over to our table and said, "You know, Ada, as I sat there and looked at all those airline presidents, I realized that not one of them ever had a bad word to say about Noel." This was a wonderful compliment from this man who had grown enough in the years to recognize the important values.

Noel was always so sort of formal and undemonstrative. Long after we were married he still ended his wireless messages to me with "Best wishes." And something else—it is really jumping ahead to 1935, but it embarrassed me no end.

Our third child was due at the end of June in 1935, and our daughter Jean and son Merrill were scheduled to have their tonsils and adenoids taken out on the fourteenth of August. As the expected birth neared, we hired a woman to come and take care of the family for one month. Well, our son Richard wasn't born until the twentieth of July, so Noel asked this woman if she would stay another month and she said yes.

Jean's tonsils were embedded, and for several weeks I had to sit up and hold her at night because if her head was down she was in great pain, and her ear began to ache badly. It was very draining on me.

On the fifteenth of August, Wiley Post and Will Rogers were killed and as a result Noel made that tremendous flight with the pictures to Seattle. He was gone three weeks, leaving me with these two sick children and a new small baby to take care of.

On August 20, the woman left! She said she had agreed to stay a month, meaning from the twentieth to the twentieth instead of the whole month of August, as we had thought. So, I had no help with all these problems, and on top of it all the office calls went through our house—believe me, it was a rough three weeks.

When Noel came back with the new plane he had purchased, piloting the first passenger flight from Seattle to Fairbanks, I was very glad and went out to the airport with the children all slicked up to meet him. He got off the plane, walked up to me, and—I couldn't believe it—*shook hands!*

We had been married for six years, but he was not going to show affection in any way in front of all those people. Aboard the plane were several Nome people who had known me from the time I was a child and they looked at one another and smiled and, I don't know what they said, but they sure thought it was funny. But I didn't.

---

33. TRAGEDY

By the end of 1929 aviation had become a permanent element of Alaska life. At that time there were fifty-seven graded landing fields in Alaska, paid for by Territorial and community funds, and the battle was well joined between flying men and dog mushers. Spoils were the mail runs that could bring aviation a steady income to pay expenses while the pioneer flyers extended freight and passenger service throughout the Territory. Thomas A. Marquam, aviation enthusiast and former Fairbanks mayor, was sent to Washington by the Territory. Marquam lobbied effectively on behalf of airmail for the northern outpost, overcoming considerable opposition in the capital to removing the colorful, historic, and romantic dog team mail runs. It was merely a "sentimental idea," he told politicians, that dog teams must be preserved, and he pointed out that the nation's capital no longer received mail by Indian canoe up the Potomac or by stagecoach from New York.

A Territorial publication bragged that Weeks Field at Fairbanks in 1929 had two two-thousand-foot gravel runways four hundred

feet wide, a beacon light to guide cross-country night flyers, and
floodlights to assist their landings. A U.S. Weather Bureau station
was established at Fairbanks in 1929. Twenty-four airplanes served
Alaska, and during 1929 they flew 338,422 air miles, carrying 3,654
passengers, 17,690 pounds of mail, and 103,043 pounds of freight.
The Territory's population was just under 50,000.

The growth of aviation in Alaska and its attendant tragedies
brought warnings. An editorial in the *News-Miner* insisted that
speed must take second place to safety. "The future of air
transport," the newspaper stated, "depends largely upon the
reduction of accidents and the increasing trustworthiness of pilots
and aircraft." A speed limit of eighty miles an hour, it said, might be
desirable while still making the airplane "much faster than any
other form of transportation."

When federal aviation inspectors first ventured into Alaska, they
were appalled when they saw the loads customarily stuffed into
aircraft there. "Pilots of Alaska," Noel said, "had been used to
putting in all they could—or thought they could—get off the
ground and then climb over the mountains with. We had experience
and we knew the limitations of our airplanes. And we weren't too
concerned about overloads because we knew about the record-
breaking flights across oceans that took off with three or four times
the normal load." But those were glamour flights, and the CAA
looked the other way. The working men of the Alaska skies,
however, were gradually convinced—by groundings usually—to
stay with the design load limits of their craft.

Part of the usual load was an extra tank or two of fuel set
somewhere in the fuselage and connected with the main tanks by
hoses and a wobble pump. When the main tanks neared depletion,
the pilot would "wobble up" some more gasoline. The CAA officials
fought to outlaw the wobble. Eventually new built-in fuel systems
outmoded it.

The Chena River describes a multiple curve like a double oxen
yoke through the heart of Fairbanks. Spanning the river at the
bottom center of the triple curve is the Cushman Street bridge, in
early days a rather lofty steel structure. The first federal inspector to
take off from the Chena with an Alaska bush pilot to check out his
water abilities was totally demoralized.

But what happened was nothing more than a routine Fairbanks

river takeoff. There was no straight stretch on which to make a takeoff run, so a pilot had to get into his plane tied up at the bridge, start the motor and let it idle, cast off and allow the current to take the plane downstream to nose in on the north bank. As the tail swung downstream, he applied power and taxied upstream rapidly enough for his water rudders to become useful, under the bridge and up the right slope of the yoke. At the top he gave it the gun and swung the craft around in a power turn with one pontoon lifted toward the sky and the fuselage tilted down toward the water.

Bouncing, spraying, straining, the craft howled down the right side of the yoke, got onto the step before reaching the bridge and then whizzed beneath the steel beams and girders with inches to spare on top and both sides. Spectators lining the bridge laughed, cheered, and slapped hats to thigh. A lightly loaded craft would take off at that point, but there were almost never any lightly loaded craft in Alaska. So the pilot held her on the step and started up the left side of the yoke, taking this curve with the left pontoon in the air. The Saint Joseph Hospital flashed by and the pilot threaded the center of the narrow stream to prevent his wings from catching on the high left bank or the birches on the right.

Then, with his right pontoon in the air and the plane straining in another full-speed turn, he careened through the curve at the left top of the yoke and disappeared. The exit, as witnessed from the Cushman Street bridge, was like the departure of Charlie Chaplin's tramp, kicking up now this leg and then that one until out of sight. Fairbanks loved it.

The federal man's panic over his first such demonstration turned into sputtering outrage when he was safely back down on the Chena. He insisted that the flip-flop, underbridge takeoffs must cease. After watching pilot after pilot successfully execute the hair-raising procedure, however, and agreeing that there seemed to be no other feasible location for the planes to tie up and take off, the inspector tabled his edict. He admitted later that on his demonstration ride, when the pilot suddenly shoved in full power, swung around with one pontoon pointing skyward and headed full speed for a certain splattering against the bridge, he would have jumped out of the airplane if he had had time. Four years later a noncommercial pilot carrying half a snootful of spirits landed upside down near the bridge. The city and the CAA cited this mishap as reason enough to close down the most exciting show in town. Grumbling, the bush pilots moved their float plane operations to a Chena stretch an inconvenient two miles upstream.

When Ben Eielson, fresh from his acclaimed work with Wilkins in the Antarctic, returned to Fairbanks in 1929, the Territory assumed that the famous flyer would join its roster of Interior pilots. But Eielson came to buy, not to fly. As representative of The Aviation Corporation of America, an aggressive holding company newly formed by Juan Trippe and Sherman Fairchild and promoted by W. A. Harriman and Lehman Brothers, Eielson was sent to look over the Alaska aviation scene and to recommend companies for purchase by Avco. He chose Anchorage Air Transport, Bennett-Rodebaugh, and Wien Alaska Airways.

That Noel Wien would sell out his prosperous company was a surprise to many Alaskans. Pressure from Avco was smooth and persuasive. The corporation owned flight schools, aircraft and engine manufacturers and airlines, and was involved in all areas of aviation activity. It soon became associated with the Cord Corporation, itself made up of many interests in the automotive and aircraft industries. Consolidation of the small Alaska flying companies under leadership of the giant corporation, the argument went, could mean only good things for Alaska and Alaskans. A newspaper story said that consolidation would bring "better service and cheaper service" to the Interior, although it did not explain how a cooling of competition could bring either, especially the latter. Sale of Wien Alaska Airways would bring Noel, Ralph, and Grant Jackson twenty-five thousand dollars each. Noel could remain in flying as a pilot for the new company, to be called Alaskan Airways, Inc. Three years after the sale he would be free to fly with any other company if he wished or to organize his own competing service. Ralph was offered employment as mechanic and back-up pilot. Grant Jackson's twenty-five thousand dollars would represent a profit of 300 percent on his year-old investment.

"We talked it over for a long time, Ada and I," Noel said. "We wanted to visit the States and for me to look around down there for opportunities in flying. We learned Ada was going to have a baby. We had never even had a honeymoon, so here was a chance to have a real one with some money to pay for it and a job whenever I wanted to come back. Ben Eielson didn't want me to go Outside at all because he thought nobody else could fly the Hamilton, especially after I checked him out in it and he had trouble landing the big ship. We decided to sell and haven't regretted it since." They stored their furniture and rented out their home. Noel had logged 2440:00 hours, 1786:40 in Alaska, when he and Ada took passage to Seattle.

Noel was a celebrity. Stories about him had appeared or would appear in *Airway Age, Aero Digest, Air Transport, Saturday Evening Post, Colliers, Argosy, Flying, National Aeronautics Review, Popular Science, Alaska Sportsman, Popular Aviation, Skyways, Flight, Fortune,* in dozens of newspaper supplements, and in foreign magazines and newspapers. Many advertisements for aircraft, oil, and flying accessories in the aviation journals carried Noel's photograph and testimonials.

Progress of the newlyweds through the States was attended by publicity ruffles and flourishes that disconcerted the modest Wien. When he and Ada debarked at Seattle they were met by reporters and photographers as if they were visiting royalty. The *Post-Intelligencer* ran a two-column photograph of Ada and Noel at the top of page one, its caption, "On Cupid's Wings," causing the usually immovable Wien to blush.

The Wiens drove cross-country along the graveled Lincoln Highway to Wayne, Michigan, and bought a brand-new Stinson Junior, NC490H, equipped with a J5 Wright 220-horsepower engine. Noel paid $8,500 for it, obtaining a $2,000 discount because the plane had been built for a man who could not pay for it at completion. The couple flew the Stinson to Minnesota, making short hops. Newspaper stories followed them. Readers in Detroit, Chicago, Milwaukee, and Minneapolis read that "the Lindy of the North" was "On a Flying Honeymoon" that was being conducted "On Wings of Love." It was almost enough to make Noel head for the Yukon. Promoters appeared and for a while Noel was back in show business, barnstorming at fairs, winning a pylon race at Chippewa Falls, appearing with his photographs of the *Elisif* fur rescue in a program titled "The Wilds of Siberia" before school and fraternal organization audiences.

Tragic news arrived from the north in November. Ben Eielson was reported missing on a flight to Siberia to locate the fur ship *Nanuk*, sister of the *Elisif*. Noel messaged The Aviation Corporation offering to help in the search, but enough planes and men already were searching. The crashed Hamilton, NC10002, Noel's "bright diamond," was found demolished on the ice, victim of fog and whiteout. Eielson's body was found near it. Killed also was Earl Borland, the mechanic who had worked for Wien. An abrupt end had come to one of early aviation's brightest careers and to one of its bravest men.

Eielson's death was the second personal blow since Noel had left Alaska. When he and Ada had passed through Anchorage on the way Outside on September 18, they were guests of Mrs. Russel Merrill at lunch. She was gay and charming, although she had not heard from her husband for three days. But that was routine. Russ had left to fly machinery to a mine across Cook Inlet. She did not know it at the chatty luncheon, but she would never hear from him. Russ had disappeared without trace forever. Sorrow was striking close to Noel and would come even closer.

Newspaper headlines continued to tell Noel's story. On April 4, 1930, a son was born to "the Lindbergh of the North" and his wife and was named Noel Merrill Wien. When the baby was eleven weeks old a page-one photo and story in the Saint Paul *Daily News* claimed a record for him, pointing out that he already had logged six hours of flying time while tucked into a clothes basket on the seat behind his famous parents. The lead story in the June 4, 1930, Saint Paul *Dispatch* announced that Noel, "the aviator who preceded Eielson in Siberia fur work," would move to Saint Paul and become chief pilot on a Saint Paul–Winnipeg route to be inaugurated by Northwest Airways.

The news had Noel going here, doing this, announcing that; but in reality he was floating. Only part of him was engaged in the going and doing. He yearned for Alaska with a fervor that he could not describe then and cannot now. "There were plenty of opportunities for flying in the States in 1930," he said, "unlike just a few years before when there wasn't anything. But I knew all along, deep down, somehow, I would go back to Alaska. I had no plans for it, but it was just a matter of time."

The time came in September. "After I waited for several months for the Northwest Airways job to begin," Noel said, "and they wouldn't put me on the payroll for even a little, I decided to go back to Alaska and fly for Alaskan Airways." Plans were made. Ada and the baby would take the train from Minneapolis to Seattle, and a boat to Alaska. Noel would fly the Stinson to Fairbanks, an adventure in itself, for the flight would take place after cold weather had come. With him would go the fourth Wien brother, Sigurd, now a twenty-six-year-old master mechanic and, as Noel had sensed several years earlier, a rare specimen of born flyer.

On October 12, Noel and Sig drove Ada and baby Merrill to Minneapolis where they were to spend a night at the home of a friend and take the train to Seattle the next morning. A phone call came from the Cook farm. Enid Wien, Noel's sister, read to Ada a telegram that had come for Noel:

RALPH KILLED KOTZEBUE CRASH LETTER FOLLOWS GOD BLESS YOU.

It was from Sam White. Stunned, Ada, Noel, and Sig said nothing. It couldn't be. Big, laughing, excitable Ralph dead. Loyal, dependable, indispensable Ralph dead. No. It just could not be. "No two people could ever have felt more deeply about anything," Ada said, "not a tear was shed, but we did not sleep much that night." The next morning the solemn group drove back to Cook to the family home. Another wire arrived saying that Julia Wien wanted her husband to be buried at Cook and that she, the two small sons, and Ralph's body would arrived in about a month.

Letters began coming to the Cook farm from everywhere. The condolences of the flying world poured in. Ralph had died in a six-place Bellanca powered by an experimental nine-cylinder, air-cooled Packard diesel engine. The oldest Wien brother had been hired by the Jesuit mission at Fairbanks to fly the aircraft, Alaska's first diesel, that had been bought for the mission by the Marquette League in the States. The plane had been christened "The Flying Pulpit." Ralph's job was to last until Brother George Feltes, a pilot, had been indoctrinated into Alaska flying. Ralph flew the plane from Fairbanks to Kotzebue to show it to the priests there.

Father W. F. Walsh, head of the Kotzebue mission, and Father Philip Delon also died when the plane crashed on approach for landing. Witnesses said the motor seemed to stop. Brother Feltes later told Sam White that the craft banked about thirty degrees on its third attempt to land and then nosed down four hundred feet straight into the ground. It was a total wreck. "Wien and Two Priests Killed in Air Crash," said a two-line banner in the *News-Miner*, and the story noted that "for the second time in less than a year a funeral plane is headed to Fairbanks." S. E. Robbins flew Ralph's body back home.

Noel believed that Ralph had left the dual controls in the plane and that one of his passengers had frozen onto the stick. "That plane was awfully hard to land," Noel said. "It had no flaps and it landed at fifty. The field was only 750 feet long. The motor idled on three of its nine cylinders and you had to throttle way down to get an idle. Then when you wanted to put power back on, there was quite a delay between throttling and the engine catching.

"Ralph was a little impatient at times and I would guess that after his second try to land he banked a little steep for his third try and the passenger was frightened and grabbed the stick.

"The picture of the crash shows the plane didn't hit in a tail-low position but was almost inverted. The tail was leaning over backward. I don't know any way a Bellanca with all that lift could crash that way without being forced. It would not spin in like that unless forced."

When the Alaska Railroad train with Julia and the two boys in the passenger car and Ralph's body in the baggage car left Fairbanks, Joe Crosson flew slow circles above it as a salute to a comrade until the train disappeared into the spruces west of the town.

"I have a wonderful memory of him," Sam White wrote Noel and Ada. "Big, kind, clean, deep thinking, honest and tolerant. He died a man's death, at the stick, and we can vision him to the last instant cool and calm, struggling for the control of the ship."

A month after he was killed Ralph returned to Cook. He was buried two days later. "It was a hurt that went deep for Noel and me," Ada said. "I never hear a train whistle but what it doesn't send shivers down my back, because I remember that shrill whistle as the train came into Cook with Ralph's family and his body.

"As Julia got down someone handed me little Bobby, who was two and a half, and he had a pilot's helmet on his head and was a carbon copy of his dad Ralph. As I held him I looked past his little face down the length of the train and saw the big box with Ralph being unloaded . . . and I can't even talk about it."

34. INTO THE THIRTIES

Without joy, Ada, Noel, and Sigurd made new plans for their trip to Alaska. They did not speak of Ralph, hoping that the pain would go down. It would not. Once again they drove to Minneapolis. Ada and the baby boarded a train for Seattle. The Associated Press reported on December 6, 1930, that Noel Wien, "the Arctic Ace," had left Minnesota in his Stinson, bound for Alaska where he had made his reputation. Beside him was brother Sig, at twenty-seven four years his junior.

A kind of genius with things mechanical and electrical, Sig had attended Dunwoodie Institute for three years. Physically and temperamentally he resembled Noel and Fritz. He listened to all Noel told him about flying in the north, and did some adapting. He was as careful as Noel, and became an excellent pilot. Like Noel, Sig was taciturn and he often exasperated people by his slowness of response in conversation. "I deeply believe, though," Ada has said, "that most of the men who truly built Alaska aviation and are still here today are the quiet, seemingly slow thinkers." For years Sig flew the Arctic routes; for five years he lived at Barrow at the top of the continent. His quiet ways and total reliability made him beloved of the Eskimos, who called him Sigwien. Hundreds of Eskimos still believe Sig Wien is one word.

Leaving Minneapolis, Noel flew the Stinson to Hatton, North Dakota, where he paid a call on Ole Eielson, Ben's father. The old man was grateful, and Noel answered many questions about his friend. Then Noel and Sig headed northwest across Saskatchewan and Alberta to Prince George in British Columbia, from where Noel planned to follow the route to Alaska that had been much talked of as a feasible one for a highway.

North of Smithers, the next stop beyond Prince George, a snowstorm caught the Stinson in a narrow canyon of the Skeena River. Their return to Smithers was a bit tentative, but Noel managed it by flying a few feet above the telegraph line and letting it guide him back to safety. Next day they made it through to Telegraph Creek. From there they passed over Atlin Lake, a lovely pencil-shaped body gouged deep into granite mountains of the Yukon Territory; then landed at Whitehorse, Dawson, and finally, on December 21, Fairbanks. In fourteen days they had made the first winter flight along the dangerous inland route, only the fourth over the talked-of international highway route. When the highway finally was built at the beginning of World War II, it did not take this easier line but barged ahead through mountains, over rivers and muskeg and other "impassable" obstacles, following a shorter route.

Since Noel had left Minneapolis, a feeling of contentment had grown within him as the western sky gradually opened before him. Reaching Fairbanks was a consummation. After fourteen months Outside, he knew he was back home. Almost everyone in the Territory knew of his return, for the "mukluk telegraph" spread the news that Noel Wien was back. Within days, a dozen job offers and business proposals had poured in. Ironically, Speed Holman, now Northwest's chief pilot, messaged from Minneapolis:

CONTRACT RECEIVED FOR TWIN CITIES WINNIPEG LINE TO START ABOUT 14 FEB STOP CAN YOU BE ON HAND AT THAT TIME AS SENIOR PILOT OF THAT RUN.

Two weeks before, while Noel was still in Minneapolis after waiting nine months, such a message might have changed the course of his life. Now it was too late. Before Noel responded, another message came from Holman:

WINNIPEG RUN STARTING FEB 3 STOP POSITION OPEN FOR YOU ON IT STOP IF YOU STILL WAITING ANSWER BY WIRE.

Noel was no longer waiting. He sent his regrets.

Ada and the baby had arrived in Fairbanks by train from Seward. Without sorting out the job and business offers, Noel put the family and Sig aboard the Stinson and set out for Nome to spend Christmas with Mr. and Mrs. Arthurs. They arrived in Nome on Christmas

Eve. Baby Merrill was hailed as a prince, not only by his overjoyed grandparents but by the general populace of the lonely Bering settlement. This indeed was a notable event: favorite daughter Ada Arthurs and her hero husband Noel Wien had returned, bringing with them a son. For the baby, Billy Arthurs had an Eskimo make a tiny wicker sled woven of hickory shipped from the States and placed on hardwood runners. It was an Alaska wintertime baby buggy.

Prospective customers besieged Noel. His noncompetitive agreement with Avco would not end for more than a year. Noel accepted a few contract hops from Alaskan Airways, Avco's name for its combined airline, flying passengers, mail, and freight to Teller, Saint Michael, and White Mountain, and bringing in a sick man from Council.

By the beginning of February Noel was ready to get back into full-time flying. He decided to accept Alaskan Airways' original offer of a job. When the noncompetitive agreement terminated in August 1932, he would see how things looked. Noel strapped the baby's sled to a strut outside the Stinson cabin and the family took off from Nome for Fairbanks on February 16. It was to be a slow trip. Winds, ceilings, snowstorms impeded the flight, and Noel put down at Ruby and spent the night. Stretching it as he so rarely did, Noel took off the next morning although he was certain the weather eastward was bad. He knew, however, that there were safe spots for precautionary landings and he knew this terrain as did no other man alive. Gradually the visibility and ceiling diminished until Noel was flying just above the Yukon's frozen surface, close to one bank, navigating by watching the trees that flashed by along one shore, a hair-raising but workable technique he had discovered. The other shore was lost in the swirling, snowy fog.

Suddenly the trees disappeared and in that split second Noel knew that somehow he had left the Yukon main bank and had begun to follow the trees along an island. Now they had disappeared with the island. There was no way to know what was ahead. The only possible safety was in altitude. He hauled back and the Stinson whined aloft into white blindness. Noel held steady, and almost immediately found a hole through which he saw the bright blueness of sky. Through this hole they rose above the solid fog and circled while Noel studied the low winter sun and scanned the white ocean below.

Far to the south the Alaska Range stood saw-toothed above the white. Noel banked right and took up an east by south course. Holes soon appeared in the overcast below, and Noel immediately recognized his position. He descended through a hole and landed at Manley Hot Springs, a dog trail roadhouse 145 air miles east of Ruby on the Tanana, ninety miles west of Fairbanks. For several hours the Wien party chatted with the roadhouse people while the sky gradually cleared. Off again and almost immediately into trouble once more. The blue disappeared and white closed in, forcing Noel down to within a few feet of the Tanana's frozen surface. His caution took over and he landed thirty miles east of Manley at the Tolovana roadhouse, where they spent the night. The ceiling had risen only a few hundred feet next morning, but Noel knew that was sufficient if he followed the Tanana and remained south of the highlands just west of Fairbanks.

The final hop was made without a scare. "But when I got on the ground," Ada said, "I started to shake. It was the first time I had been frightened with Noel. It hit me that Merrill was with us. What right did I have to put this little life in danger?" Merrill continued to fly with his parents, nevertheless. He obtained private and commercial licenses at the minimum legal ages, as did his younger brother Richard; both learned to be excellent bush pilots, and Merrill later became a jet pilot for Wien Consolidated Airlines. Cradled in the cockpits and cabins of early vintage airplanes, the Wien sons never knew any way of life but that of flying.

Ada and Noel, with Merrill and Sigurd, moved back into the house on Fourth near Cowles in Fairbanks. Noel sold the Stinson to Alaskan Airways and went to work for that company. New aircraft had come into service and Noel happily tested and flew the Fairchild 71, which became a trusted workhorse of the North; the Stinson R; Loening's fine amphibian; and Wacos, Eaglerocks, and Swallows.

Noel was Alaskan Airways' "celebrity" pilot. Passengers asked for him. Alaska's governor and other state officials, visiting functionaries, and dignitaries from Outside wanted the famous Noel Wien as their pilot. He flew to within one thousand feet of the boiling

Iliamna crater where he captured dramatic photographs of the erupting volcano. So well known was the "Lindbergh of the North" that he was named as pilot of flights he did not make. One story in Stateside newspapers told how the "Arctic Ace" was at the stick while an official of The Aviation Corporation made a fourteen-thousand-mile tour of Avco facilities in Alaska. The pilot was not Noel but Joe Crosson. Writer of the story was one Ernie Pyle.

In between these assignments, Wien worked steadily as a bush pilot, flying the nonglamour routes that his pioneering had made routine. On July 4, 1931, he put on a holiday flying exhibition over Anchorage in an amphibian, making the portly craft perform like a dancing Percheron. It was seven years to the day since Noel had shown Anchorage its first stunt flying. Season followed season, marked by changes from wheels to floats to skis. With each change, the cautious Wien made four or five practice landings to become familiar again with the changed configuration.

Noel flew his last hop for Alaskan Airways on January 19, 1932, taking two passengers and 800 pounds of freight to Chandalar, where the temperature was fifty-two below. He decided to remain grounded during the winter. Seven months later, a page-one story in the August 6 *News-Miner* was headed, "Noel Wien Back in Flying Game/Ace Aviator Reenters Commercial Aviation." An advertisement inside the paper announced formation of Wien Airways of Alaska, Inc., and offered "passenger and express service to any section of Alaska at reasonable rates. Six-place Bellanca Pacemaker airplane with Wasp Junior 300 horsepower engine especially equipped for large freight loads and long distance flights. Address all communications to Fairbanks Alaska. Phone Noel Wien's residence or Wien Airways hangar." °

Wien's noncompetitive agreement with Avco had expired with the coming of August 1932. His new company, in which Mr. and Mrs. Arthurs and Ada made a financial investment, built a hangar at old Weeks Field and bought the Bellanca Pacemaker from Art Woodley for eleven thousand dollars. A newcomer pilot then, Woodley later organized Pacific Northern Airways and after World War II merged it with Western Air Lines, of which he became vice-president.

° This is the first time the word "engine" instead of "motor" appeared in stories and advertisements concerning Noel.

The Pacemaker was another in the series of great aircraft that Noel flew in his long career. "It had 127 hours on it when we bought it," Noel said, "and I operated it for three years continuously, winter and summer. It was a high-performing plane with a top speed of 145 and cruised at 120, and it was really built to lift at lower speeds, more like a STOL plane.° It could carry almost everything you could get into it, either on skis or wheels. It could take one thousand pounds into six-hundred-foot fields at three-thousand-foot altitude."

In November Mr. and Mrs. Arthurs moved from Nome to Fairbanks. Mrs. Arthurs became the bookkeeper at Wien's downtown office and Billy a helper and mechanic at Weeks Field. "No more skilled pilot than Noel Wien ever handled an airplane," a *News-Miner* story said. "He is the veteran of all Alaska aviators from point of service, having started his flying career in the Territory in 1924." Noel's log and the newspapers reported day after day on his flights: freight and passengers to almost every locality in the Interior; a frozen body from Circle to Fairbanks; an ailing man to see the nearest dentist at Whitehorse in the Yukon; a planeload of sightseers to seven thousand feet above Fairbanks on the year's longest day to see the midnight sun still aloft beyond the Yukon Highlands; six hundred pounds of gold dust to Anchorage; a desperately ill man all the way to Seattle; a flight to twenty thousand feet above Fairbanks to record temperatures at each thousand-foot level for the U.S. Weather Bureau; a new record of 3:15 from Valdez to Fairbanks; a trapper and his dog team into fifty-six-below at Wiseman; the U.S. marshal to Fort Yukon to bring in a desperado; into seventy-below at McGrath; and the always amusing entry of "from Eagle to Chicken," from the sublime to the ridiculous, as it were.

On July 20, 1933, Noel flew a geologist to Ruby. Ada went along, her first flight with her husband since the birth of their daughter Jean in January. They were leaving the roadhouse down by the river when they saw a sight that made even Wien start with excitement. A white, high-winged monoplane flew over them so low that it barely cleared the 300-foot-high bluff above Ruby on which the local airfield was located. Noel recognized the craft instantly as the

° STOL, a word not in use in 1932, stands for Short TakeOff and Landing.

Lockheed Vega *Winnie Mae*, the famous plane of Wiley Post, who was attempting a solo around-the-world flight from west to east. On this flight Post was to become the first person to circle the globe in less than eight days, but when he flew over Ruby he was in trouble and the effort nearly ended in disaster in Alaska's Interior.

He was so low I could see the writing on the side: the *"Winnie Mae."* He just cleared the hills. It took us an hour and a half to get to the top of the hill and the airfield at Ruby. Post's Vega cruised at about 150, so I figured he would already be in Fairbanks by the time we got to our Bellanca. We were half an hour out, about fifty-five miles up the Yukon at twenty-five hundred feet when Ada said, "Look, what's that sea gull doing down there like that?"

I banked over and looked down and saw something white flying along very low. "It's not flapping its wings," Ada said. I kept looking and suddenly realized it was Wiley Post's Vega. Something was wrong, because he'd passed over Ruby about two hours before and should have been in Fairbanks for his scheduled stop long ago.

He seemed to be on course for Fairbanks, but I decided to help if I could. I dove the Bellanca down, hoping to get in front of him to show him the way, but the Bellanca couldn't make his cruising speed even though it was diving wide open. He pulled ahead of us very low and after a while disappeared. About fifty miles from Fairbanks we went into solid rain and some low clouds. We knew the route and continued on across the Tanana, then south to Nenana and east to Fairbanks; but I wondered what had happened to Wiley Post.

When we landed we expected to see the *Winnie Mae* on the ground surrounded by people; but instead there wasn't any white plane, and some of the awaiting crowd rushed up to us, thinking we must be Wiley Post. We told them we'd seen Post and figured that since he hadn't arrived, he must be going around in big circles on his autopilot. He had one of the first autopilots put in. Thinking back over his low flight over Ruby, I thought he must have been asleep and must have made a big circle somewhere south of the Yukon. I knew something was wrong. There had been no message about where he was, so Wiley Post was missing.

Later that day the Signal Corps reported by radio that Post had landed on a 700-foot field at Flat and nosed over. He cracked his landing gear and ruined his propeller, which was one of the first controllable propellers.

Joe Crosson took off from Fairbanks in a float Fairchild 71 with a new propeller, a fixed-pitch one because we didn't have any other kind in Alaska. The next day, after Wiley got a little sleep and some miners welded his landing gear back in shape, Wiley came in. The ceiling was so low that Wiley followed the float Fairchild, throttling the Vega back to ninety or so, almost his stalling speed. But they made it.

"Boy," he told me, "I sure wish you could have caught me. I was more than half asleep and so dizzy I was seeing five Yukon Rivers."

Even after losing this time and having the old propeller put on his ship, Wiley Post went on and set his fine record for around the world.

Despite the multiple dangers of Alaska flying and the loss of many pilots, it was not until September 1933 that the first commercial passenger death occurred in the Territory. A plane flown by Ed Young of Pacific Alaska Airways crashed at Livengood, killing Young and two others. Young was the brave man who had offered to search for Noel when Noel had gone down in the Toklat in 1925. It was Noel who nine years later flew to Livengood to return Young's body to Fairbanks.

Aviation in the Territory flourished in the thirties. From 22 aircraft in 1931, the industry grew to 31 planes operated by 12 companies in 1932, flying 942,176 passenger miles and 496,680 pounds of cargo. In the deep Depression days of 1933 the industry expanded further to 42 airplanes flying 1,222,510 passenger miles and carrying 785,586 pounds of mail and freight.

"You would hire a pilot," Ada said, "and he would stay with you just long enough to save money to buy a plane and start his own business. Then they hired pilots and had the same thing happen to them. Sometimes it seemed there were more plane-owner pilots than passengers. It became a tough, cutthroat game and appeared that no one was going to make a living. The operators formed an organization, a sort of gentleman's agreement setting fares, freight rates, and charter rates. Suddenly one operator seemed to be getting all the business. He had been the organizer of the agreement, and now he was cutting all his prices."

The number of air transport companies was reduced to 34 by 1936, but their 79 aircraft flew 16,982 passengers more than three million miles and hauled more than two million pounds of freight. The next year Governor John W. Troy reported that "Alaskan aviation is out of the pioneering stage." It was then composed of 40 companies, 101 airplanes, 60 transport pilots, 3 private pilots, and more than 100 landing fields. A Seattle newspaper quoted Noel as saying that the Fairbanks-Nome trip that once cost $750 by dog team could now be made for $100 by airplane.

Wien bought a newspaper ad that year to wish Alaskans Merry Christmas from its pilots Noel Wien, John Lynn, James Dodson, and Herman Lerdahl; mechanics Sigurd Wien, Oscar Bredlie, Milton Flora, and James Stewart; and office personnel Arthur Stamp, Marie Quirk, and Al Hjellen. By then the line was operating eight aircraft from two main bases, Fairbanks and Nome.

In 1938 the Civil Aeronautics Authority shipped to Alaska transmitters for two meteorological stations. The Alaska Aeronautics and Communications Commission established four other stations, and by early 1939 eight-hour weather broadcasts were going out daily from Anchorage, Fairbanks, Juneau, Cordova, Nome, and Gravina Island near Ketchikan. A decision was made to establish radio ranges for aerial navigation on Gravina Island and on Ralston Island near Juneau, and at two other locations to be chosen later. There were then 175 aircraft in Alaska.

In 1936, Noel had already installed radio transmitters and receivers in his airplane and in the Wien home, among the first air-to-ground radio link-ups in Alaska. For the first time, Ada said, she knew where her husband was and that he was alive and safe, "at least part of the time." Ada was a bookkeeper, secretary, and buffer between her husband and the numerous customers who demanded personal service by none other than the famous Noel Wien himself.

35. NIGHT RACE

Newspapers like to claim that "the nation was shocked" and "the nation mourns" when they report the death of a famous person. The clichés came nearer the truth than usual in mid-August of 1935 when word reached the States that Wiley Post and his friend Will Rogers had died in an Alaska plane crash. Post was internationally known as a daring flyer whose around-the-world and high-altitude flights had contributed to the advancement of aviation. Rogers had earned unique esteem from his fellow Americans. Beginning as a rodeo performer, Rogers projected such an endearing personality and incisive wit through stage productions, motion pictures, radio shows, and his newspaper column that his fans included both the average, entertainment-seeking moviegoer and the more literate connoisseur of irony. Probably no public figure of today occupies quite the place in the public regard that Will Rogers did in 1935.

On what was reported as a leisurely sightseeing tour, Rogers and Post spun in when the engine of Post's Lockheed Orion failed on takeoff from a lagoon fifteen miles south of Barrow. The craft had been made cumbersome by the addition of floats despite, it is said, the warnings of some float experts in Seattle. An Eskimo witness of the crash ran all the way to Barrow to report the deaths. There was shock; there was mourning.

News of the tragedy overwhelmed another news break that occurred the same day. A full-page ad in the Nome *Daily Nugget* and other Alaska newspapers announced the merger of Wien Airways and Northern Air Transport of Nome into Northern Air Transport, Inc. The two stories were also soon to merge.

President of the new company was Victor Ross, then about forty, a short, thin man who had been chief mechanic for the Road Commission at Nome when Noel established the first flying service there in 1927. Noel was vice-president of the new NAT company and was the only member of the firm mentioned in most news stories that reported the merger. Two other pilots, Chet Brown and Jack Hermann, were among stockholders and employees. There was a pooling of equipment and personnel, and Wien agreed to guarantee $29,500 in NAT debts.

The firm lasted only a few months. "Vic Ross was a very good pilot," Noel said, "but he was not really in love with flying, and you had to be to stick with flying in Alaska. Everybody in those little companies had to be a flyer, a mechanic, or a good bookkeeper. They couldn't get by with a man who wasn't any of these things but was drawing a salary. Finally I offered to sell out to them but they said, 'No, we'll sell out to you.' " Wien Alaska Airways, Inc., was the successor. It took Noel four years of hard work to get into the black and out of debt.

Meanwhile on the day when Wiley Post and Will Rogers died and the merger was announced, the new company received its first job: obtain photographs of the crash and fly them to Seattle for delivery to International News Service. This became one wild scramble for a scoop between Hearst's International and the Associated Press, carried to the ends of the earth with almost no regard for expense—a practice customary in those days of shoot-'em-up journalism.

The great photo race started with Chet Brown in a float-equipped Bellanca taking Alfred Lomen and his photographer Emil Jacobs from Nome to the crash scene, refueling at Kotzebue. Lomen had obtained the INS photo job and hired Noel's NAT. Hoping to make Fairbanks in a time-saving single hop, Brown then flew up to Barrow to refuel and found no aviation-grade fuel available. He took on low-grade gasoline and took off headlong for Fairbanks.

It was now the night of August 16, the day after the fatal crash. There is no darkness in August at that latitude; but fog, low ceilings, rain, and aching fatigue plagued the pilot. He pushed on, knowing the stakes, and arrived at Fairbanks with the precious photo film at 2:00 P.M., August 17. He was exhausted, in no shape to continue to Seattle, so Noel, himself weary from overnight flights to Dawson and back, had to take over. Vic Ross would copilot.

Noel's Bellanca was filled to capacity with 112 gallons of gasoline while Noel looked over maps trying to improvise a safe route. Ten five-gallon cans of fuel were loaded into the cabin. Noel decided there was no safe route. His Bellanca was wheel-equipped. He would not trust Brown's float ship and he would not take his own without floats down the shorter route from Juneau to Seattle. The only other way was overland and among the skyscraping granite of the Canadian Rockies to Whitehorse, Prince George, then Seattle, a distance of eighteen hundred miles. Only a master innovator would even have thought of such a route. In those days of routine daily forced landings, no one had ever attempted it before: all Alaska-Seattle flights went on floats along the coast.

The bodies of Post and Rogers had arrived in Fairbanks that same morning of August 17 aboard a Fairchild 71 piloted by Joe Crosson of Pacific Alaska Airways, by then a subsidiary of Pan American Airways. The bodies were removed to a hangar while a Lockheed Electra twin-engined craft was fitted out for flying them down to the States. At the moment that Chet Brown was arriving at Fairbanks with the INS film, the PAA Fairchild was taking off from the Chena River at Fairbanks with photos ordered by the Associated Press and brought to Fairbanks with the bodies. Pilot Alex Holden was directed to deliver the film in Juneau, 700 miles southeast, for transfer to a fast Lockheed Vega which, although impeded by floats, would still outcruise Noel's Bellanca by thirty miles an hour to Seattle, a distance of 900 miles. Holden took off from Fairbanks without even removing the blood-soaked newspapers in which the two bodies had been wrapped in the Fairchild.

The competition had a head start, as well as a shorter trip and a faster aircraft. And then Noel's problems became more acute when Al Lomen announced that he was going along to Seattle. Lomen, at forty-five, was short and chunky. His 180 pounds—the weight of thirty gallons of gasoline—could make a difference in winning or losing the race. Noel told him so.

"I'm in charge of this charter," Lomen sputtered. "If I don't go, then the plane doesn't go." The Nome entrepreneur and photographer, who had seen Noel routinely accomplish the impossible for years, confidently expected him to get to Seattle first no matter what the handicaps. Lomen wanted to deliver his film in person.

With Lomen clutching the film among the extra gasoline cans,

Noel raised the Bellanca from Weeks Field at 2:30 P.M., a half hour after Holden had started for Juneau. With Vic Ross in the right seat, Noel would fly to Whitehorse and then to Prince George, places he had been before. From Prince George he would strike out directly for Seattle, a 475-mile stretch that nobody had flown before and along most of which there was no possibility for a safe landing should something go wrong. The course Noel plotted in his mind was 600 miles southeast to Whitehorse, 740 to Prince George, then 475 south to Seattle.

They flew up the Tanana with the highlands to their left and the Alaska Range peaks to the distant right, passed the Delta River and the Nabesna, and at the one hundred forty-first meridian left Alaska and entered Canada's Yukon Territory into a narrow canyon leading to claw-shaped Kluane Lake. To their right now, so unbelievably high in the sky that it appeared to be a cloud, the white tip of Mount Saint Elias hung detached above the haze at eighteen thousand feet.

They had come a little more than half their first leg to Whitehorse, and Noel told Lomen to open a gas can and insert the hose. Noel stroked the wobble pump, transferring gasoline from the can to the Bellanca's tanks. Then he searched closely the obscured land below and the air about him. Holden would be flying this same stretch for 400 miles, and Noel was hoping to catch sight of his competition. Holden's Fairchild had taken some rough treatment and was not the speediest 71 around. Noel just might catch it.

Thirty miles southeast of Kluane Noel turned east for the final 100 miles to Whitehorse. From here Holden would have continued southeast to Haines and then followed the fjord called Lynn Canal to Juneau. Although Noel could not know it, luck was joining the race, and on his side. Holden had landed on Kluane Lake, refueled at Burwash Landing, and taken off before the Bellanca reached the lake. But he found a violent storm blowing into his face when he turned into Chilkat Pass for his leg through the mountains to Haines. He turned back, and he and his mechanic Lloyd Jarman waited at Burwash until three the next morning, listening to wolves howling on the hills and wondering where Wien was in his dash to Seattle. They did not know that Noel intended to fly inland—who would have expected that?—so they assumed he also had met the monster winds howling up the Chilkat and had had to turn back. But where was he?

He was almost to Prince George. Hours before, while Holden was trying to fight his way through the Chilkat, Noel had overflown Kluane and made his left turn toward Whitehorse; at 7:25 P.M. Noel cleared customs, topped off the Bellanca's tanks and the spare cans. Then he relaxed against a hangar wall.

Relaxed? At a time like this? Lomen, even though he had known Noel since his first days at Nome and was well aware that some mistakenly claimed Noel was a slugabed, was staggered. "Let's go, Wien!" he shouted. "We don't have time to waste sitting around here."

Calmly Noel explained that there was no use going on just then. Although it was still light at Whitehorse, if they left then it would be dark when they arrived at Prince George. The airfield there was not lighted and Noel could not land on it in the dark. It would soon be dark at Whitehorse, but it would lighten about 4:00 A.M. They would leave then. Besides, Noel said in what was an unusually long speech for him, he was tired. He could not stand a flight from Fairbanks to Seattle without rest. He had flown all the previous night. All things considered, this was the best place to rest along the route. He sat.

Ten o'clock neared and it was dark. Noel relaxed. Lomen began pacing. Finally he stopped in front of Wien and shook him by the shoulder.

"We have to go on," he told Noel. "I don't care about all those things. We have to go on."

"Well, besides all those things," Noel told the agitated man, "it's dark here now and there aren't any lights on the field. This is a real short field, only two thousand feet long, and it's twenty-five hundred feet in altitude. We'll have a long takeoff run in the dark. I don't think we could make it."

Lomen, shouting again, said, "If we don't go now, then we'll just wait for light and go back to Fairbanks. It's all over and we've lost. It won't do me any good to get these pictures to Seattle after the other people have been there twelve hours or so."

Vic Ross, Noel's copilot and NAT partner, took no part in the dispute. He left the decision to Noel's experience. But the PAA

station manager at Whitehorse entered the discussion and offered to
place his automobile at the end of the field and turn on its lights if
Noel decided to take off. Obviously, this good chap was unaware
that his own company was racing the Wien Bellanca to Seattle with
film for a competing news service.

"All right, that's fine!" Lomen said. "See?" he added, turning to
Noel. "We can at least get out of here."

Noel was not at all sure. The auto lights could not get the
Bellanca with its load of 162 gallons of gasoline and its three men off
the ground, but at least they would let the pilot know where the
end of the field was. That might be of some help.

Noel decided to try it. The PAA man drove his car to the other
end, turned it around, and aimed its lights down the runway toward
the Bellanca. The three men got aboard.

"I didn't even have any flaps," Noel said. "I got the tail up right
away so the nose was almost pointing down. I always did this on a
short field, if it was hard. Most pilots thought they had to keep the
tail down and get lift on the wings. But I found it was better the
other way, because I could get up good speed sooner and then ease
back on the stick and be in the air. I kept the tail down only on soft
fields, where you had to keep it almost three-points all the way to
keep the propeller from digging in."

As in the newsreels of those old days, the loaded Bellanca
bounded through the blackness, flame crackling from the exhausts,
tail up, wheels leaving the ground briefly and settling heavily back
again. The two thousand feet rapidly swished beneath the plane
while the lights of the station manager's auto grew larger and larger
ahead. When he felt life in his craft, Noel gently hauled back and
the plane roared off the ground, skimming over the auto lights and
the manager, who crouched and waved at the same time. It was
10:45 P.M., August 17, two days since Post and Rogers had died.

Noel leveled to gain speed and then put the Bellanca into a gentle
climb, turning to a magnetic heading of about 100 degrees. He had
a gyro for holding course, a turn-and-bank indicator for flying level
when there was no visibility. He needed both on this trip. The night
was clear, but there was no moon. Only faint starlight glowed and
was no good for illuminating the ground directly below, only for
outlining the crags ahead and to both sides. Noel had to use the
turn-and-bank to fly straight and level. And he had to maintain his

compass heading and resist the urge to try to identify and follow the faint terrain features below. East and south of Whitehorse there were two large lakes, Atlin and Teslin, and a dozen smaller ones, all more or less pencil-shaped and pointing every which way. With the lack of light he easily could have mistaken one for another and, had he followed the wrong one, ended up hopelessly lost. He disliked night flying except with a full moon. But here he was flying in blackness over mountain country that matched any in the world for inhospitality to aircraft. He had let an insistent customer push him into a flight that all his knowledge told him should not be attempted. He regretted it.

The distance was 740 miles from Whitehorse to Prince George. He flew at eight thousand feet, holding about 100 degrees, trying to maintain a constant distance from the peaks of the Coast Mountains that were faint silhouettes in the dark sky. He could see nothing below. On regular order, Lomen dipped the hose into a can and Noel wobbled fuel into the plane's tanks.

Noel kept the Wasp turning at 1650, resisting the impulse to throttle to full power. He had fuel enough to fly all out, but his long habit of babying his equipment could not be broken. At 1650 he would burn fourteen gallons an hour.

A surge of pleasure came with the recognition that his navigation, clairvoyant as it was, was on the nose: a little more than two hours out of Whitehorse he picked up in the starlight the faint outline of Edziza Peak in British Columbia. It was to his left, where it should be, its 9,100-foot thrust standing alone above a 5,000-foot plateau about twenty-five miles southeast of Telegraph Creek on the Stikine. He had flown 270 miles, and this was his first checkpoint. On the nose. Edziza's snowfield shone dully in the feeble light.

Noel turned a few degrees left beyond Edziza. He would cross the Skeena a few miles beyond Edziza but he was not certain he could see it. The rough land below lay in darkness. He did not see the Skeena. A checkpoint he could not miss, though, was the group of thin lakes, much like Atlin, Teslin, and their companions. He should reach the first one, Takla, about 2:15 after passing Edziza. The others would be ahead and to the right, lying haphazard like strands of spaghetti thrown onto the ground. They should reflect the starlight, weak as it was.

He sighted them! Steel-colored slivers that told him he was still on course. Now he felt safe. A hundred or so miles east of the lakes was the broad valley cut by the Findlay and Parsnip rivers. He would turn left a little, pick up the valley, and fly south to Prince George. A yellow glow to the left told him dawn was coming. After a flight of 7:15 he landed at Prince George at 6:00 A.M., fifteen and a half hours and 1,340 miles out of Fairbanks, and nearly forty-eight hours since he had slept.

There was no way of knowing, of course, but Alex Holden in the opposition PAA Fairchild was still about an hour and a half the other side of Juneau. Noel and the INS film were well ahead in the race, but the edge might not last. Holden landed at Juneau at 7:30 A.M. and his AP film was hastily handed to pilot Bob Ellis who took off immediately in the speedy Vega.° Even on floats it cruised about five miles an hour faster than the Wien Bellanca on wheels. But Ellis had 900 miles to cover to reach Seattle. Even flat out, it would take him 6:30, yet PAA swaggered with confidence. None of its people had reported sighting Wien at any station in Alaska. Obviously the cautious Wien had decided to wait even longer, wherever he had sat down, for the Chilkat weather to subside. His fuddy-duddy style of flying would cost him this time.

At that moment Noel had only half as far to go to reach Seattle as did his opposition. But he had been at Prince George an hour and a half and now it looked as if he could be there much longer. He had spent a half hour poking about the airfield trying to find a customs officer. He would be checking out of Canada here. At seven he found someone who knew the name and home telephone number of the local customs official. Noel called. The official informed Wien that (1) he had regular hours; (2) the present time was not among them; (3) he would not consider arriving at the field before his appointed time; and (4) he did not at all appreciate being disturbed at home at that hour. At this news Al Lomen nearly dropped dead from acute outrage. Noel shrugged.

At 8:00 A.M. the customs man arrived at the airfield. When Noel told him what the aircraft was carrying, from where to where, the man said, "Why, my good fellow, you have no need for customs. There is nothing at all to clear with me." He seemed pleased to be delivering the tidings that the Bellanca and its film had lost two hours for nothing.

° Ellis came to Alaska in 1929 and later founded an air service out of Ketchikan.

Tanks and cabin cans had been topped. Noel, Lomen, and Ross piled back into the airplane and Noel took off to follow the Fraser River south and then west to its mouth in the Strait of Georgia at Vancouver, ninety miles north of Seattle. None of the three men now had much confidence that they could win the race. Bad enough to lose out on flying strategy and ability; unbearable to lose by needlessly wasting time.

As they approached Williams Lake, Noel saw ahead a layer of clouds that appeared to be quite low. When he reached Williams he found that the five-thousand to six-thousand-foot mountaintops bordering the river were in clouds. Worse, a thin layer seemed to be forming below. If that layer became solid, Noel thought, and the overhead one lowered, he could be forced to turn back. He would not fly through a socked-in canyon that twisted in its course. He wondered also about conditions at Seattle. Its notorious morning fog often lasted long enough to become afternoon fog. The layer below remained broken, and Noel caught occasional glimpses of the river below. The overcast remained at a kindly altitude. They flew on, hoping and wobbling.

About three hours out of Prince George, Noel reached Hope and made the sharp right turn with the Fraser River. When they reached the flat land that stretches from east of Chilliwack to the great sound, Wien saw with a flood of relief that there was no coastal fog. He left the river, turned south over the flat land, skirting the Skagit Range and Mount Baker, past Abbotsford and into the United States over Bellingham and Everett, searching ahead for signs of Seattle fog.

There was no fog. Seattle sparkled in a noon sun. Noel put the Bellanca down at Boeing Field at 12:30 P.M. Seattle time, less than twenty hours after leaving Fairbanks. Before he shut down the Wasp, the cabin door was jerked open, identifications exchanged, and the film snatched from Lomen's hands.

As far as anyone at Boeing knew, the PAA Vega had not yet arrived. It did not reach Seattle until mid-afternoon. By then the INS photos of Wiley Post's wrecked Orion, and of Post and Rogers in their last poses before leaving Fairbanks, were on the street in the Seattle *Post-Intelligencer*, and the film was on its way to New York for worldwide INS distribution. The INS scoop was voted the biggest of the year and the Post-Rogers crash was voted the year's second top news story, outranked by Mussolini's war on Ethiopia.

No public votes were taken on Noel's achievement, but among flying men it rates to this day as a classic. Alaska's most conservative pilot had staked everything and pioneered an overland route from Alaska to Seattle. Even in 1940, the flight from Fairbanks to Seattle took two full days, requiring a hop down to Juneau and then one by Pan American Sikorsky S-42 flying boat to Seattle. Wien, in covering the eighteen hundred miles in 16:25 flying time, more than five hours of it in darkness, had made not one false turning, had lost not a mile or a minute in the air. And the flight had not been made after laborious planning by a force of aviators and geographers, but by a lone, tired man on the spur of the moment and in the heat of fierce competition.

36. TRI-MOTOR

For anybody but Noel Wien, the stay in Seattle and the trip back to Fairbanks could have been only the dullest anticlimax. True to character, however, Noel regarded his pathfinding flight south as routine. In later years he more clearly remembered details of the hours after arriving in Seattle than those of the hazardous dash from Fairbanks. This was because he saw, coveted, and bought during those later hours the airplane that became perhaps the one favorite machine of the scores that he flew during a long career. No others, save the Fokker F. III, the Hamilton Metalplane, and the Bellanca Pacemaker, came close.

First, though, he and Vic Ross collected the thirty-five-hundred-dollar fee that Al Lomen had offered them for delivering the Post-Rogers film to Seattle. An INS newsman asked Noel if he had any personal film of Post and Rogers. He had 100 feet of 16mm movie film and a pack of stills he had made of the two men during the minutes before their Fairbanks takeoff. The newsman offered him one hundred dollars for all of it. Of the thousands of photographs Wien took during his decades in Alaska, these were the only ones he ever sold. Over the years he gave away prints—others were appropriated by acquaintances—that later became priceless, many of them still appearing in new publications with credit given to this and that "Collection," without explanation that the originals were collected from Noel Wien. One of his Post-Rogers stills was used as a full-page photo in the Hearst papers. He could have gotten one hundred dollars for that shot alone. "Over the years," he admitted, "inexperience cost us an awful lot of money."

Noel was satisfied at the time, however. Besides, as soon as he pocketed the hundred dollars his full attention was seized by two lovely aircraft parked on the ramp. They were Ford Tri-Motor transports, the greatest aircraft of their age, old reliable workhorses now being pushed out of first-class service by the Boeing 247, the Lockheed Model 10, and soon by the DC-2 and DC-3. They were model 5-ATs, the second, larger version of the 198 Tri-Motors built by Ford between 1926 and 1933. They were owned by Northwest Airways and both were for sale.

One of the corrugated birds—NC8419—was fitted with just about everything an Alaska bush pilot could dream up for his ideal aircraft. It had two extra 100-gallon fuel tanks in the wings, giving it a total fuel capacity of 555 gallons; a Western Electric radio; twelve passenger seats; three 420-horsepower Pratt and Whitney Wasps; full instrumentation; air wheels, those sixteen-inch-wide balloon jobs that supported a craft on mushy ground; a certified load capacity of thirty-three hundred pounds, which Noel calculated was far under what it could safely carry; and, best of all, disc brakes that could bring the big plane to a quick stop on short fields. Its price was $7,500. The reorganized Northern Air Transport, Inc., only three days old when its president Ross and vice-president Wien arrived in Seattle, went multi-engined. The thirty-five-hundred-dollar film fee became a down payment on NC8419, and Noel transitioned to multi-engine during an hour and ten minutes of familiarization by a Northwest pilot.

Seattle fog closed in and not until August 28 could Noel raise the Tri-Motor into the air for the first Seattle-Fairbanks passenger flight.

Vic Ross was copilot. Passengers were Al, Ralph, Rosemary, and Lucille Lomen (the Lomens got around), and several others, who deplaned at stops en route. When NC8419 winged into Fairbanks in all her corrugated magnificence on August 31, it was by far the largest aircraft ever to have landed there.

Jack Hermann by coincidence was in Seattle on his honeymoon. He and his bride flew Noel's Bellanca back home. Leaving Seattle at the same time was Ray Petersen of Bethel Airways, who had begun flying in Alaska in 1934. Petersen later was a founder of Northern Consolidated Airline and became president and general manager of Wien Consolidated Airlines when Northern and Wien Airways merged in 1968. The line became known as Wien Air Alaska in 1973.

We nearly lost the Tri-Motor in the spring of 1938. I flew the Ford to Harding Lake, about forty miles southeast of Fairbanks, landed on wheels, and we changed to the skis. Then we brought our twelve passengers and the freight out by trucks and loaded up. I started to taxi about three miles across the lake so we could take off into the wind. In addition to the twelve passengers, I had full tanks of 555 gallons, and about one thousand pounds of baggage and freight.

The ice was three feet thick. But hidden under fresh snow from the night before was a long, deep crack that had been made by an earthquake during the winter. The ice in this crack had become honeycombed and soft from sun rays of the previous few days. If I'd taxied real fast, with the tail wind, I would have gone over this crack fast enough to have made it onto the solid ice. But, taxiing slowly, about half a mile out, I went through with the skis. Those skis were wide and long and distributed the weight over quite an area; yet we broke through the soft ice in the crack.

Down we went. As we sank down to the engines, I called to the passengers to get out. They opened the door and walked out on the ice without so much as getting their feet wet. The side engines caught on the ice and I thought we'd stop there. But she began slipping under some more. I opened the trap door above the pilot, and my copilot and I climbed out and slid over the side at the rear.

In five minutes the Ford slipped clear under down to the wings.

The nose and all three engines were under, with just the wings on the surface and the tail sticking up. That was a sad feeling, standing there and looking at that. There was no telling what damage was under the ice.

Well, we got word back to town. The passengers were taken back to Fairbanks. Ada called Sam White and some other friends, and fourteen men came out to help. People were always there to help in emergencies.

We had the use of a nice building at the lake, a Boy Scout building that they used in the summer, with a large wood-burning range and a lot of tables. Ada came out to do the cooking.

I loved that Ford, Ada said, and so did each of our three children. As soon as word was received in town, friends gathered from all corners. Men quit their jobs for the time being and went to Harding Lake. After their first night, I made arrangements for the care of the children, shopped for groceries, and hopped a truck going that way. The men were not looking forward to another meal of scorched stew. I would cook for them.

For five days and five nights those men worked dangerously over a hole surrounded by black, rotten ice, over forty feet of water. They rested twice a day, for a few hours each time. I served three meals a day in the Scout camp and carried out two lunches a day and served them on the ice.

We all became too tired to keep going, but somehow we did. There never was a cross word; in spite of it all, we laughed a lot. Those men could not have been induced to do that hard, dangerous work for any sum of money. But for friendship they placed no value on their lives or time. I shall never forget those five nights and days. No good time ever brought me so much satisfaction as did this bad time.

One of the men who came, Noel recalled, had experience with tripods and derricks and cables and winches. He also brought out many heavy timbers, about two by twelve by twenty feet. Many spruce poles were cut.

We had long daylight hours in May, so we were able to work from two or three in the morning until eleven at night. The sun was beating down almost all the time. The metal airplane was reflecting it, and we had to work fast before the whole ship disappeared in the lake.

Two tripods were stood up on the heavy timbers laid out around the hole in the ice. One tripod was at the front of the ship and one at the back. A cable was attached to the shaft of the center engine, and the rear cable was put around the tail of the fuselage.

Gradually we hauled and raised the ship, inch by inch. The motors slowly came up, dripping water. We worked for three days, twenty hours a day. The ice was getting soft and bad, and we had trouble keeping the timbers from slipping into the hole. At the end of the fourth day the skis were up high enough for logs to be shoved under them. Getting timbers to hold lengthwise and crosswise long enough to take the entire weight of the airplane caused us a lot of trouble.

We finally made it, and a truck hauled the ship to the heavy ice. During the work many of the fellows fell in the hole. They got out in a hurry.

Then we had the problem of getting the three engines checked out. The magnetos had to be taken to Fairbanks to be cleared out. We found the wiring system soaked pretty badly, the spark plugs were bad, and the three propellers were bent.

When we felt we were able to, I took off and flew the ship back to Fairbanks with all three engines sputtering. Even when I arrived over Fairbanks twenty minutes later, the engines were still sputtering. Our shop finally got everything working perfectly again, after I had thought we weren't going to be able to save the old Tri-Motor.

In five years Noel put in several thousand hours flying the Tri-Motor. On "days off," he would take the family for a hop. Son Merrill and his little brother Richard took turns sitting in their father's lap, as groundling sons do in automobiles, and working the ailerons and elevators with the Model-T wheel. The plane was sold in 1940 to Alaska Airlines. "You know," Noel said, "that 1929 airplane was one of the finest ships ever built. It still could be used very efficiently even today for freight and hauling in the bush."

And it was in the Tri-Motor that Noel made perhaps the most spectacular takeoff in the history of northern aviation, one that is still memorialized whenever old-timers get together. In May 1936

Bessie Creek field at Nome was only partly thawed and partly dried. Gravel showed through on the takeoff area of the strip where snow had been cleared. Here and there, however, was a puddle of half-frozen water up to eight inches deep. Snow still remained on the far end of the strip, and was piled alongside the field into heavy drifts sculptured by the Bering winter winds.

A row of airplanes was parked on each side of the strip at the takeoff end. Noel pushed about three-quarters power in and began his roll carefully between the lines of aircraft. He intended to give full power when he had cleared them.

With a jar the right main gear dropped into one of the deeper water holes and Noel felt his huge bird jerk to the right and take aim at the lined-up airplanes.

Instantly he cut power on his left engine and jammed home the throttle of the right engine to full power, in order to bring the plane back to the left and straighten it out. But the right engine did not take: it had been called upon too abruptly; it just idled.

Noel had full power on his center engine, idling power on the right, and half power on the left. The plane was moving too fast now for him to take a hand off the wheel in order to jiggle the right throttle and coax the engine up to the full power he needed for symmetry. He had gone too far to chop all power. His brand new copilot just sat and observed the master's unusual maneuvering.

At just under takeoff speed the Tri-Motor flashed in a swooping turn beyond the parked aircraft, reached the uncleared part of the strip, and began carving two wide circles into the snow, continuing its curving, roaring dash onto the tundra and among the dangerous drifts there.

Noel had to keep elevator in or let the wheels sink into the deep snow. The right propeller turned daintily, giving no help. He couldn't chop power now, he was half flying. If he chopped power, the big ship would stop and sink into the snow over its wheels. Doing his best to avoid the more menacing drifts, Noel continued the careen and felt the Tri-Motor wanting to take off.

At just that instant, the right engine roared back into life. Noel straightened with rudder and took off, matter of factly setting course for the States.

Sam White, coming in to land a half hour later, saw two deep troughs cut through the snow on and about the Bessie Creek field, marking out about 120 degrees of a circle. He thought about that. Certainly no airplane would be running around like that—couldn't, anyway, in that deep snow. He couldn't figure it out. In the air over Norton Sound to the south, Noel's new copilot had said not a word about their unusual departure. After all, maybe that boomeranging kind of takeoff was the way you did it when you were the Lindbergh of the North.

---

37. ONE-EYED PILOT
WITH A LIMP

Weather, topography, finances, unfair competitors, creaking equipment, and predatory mosquitoes. These were Noel's early adversaries. Poor health joined this list in the 1930s. But in his phlegmatic way Noel kept silent and prevailed over two crippling afflictions that would have retired even some persons in sedentary jobs.

By 1935 Noel had flown four years without a vacation. The family back in Minnesota had not seen Jean, now two, or Richard, the three-month-old baby, so the Noel Wiens decided to spend Christmas on the farm at Cook. In October the five went by ship from Seward to Seattle, where they spent a few days visiting friends and having the children examined by a pediatrician. In 1935 making a long trip with three youngsters was no small undertaking. Diapers then were made of outing flannel, and washing them was a chore no present-day, total-electric mother can imagine. There were no jars or plastic tubes of instant baby food, either. Everything for Richard had to be cooked, ground, mashed, or pulverized, and carried about, by mother herself.

From Seattle a long train ride took the family to Fargo, and a short one aboard a car with a coal stove that emitted only feeble heat took them to Cook. In February, after a pleasant visit, they began the return to Alaska. Noel developed a toothache, with much swelling, in Seattle. In agony, he went to a dentist to have the tooth pulled. Instead, the dentist drilled and filled, inflicting almost unbearable pain. Gradually the tooth stopped aching, but another pain, an insistent ache in his back and down his legs, came to take its place. Shepherding his family, Noel dragged himself aboard the boat for Alaska and headed home.

The children and I were very seasick, Ada said. Noel was not, but his back hurt so badly he was in agony. Yet he stood up most of the time caring for us, and I marveled how he could do it. He said he was more comfortable standing. He would lean his head on the upper bunk and take a nap standing up.

On the train he sat a little, with his right leg out in the aisle; but he walked up and down more than he sat, bent over and favoring his back and right leg. When we arrived in Fairbanks, he collapsed and went to bed. He kept thinking about the bad tooth. After a week in bed he said, "I've got to get to a dentist. I want that tooth pulled." Noel was the only one who could fly the Ford Tri-Motor, and it had been sitting on the ground the whole time we had been gone, from October to March. Waiting were hauls that only he could make.

The pain was excruciating, but we got him into the car and to the dentist and the tooth was pulled. Almost immediately Noel seemed to get better and in a few days the pain was gone. He walked with a limp from then on, and he found out he had almost no strength in the toes of his right foot, that he could not press down with them.

One night I noticed that his right leg was different. It had always been a little heavier muscled, but now the calf had shrunk and the leg was absolutely straight in the back like a stovepipe. If he started walking on his right toes, he would nearly fall down.

Four years later Ada and Noel underwent medical examinations at a Seattle clinic. A physician, medical record form on lap, pencil in hand, matter of factly asked Noel when he had had polio. "Polio? Why, I've never had polio," Noel answered.

He was told that indeed he had. His limp and the shape of his right leg gave testimony. Further questioning elicited the story of

the toothache and backache four years before. That was when he
had been afflicted with polio, he was told. The physician was
astounded that Noel had been able to continue work as a flyer, and,
moreover, as a flyer in Alaska. That he had survived polio was
wonder enough.

But to Noel, poliomyelitis had been only a backache, another
routine obstacle to be overcome calmly. What did the people in
Alaska, prospective customers, think about his limp? Just a little
problem stemming from that backache he had awhile before. Did
they worry about flying with him after seeing him almost fall flat
when he stood and began walking? He stopped striding out on his
right foot and nobody noticed. How did the bad leg impair his flying
ability? Not at all.

"Oh, there was that one time," Noel remembered. "You needed
to brake a Cessna Airmaster smoothly, and it had toe brakes on the
rudder pedal that had to be stepped on. I came in one day with a
heavy load in the tail and was almost stopped when I lost the right
brake. I just couldn't keep my toes pressed against the pedal top.
We ground looped quick as a flash, spun clear around, and stopped
facing down hill. No damage done, though."

Noel's only official reprimand in a lifetime of flying resulted as
much from his honesty as from his piloting a Fairchild into the trees
off the runway at Chena Hot Springs. His withered leg played no
part.

"It was the fall of 1937," Ada said. "I was on my knees scrubbing
the kitchen floor when Noel came to the door and said he had a
flight to Chena to pick up a passenger. The floor between us was
covered with suds, and this was the first and only time in our lives
that I did not give him a hug and a kiss and tell him to be careful
when he set out on a flight. I thought by telling him it would make
him more conscious of his responsibility to me and to our family and
himself.

"Anyway, I just looked up from my scrubbing and said, 'All right.'
He did not come back that day. Then the weather turned bad and
they could not search for him for four days. You can be sure I
suffered tortures. I was sure that he was lost because I had not given
him our special blessing. I never missed it after that."

Noel did not return because the Fairchild 71 had been speared by
a spruce. It was not a good lifting plane, but Noel thought it would

be suitable for carrying out one passenger from the Chena strip. When he reached the springs, however, he found three men waiting to be flown out to Fairbanks. The day was young, the steam rising from the springs into the brisk fall air was inviting, so Noel decided to take the baths. When he had finished, he found six passengers now waiting for him.

"I didn't like this one bit," Noel said, "but I guess the steamy bath had made me lazy-minded. I set the prop up to get a better takeoff and then began my run. The engine ran fine, but after we lifted off there just wasn't any more lift. We sailed down the runway a few feet in the air and I knew I had to make a controlled crash. We were too far down to land on the field.

"I shut the power off and flared. We skinned through some trees, but then we hit some and a big one stuck right through the wing beside the fuselage. It was a real close call, but only a few scratches were put on my passengers."

They were the only injuries any passenger ever suffered while flying with Noel Wien.

When the weather cleared, Noel and his aborted fares were brought into Fairbanks and Noel faced a session with the CAA man on the spot. Noel reconstructed every second of the ill-fated takeoff, as eager as the CAA man to figure out the cause of the crack-up.

"You know," he mused out loud at the end of the interview, "it had gotten colder while I was taking the baths. Maybe the cold and the steam from the springs put some frost on the wings."

This innocent honesty cost him. When the judgment came down from the CAA, it ordered Noel grounded for fifteen days for taking off with frost on his wings. "They really shouldn't have done that," Noel said, "grounding me for frost that I couldn't see and they really didn't know was there. But I had busted the airplane considerably and the man figured I should be punished."

The fifteen days were tough ones for the pilot. He told no one about the grounding. Only he could fly the Tri-Motor, and he had to turn down flight after paying flight in the big ship. He claimed he was busy with important company affairs, and, in truth, there always were ground duties waiting to be performed. Company people wondered why he was not flying. Ada wondered.

"He kept so quiet," Ada said, "that even I did not know. I had to answer the phone and make excuses for why he couldn't take jobs.

It was several years before I learned he had been grounded officially. He could just as easily have told the CAA man that the engine quit. But he was like a little boy who tells all the truth and then gets punished unjustly."

During that same year the Wiens realized that they had outgrown their home, in which they had lived since they were first married. The place had originally been a one-room log cabin. In the years previous to their purchase, a second room had been added and, later, two frame bedrooms had been built on the side. The whole structure had been raised a foot so that a shallow basement could be dug beneath the central room. In this basement was placed a "furnace," consisting of an oil drum with an opening at one end for the insertion of logs for burning and a duct leading from the other end to the central room above.

Such a heating system required constant vigilance during Fairbanks winters. First, if a home fire was allowed to die out at forty below or colder, everything in the house would freeze, causing damage and countless irritations. Second, it was a fire hazard. Homes and buildings regularly burned down because heating sources were neglected for a moment.

"During the winters when Noel would be stuck out in the bush," Ada said, "I would have to stay up until midnight to stoke the furnace with logs for a last time, watch it for a few minutes, and then go to bed. Then I would have to get up at four or five in the morning and stoke it again. The fire danger was a constant worry for everybody in Fairbanks."

Other improvements to the house had been sinking of a well in the basement and conversion of Ada's pantry into an indoor bath and toilet, the most luxurious delight a sourdough could dream of. The tiny "master" bedroom was crammed with bed, desks, dressers, and a wardrobe closet. The even tinier second bedroom was crammed with Merrill, Richard, and Jean, assembled in a double-decked bunk and a crib.

Five people in less than one thousand square feet did not rattle. Something had to be done. For five hundred dollars Ada and Noel bought a lot at the edge of town on Ninth and Kellum and built a story-and-a-half house that Ada designed from pictures in magazines.° Downstairs were a parlor, dining room, kitchen, study,

° Now well inside town, it became the residence of the Episcopal bishop of Alaska.

bedroom, and a bath. Upstairs were three bedrooms, a bath, and sewing room. There were thirteen closets.

In the yard Ada and Noel planted trees from the Interior forests—spruce, birch, and tamarack—and around the house they planted wild rose, Hudson's Bay tea, and high bush cranberry as shrubs. The family moved in on November 9, 1937, with siding not yet nailed to the outside and only the kitchen and downstairs bath finished on the inside. They propped up wallboard, hung blankets and canvas for privacy, and settled into the downstairs. A wood furnace in the basement kept them cozy through the winter.

After a year they borrowed five thousand dollars at 8 percent interest to finish the rest of the house, something many an Alaskan never does. He first builds a basement, covers it over with wood and piled dirt, and moves in his family, telling himself and friends that "as soon as he can" he will finish it. Because of high costs and the difficulty of construction in permafrost and unfriendly weather, thousands of Alaskans live forever in these dugouts that they always intended to finish. But Noel and Ada did finish their home.

Even though the well for the new home was sunk to fifty feet, it still brought forth only the brown Fairbanks water "too thick to drink and too thin to plow." Despite filters and water softeners, pipes clogged with impurities. One frigid November night in 1938, Noel came home from flying, put the car in the basement garage, and removed his mukluks and parka. A plumber was there banging around on the pipes trying to get a flow started. He asked Noel to buck with a sledge while he pounded. Noel did. At the first lick something hit Noel in the right eye, causing a piercing pain. The hurt was so intense that Noel went upstairs and lay on his bed, blinking and streaming tears.

A doctor examined Noel, said he could not see anything in the eye, and gave him some eyewash. Noel had a sleepless night. The next day he went back and the eye specialist took X rays, but said he couldn't tell whether there was anything in the eye.

"Noel stayed home some three or four days," Ada said, "and we washed the eye out with boric acid. There was flying to do, so he got up and flew. For about a month the eye bothered him, not as steadily as at first, but at the end of a day of flying it would be irritated and he would lie down and we would put boric acid compresses on.

"About the first of February in 1939, some three months after the accident, it started to get worse. Noel went to the only other doctor in Fairbanks, who took X rays, saw a metal chip, and told Noel, 'You have to get to Seattle immediately, where they have powerful magnets and eye specialists. I'll wire and make an appointment for you.' "

Pan American had started Lockheed Electra flights from Fairbanks to Juneau, so Noel boarded one and then took a boat to Seattle. The specialist there said the piece of metal had gone in at the outer edge of the iris and was in the middle of the eye. He said it had to come out immediately.

Two doctors operated. They held Noel's head in a vice and gave him only a local anesthetic. He was conscious and heard the two doctors get into an argument about what to do. One of them charged the other with cutting into the wrong place. It was extremely painful.

They put a patch over the eye and told Noel to come back in three days. When they took the patch off, all he could see was something like waves or "clouds going past" the eye. They assured him that in time he would get his sight back.

"Noel held to this hope," Ada said, "because he could not believe that doctors would lie to him. When the bill came from Seattle it was for only fifty dollars. Noel still could not see through the eye. He said, 'This is one bill we are not going to pay.' He remembered the argument the doctors had while he was on the table.

"After a while a credit company in Fairbanks telephoned and said we had to pay or they would sue us. We told them in no uncertain terms that we were not going to pay. We tried to forget it and not to hold bitterness."

Forgetting the injury that had been done him by the bungling physicians was one thing; forgetting the loss of sight in an eye was impossible. A bush aviator, flying into mountain strips where inches determine life or death, is dependent upon his depth perception. Depth perception requires two working eyes. Almost anyone will tell you that a one-eyed bush pilot is about as functional as a one-armed kayak paddler.

But Noel continued to fly successfully, safely, and, amazingly, he took even this adjustment in stride with the same calm fortitude he mustered for the minor harassments of life. The story of the one-eyed bush pilot never became public knowledge.

I didn't lose any job. The local doctors didn't want talk about it going around town, because they hadn't come out too well in the story. One of them arranged for me to get a waiver through Washington when I went up for my CAA physical every year.

Before the operation the eye would get red and watery and hurt sometimes, but I'd just say that I got something in it. After the operation I couldn't see at all, but nobody but Fritz and Sam White and one or two other closest friends knew it. Not even the children.

I had to use a slightly different procedure in landing the Tri-Motor on short fields with only one eye. I found that my lack of depth perception didn't matter when I looked straight ahead but that it was noticeable when I looked straight down. So I had to come in higher and get lined up way out. I couldn't clip the trees like before and then clear the creek bed dropoff by six inches, like Fritz said I used to do. I had to clear by two or three feet.

After I lost the eye I flew a gold dredge into Taylor, making sixteen flights into the fourteen-hundred-foot field. I would come in at stalling speed, nose up, and, with power on, let it stall about three feet off the ground. When I felt the stall, I'd give it a little gun to take the bounce out. I'd hit harder than before, but it never seemed to hurt. There was no chance to go around if I thought I was going to land too long. All those three-hundred-foot landings I made with the old Standard back in the twenties were mighty good experience for this.

The useless eye was removed in Seattle nine years later, in 1946, after an infection set in. It was an emergency operation hastily scheduled before sympathetic infection could attack his good eye and lead to total blindness. A glass eye was inserted.

"This, more than anything in Noel's life, changed him," Ada said. "He had the most beautiful soft, blue-gray eyes, and he held them wide open. My mother used to talk about Noel's clean, clear, unwavering look.

"The false eye changed his looks and personality completely. He started squinting and he got in the habit of talking to people with his cheek resting on his hand and his fingers pushing the lower eyelid closed. He stopped looking at people when he talked with them."

But it did not change his means of livelihood. Noel flew as a commercial pilot—a limping, one-eyed pilot—through the 1940s and into the fifties. Every year even into the 1970s he returned to Fairbanks each May to take the necessary physical to retain his commercial pilot's license. Although he had not flown as a commercial flyer since 1955, he was as proud of that annual slip of medical paper as he was of any of his flying records.

38. OUR BABY STILL

By 1938, Wien's four pilots were operating eight aircraft on a dozen routes in all directions from Fairbanks but south. Eight of the routes were mail runs, most valued because the post office paid a good part of the expenses. Among the pilots now was brother Sig Wien, who had obtained his commercial rating at Fairbanks in 1937 and was a full-fledged transport pilot. Already he had made a name for himself as a daring and resourceful flyer in the Arctic.

There was no doubt that Wien Alaska Airlines was over the hump. Its wings were a familiar sight to the townsmen, villagers, lonely trappers and miners, and Indians and Eskimos of the Great Land. Although he paid his pilots 20 percent of the gross that they hauled, Noel still took only $500 a month for himself. Profits piled up until the airline showed a net worth of about $150,000. Surely Noel had found a glory hole in the Alaska sky.

But good fortune was not to last. Ada became increasingly unwell during the spring and summer of 1939. Early in November she suddenly felt worse. The doctor diagnosed it as typhoid fever.

The old-fashioned treatment for typhoid was turpentine stoops. We got a special nurse, Ada recalled, and she made the stoops, taking a piece of canvas about eighteen by twenty-four inches, making a deep hem in each side, and slipping sticks through the hems. She dipped this into a deep kettle of boiling turpentine and water and wrung it out with the sticks and put them on my back and stomach.

For the next nine weeks I had a fever of 102 to 104 degrees, and I could not keep anything on my stomach. My mother and Fritz's wife and the Pete Grandisons each took one of our children. I would have chills, which I later learned the doctor called "death chills," as I wasn't expected to live out the day each time I had them.

I got weaker and thinner, not eating, and went down from 145 pounds to eighty. During the first weeks they sent to Juneau for a government man to come up and make tests for typhoid; the results were negative, but the local doctor still kept saying it was typhoid. I was on morphine and sometimes hardly knew anybody, but the pain was still terrible.

They didn't quarantine Noel, and he kept on working. We had two nurses, one of them coming on at eleven at night and the other coming during the day and leaving at seven. Noel or somebody would stay with me for the four hours until the night nurse came.

In April, when I was beginning to get my full strength back, the children came down with the measles and so did I. My temperature went to 105 and I was delirious and sicker than the children. Then the children caught another kind of measles and I started coming down with them, too. The doctors told Noel he had better take me to the States or they did not think I would survive, as I was only skin and bones.

Through the long ordeal Noel had remained stoical, showing Ada so little emotion that often in lucid moments she wondered if he cared at all that she was dying. He cared deeply. "But I felt I shouldn't panic," he said, "or get into such a state that I couldn't go visit the children or run the house or the company."

Running the company was a special problem, for during Ada's illness two of the four pilots—Sig and Herman Lerdahl—went on vacation, leaving the entire system to Noel and Herm Joslyn. Often

Joslyn carried the burden alone, because on very bad days Noel remained at Ada's bedside. Joslyn kept Wien Alaska flying.°

On July 4, 1940, Noel left Alaska to take his wife south to warmth and, they hoped, renewed health. All of their savings had gone to pay medical bills. They would not borrow. To finance the Outside trip they sold their stock in Wien Alaska Airlines to Sig. The price was fifteen thousand dollars, the cash amount that Noel and Ada had put into the company, representing a fraction of what their interest was worth and giving Noel nothing for his years of trail-blazing toil.

Noel and Ada went to Seattle. Merrill stayed with the Fritz Wiens, Jean and Richard with Mr. and Mrs. Arthurs. At a Seattle clinic Ada's troubles were blamed on a staph infection and Noel learned that he had had polio five years before. They were advised to go to southern California so Ada could bake in the sunshine and receive treatment. They took an apartment in Hollywood and spent their days at the beach. After ten weeks, Ada's physician thought she was able to return to Alaska.

"I guess there was no time in my life," Ada said, "when I was so blinded by excitement than the moment when I arrived back home and saw the children again. Merrill was on the roof of the hangar jumping up and down. If there is anything in our life to resent, it is that we had to be separated from our children for almost a year."

Noel and Ada flew back to Alaska in a Gullwing Stinson from Seattle for delivery to Wien Airways. But there was an adjustment in attitude to make when they returned to Alaska. "When we sold our interest in the airline," Ada said, "it was like our child being married and being no longer under our control. But we continued to do everything we could for the good of the company, just as for our children.

"Through the ups and downs, from 1940 on, when Wien Alaska Airlines was no longer Noel's and my child alone, we grieved and were elated. It took us some time to realize we were no longer the guiding force. But we still had that warm feeling that you have toward your children when they are married. They're still your children. Wien Airlines was still our baby."

The father of Alaska bush flying returned to Fairbanks as a

° Joslyn became a Pan American captain, retiring in the 1960s. He received a heart transplant at Stanford University in 1971 and died a short time after.

vice-president of the company he had founded. Through the 1940s and into the fifties he flew for the airline, often in DC-3s hauling supplies, equipment, and men for the military build-up during World War II. He stopped logging flying time at just over 11,600 hours. In the 1950s he often flew single-engined planes on the bush runs, where he had started it all thirty years before. At such places as Hogatza, Umiat, and Allakaket, a portly, graying pilot would emerge from his just-landed Cessna and begin unloading the beans, calico, hardware, and mail. It was the world-famous Noel Wien still doing what he loved best—flying every day.

In 1956, five years after passing his check for an instrument rating, Noel had his last forced landing. On a flight delivering mail to Circle Hot Springs, the engine of his Cessna 170B conked out. He picked up his radio microphone and calmly broadcast a mayday, giving his identification and location. Ten minutes after he had made his landing on the ice of a mountain creek, the U.S. Air Force Search and Rescue already had an airplane in the air.

Remember the Toklat, Lake Minchumina, and the Arctic Plain—and a dozen other places—where he had gone down, not to be heard from for days or weeks? Pilot Ed Parsons flew directly to Noel's downed plane on Deadwood Creek. Parsons saw that he could not land his Stinson 104, cut his engine, and shouted encouragement to Noel. Then he flew on to Circle. Within three hours of Noel's landing, a high-wheeled snow vehicle came mushing through the snow and over rocks and brush to pick him up. Radio, which Noel introduced into Alaska aviation in the late 1930s by installing the first air-to-ground system, was responsible for the miracle.

39. SINCE

Alaska today has the country's highest ratio of aircraft and pilots to residents, and planes from four continents daily fly her skies and stop at her airports. Yet the Great Land did not reach the eminence as a crossroads of the air that some early visionaries forecast for her. Some predicted that all aircraft westbound for the Orient would have to fly the North Pacific land rim, in which Alaska is the keystone. In the 1930s, around-the-world and other distance flyers used Alaska because it was a land base on a northern great circle route to the Orient. Wiley Post and Harold Gatty made a refueling stop in Alaska in 1931, Post did so on his solo flight in 1935, and Howard Hughes landed at Fairbanks on his record-breaking flight of 1938. Lindbergh sought routes to the East through Alaska. During World War II thousands of American planes were flown to Fairbanks and delivered to Russian pilots for use against the Germans on the eastern front. The coming of jets with their great speed, distance, and altitude capabilities, however, made refueling a less crucial factor in distance flying. Jets can hop from anywhere to almost anywhere, and they fly as much by pressure differentials and high-altitude winds as by great circles.

Nevertheless, Anchorage International Airport is a colorful and cosmopolitan hive where any day one may see aircraft from almost the world over. Twenty-three international airlines fly into Anchorage, and in 1972 a total of 1.6 million passengers and 108.3 million pounds of freight moved through the airport. Alaska in 1972 had 762 air terminals, making the state second only to Texas in this statistic and ahead of such giants as California, Illinois, and Pennsylvania. Alaska's population of 300,000 was a fraction of theirs. Over the state there are 185 air taxi operators flying from 90 different locations. Twenty-seven contract carriers work from 9 bases. All together during 1971, these contract carriers flew 23 million air miles, carried 586,000 passengers and 126 million pounds of freight, and grossed $28 million.

Old Weeks Field, the combination ball park and landing field that was the cradle of Alaska aerial transport, was closed in 1951. Fairbanks aviation, except for some private craft, moved a few miles west to a new facility now known as Fairbanks International Airport. At Kotzebue, Ralph Wien Memorial Airport was dedicated in 1951 by Governor Ernest Gruening.

Through the 1960s and into the 1970s Noel Wien worked for the Wien company in public relations. He represented the firm at meetings, domestic and foreign. At home he was pointed out to awed tourists as a state resource rivaling Mount McKinley and the northern lights.

In 1962 the University of Alaska awarded Noel an honorary doctor of science degree, and in 1964 hundreds of persons, some from as far away as New York, attended a testimonial banquet in Fairbanks noting his fortieth anniversary as an Alaska aviator. At this occasion the president-emeritus of the University of Alaska, Dr. Ernest Patty, who as an early-day mining man had used Noel extensively for flights into camps on the Yukon River, said: "I remember Noel as a handsome dashing young fellow [engaged in] dangerous and intrepid bush flying. He had an uncanny ability in handling a plane and in knowing his limitations. He was cautious but when the chips were down on some mercy flight he would nose into the toughest weather. He made many flights to our mining camps and the men would say, 'That's Noel Wien. I can tell by the way he sets the plane down.' "

On his birthday in 1964, Noel and Sam White went flying. A Fairbanks news story reported that "Noel Wien, one of the two remaining Alaska pilots of 1920s vintage, celebrated his 65th birthday by practicing landings and takeoffs in the other's old L-5 airplane. Wien skillfully went through the routine three times . . . in Sam O. White's tandem seated World War II liaison craft on floats. . . ."

Wien Air Alaska merged with Northern Consolidated Airlines in 1968 to form Wien Consolidated Airlines with Sig Wien as

Pioneer Bush Pilot

chairman, Ray Petersen as president, and Noel and Fritz among board members. The name was changed back to Wien Air Alaska in 1973. By then the line had more than 800 employees and nearly 10,000 route miles, serving 190 airfields in Alaska and one at Whitehorse in Canada's Yukon Territory. Wien operated five Boeing 737 jet transports and various Fairchild F-27s, De Havilland Twin Otter propjets, Grumman Mallard twin-engined amphibians, Pilatus Porter single propjets, and Short-Harland Skyvan twin propjet cargo craft. In 1972 Wien grossed $23.6 million.

Noel was invited in 1968 to an Explorers Club dinner in New York honoring the aviation industry. Among other special guests were Bernt Balchen, Jacqueline Cochran, Alexander de Seversky, Jimmy Doolittle, Grover Loening, William T. Piper, Bob Reeve, Eddie Rickenbacker, Juan Trippe, Roscoe Turner, Clarence Chamberlin, Emil Laird, Edward Link, and Leigh Wade, Noel's erstwhile colleague in the aborted Pope polar expedition of 1926.

Noel remained active into the 1970s not only as a company director but also in civic affairs, serving at various times on chamber of commerce committees, as a member of the Alaska Aeronautics and Communications Commission, and on the Fairbanks draft board.

Ada kept the pace, filling speaking engagements and in 1955 becoming one of six women among fifty-five persons elected delegates to the constitutional convention to draft the constitution for the proposed state of Alaska. In 1957 Noel and Ada were invited to President Eisenhower's second inauguration, but they were not able to attend. Noel was elected to the OX-5 Club's hall of fame in 1973.

Sons Merrill and Richard Wien soloed on their sixteenth birthdays and earned other flight ratings at the minimum age or experience level. At age twenty Merrill became by a few days the youngest copilot on Pan American Airways' roster up to that time. He later served five years as an Air Force pilot and then returned to flying in Alaska. He and Richard rose to be captains for the Wien airline. Richard left the company in 1969 to become president of a helicopter and air taxi service, Merric, Inc., which he and Merrill had formed and built in their spare time. He is a leader in Alaska civic and professional organizations.

The Wien line is further guaranteed continuance in Alaska by

Bob Wien, Ralph's son, who is a Wien Air Alaska captain, and *his* two sons, who also soloed on their sixteenth birthdays. In fact, Bob, Jr., grandson of Ralph, was hired as a pilot for Wien Air Alaska in April 1974.

Noel and Ada are now living in the Seattle area, near their daughter Jean, her husband, and their children. In 1974 Noel was still making monthly flights to Alaska to attend Wien board meetings. Everywhere he went he was sought out by reporters for comments on aviation events and for reminiscences of the past. Noel, Fritz, and Sig currently are directors of Wien Air Alaska, Inc.

During visits to Fairbanks the old hero could observe the roaring bustle of an airport through which nearly 300,000 passengers and more than 113 million pounds of freight passed in 1972. In the peak year of the oil-field build-up in the Arctic, 1969, these figures were 315,000 persons and 240 million pounds. Without air transport, in a land more than twice the size of Texas but with only 6,000 miles of roads (fewer than in some cities Outside), such a flow would have taken years. The muskeg is impassable in summer, so alternate transport during that season would have been boat to Barrow, Prudhoe Bay, or Barter Island. During the winter, tractor-towed freight sledges would lumber over an ice road, laboriously chipped out over mountains and muskeg. But many days would have been used to move by water and ice what the HC-130 Hercules propjets and the Boeing 737s moved in hours, each plane often able to complete four round trips from Fairbanks to the Arctic coast in a day.

During visits to Anchorage, the man who started it all often paused to watch the storm of activity he begat in one old Standard biplane with flapping fabric a half century before. In one afternoon he might see aircraft carrying the flags of France, Great Britain, Canada, Japan, Holland, Korea, Germany, Belgium, Sweden, Brazil, the Philippines, and, of course, the United States. As he watched, and as he looked back down the years, Noel Wien did not see world commerce and dollar signs. Nor did he see the great pioneer flights that he made. Not the smoke pall that nearly ended in disaster his flight from Anchorage to Fairbanks in 1924; or the frenzy of Wiseman residents when he lighted there on the first flight beyond the Arctic Circle in 1925; the agony of the "impossible" walk from the rotting Toklat muskeg, the survival at Lake Minchumina, and the search for Russ Merrill; the selflessness of the uncounted mercy flights; the ingenuity and courage of choosing and executing an overland flight through Canada's jagged peaks to win the race with Wiley Post–Will Rogers photographs; the remarkable navigatory ability that took him 600 uncharted miles directly to the icebound *Elisif* off Siberia.

He saw instead people, the good people of the Great Land, those rich and poor, old and young from whom the warmth of good will and love radiated during adversities to make bearable the almost unbearable life on the icy frontier. Typically he remembered the sacrifice of time and jobs made by the men who saved the Tri-Motor from sinking into Harding Lake more vividly than he recalled the drama of the rescue itself. Were he to live it over again, he would do nothing differently. There were no regrets.

The records were now dim memories in which only the human warmth remained as lasting value.

INDEX